Just Plane Crazy

Biography of BOBBI TROUT

by
Donna Veca and Skip Mazzio

As Compiled by:
Carol L. Osborne
Aviation Historian

OSBORNE PUBLISHER, INCORPORATED   1987   Santa Clara, California

Just Plane Crazy

Biography of BOBBI TROUT

Published in the United States by
Osborne Publisher, Incorporated, Santa Clara, California 95051.

Library of Congress Cataloging in Publication Data

Library of Congress Catalog Card Number:

Veca, Donna, 1936–
Mazzio, Skip, 1922–
Osborne, Carol, 1946–

JUST PLANE CRAZY
Biography of Bobbi Trout

1. Trout, Bobbi Evelyn 1906–
2. Title
3. Women in aeronautics
4. Women air pilots—United States—Biography
5. Biography
6. Aviation History

Library of Congress Cataloging-in-Publication Data

```
Veca, Donna, 1936-
   Just plane crazy.

   Bibliography: p.
   Includes index.
   1. Trout, Evelyn, 1906-      . 2. Air pilots--
United States--Biography.  I. Mazzio, Skip, 1922-
II. Osborne, Carol L., 1946-      . III. Title.
IV. Title: Just plane crazy.
TL540.T73V43  1987     629.13'092'4 [B]     87-7886
ISBN 0-940997-01-0
```

International Standard Book Number 0-940997-01-0

Manufactured in the United States of America

12 11 10 9 8 7 6 5 4 3 2 1

First Edition
May 1987

Table of Contents

Acknowledgments

Without the assistance of the following people this book could not exist as you see it today. I would like to offer each of them a very special and heartfelt thank you:

Carol "Petey" Johnston for her professional preparation of camera ready art work.

Willys Peck, Copy Editor of the San Jose Mercury News for his editorial reviews, suggestions and support.

George Akimoto for his paintings used on the cover of *Just Plane Crazy* and *Amelia, My Courageous Sister.*

Rochelle Anderson for help with the many captions associated with each and every photograph, the newspaper clippings, and especially her assistance with proof reading the final copy before it went to press.

Jay McKendry and Jake White of CBM Type for their help in typeset design and their valuable suggestions.

OX5 Aviation Pioneers, for loaning their photographs and complete support of Bobbi's video tape interview project.

Marty Blaker for his editorial and writing assistance.

Carol Osborne, Aviation Historian, for her efforts, without which this book couldn't have been published.

Bobbi Trout, who devoted limitless hours to the preparation and layout of this book. She also provided and authenticated all of the historic data contained in *Just Plane Crazy.*

Skip Mazzio and Donna Veca

FOREWORD

Just Plane Crazy is not just another biography of a pioneer aviatrix. It's a personalized and highly entertaining account of the unusual life of an unusual lady flier who "was there" when much of aviation history was being made.

From her first solo flight on April 30, 1928, Bobbi Trout went on to compile an amazing list of aviation records, stretching her flying endurance record times from 12 hours 11 minutes in 1929 to 122 hours 50 minutes, with aviatrix Edna May Cooper, a new refueling endurance record for women.

Perhaps you remember Bobbi as a competitor in the National Women's Air Derby (Powder Puff Derby) from Santa Monica, California, to Cleveland, Ohio, pitting her piloting skills against such other famous women flyers as Amelia Earhart, Pancho Barnes, Gladys O'Donnell, Ruth Nichols, and Louise Thaden. Due to engine troubles, she didn't win, but people loved her for her courage.

An expert mechanic as well as a pilot, Bobbi was not afraid to tear into her engine and fix a broken con rod to stay in competition.

Perhaps more important than her record-setting flights was Bobbi's love of adventure that knew no bounds. In this book we get a close personal look at this amazing lady, thanks to the bright style of its authors, Donna Veca and Skip Mazzio, who really bring the story to life with interesting and amusing anecdotes.

We learn her real first name was Evelyn, and that she adopted the nickname Bobbi when friends teased her for having her hair bobbed in the fashion of movie star Irene Castle. "Just call me Bobbi," she smiled.

She made up her mind to become a pilot at the age of 12, when she heard a Jenny flying overhead one day in 1918, when World War I barnstormers were bringing flying to grassroots America.

Her interest in aviation history was stimulated in the early 1970s when she received a call from Professor David D. Hatfield of Northrop University in Inglewood, California. He wanted to give her a well-illustrated book on the subject that he had compiled. It included many pictures of Bobbi he had taken of her during her flights.

Professor Hatfield passed away on June 21, 1981, and willed his important collection to Carol Osborne, a good friend and aviation historian in her own right. Carol contacted Bobbi for assistance in adding to the Hatfield Collection, and soon they became inseparable friends.

Since then Bobbi and Carol have interviewed hundreds of aviation pioneers to enlarge this important library of materials, which forms the basis for this present work, *Just Plane Crazy*.

I feel honored to have been able to assist these lovely ladies in their work with contributions from my own aviation historical collection, assembled over the past half century. Much of it has never been published, but I am completing a manuscript, *America Grows Wings*, tracing the early history of aeronautics in this country, much of it prior to the Wright Brothers' flights at Kitty Hawk in 1903.

But for good fun, and to enlarge your own knowledge of early aviation, through the eyes of Bobbi Trout, I'll bet you can't put this volume down once you read the first few pages!

—Don Dwiggins

FOREWORD

Readers of *Just Plane Crazy* and its companion publication, *Amelia, My Courageous Sister*, will be struck by the similarity in careers between Bobbi Trout and Amelia Earhart.

Though almost a decade apart in years, they were friends and they were both leading figures in what many historians regard as the Golden Age of Flying.

They had mutual ties with Canada; they both had musical interests; and they both experienced similar family strains during their formative years.

Most striking, though, is the passion they shared for flying at a time when relatively few men, and even fewer women, chose to make their careers in aviation.

We of the Early Birds of Aviation, those who soloed before December 17, 1916, the thirteenth anniversary of the Wright Brothers' first flight at Kitty Hawk, have a special appreciation of the achievements of these two women.

But everyone whose lives have been touched by the science of aviation, and that means just about everyone, owes a debt to people like Bobbi Trout and Amelia Earhart, whose adventurous spirits helped advance that science to its present state.

This is a story of high adventure. Read it and savor its message.

Forrest E. Wysong, President
The Early Birds of Aviation, Inc.

This book is dedicated to my wonderful long time friend, Edie Curtis, whom I met in 1934. She untiringly helped me with this book until her untimely death in 1982.

Edie named it: Just Plane Crazy

Edie Curtis modeling for Eastman Kodak in the 1920's.

Chapter One

The Early Years

"I DID too build it all by myself." Nine-year-old Bobbi Evelyn Trout glared at Johnny Brown, who had just coasted down the snow covered hill in midtown Oak Creek, Colorado. Johnny had just made the accusation that girls can't build things like that. Bobbi firmly defended herself against the neighborhood kids who questioned Bobbi's ability to make her bobsled. Her younger brother, Denny, who at five was her constant companion and confidant, confirmed Bobbi's statement.

"Evelyn did too build it," he insisted. "My sister builds lots of things." Bobbi marched the two neighborhood boys to her grandmother's to prove it.

"Why, Evelyn did," her grandmother said. "I gave her a set of tools a while back. Isn't she getting good with them?" Bobbi always asked for tools. When her birthday, Christmas, and other events came around, she wanted a square, a pair of pliers, a hammer, a screwdriver, nails —just tools. She started building things when she was only five years old; Bobbi thought dolls were silly and a waste of time.

Bobbi was the natural leader of the neighborhood children. She had them all out digging in the hills around Oak Creek, Colorado, where they lived, looking for gold. She had them digging a tunnel from the creek bank, under city hall, and when they were discovered by the town judge, he told Bobbi and her group to stop before city hall sank.

Bobbi Evelyn Trout was born in Greenup, Illinois, on January 7, 1906. Greenup was founded by Bobbi's grandfather, Dr. William Orlando Denman, and three of his family relatives: the Conzets, the Lyons, and the Arthurs. Dr. Denman and his wife, Zapporah Stevens, had five girls, including Bobbi's mother, Lola.

1914 "Bobbi" Evelyn Trout stars as "the preacher" in a Tom Thumb wedding in the Queen Theatre, Oak Creek, Colorado.

Evelyn Trout was Bobbi's given name. She was named Evelyn because her mother received a calender that pictured a beautiful red-headed woman named Evelyn on the cover. Bobbi was different from most girls. Since her grandfather had all girls, but wanted a boy so badly, Bobbi's mother prayed her firstborn would be a boy. Instead she got a tomboy.

Bobbi remembers being told about her first business experience at age five or six. She was with Denny, named Denman after his mother's maiden name, in Greenup to visit their Grandfather Denman and his second wife, Mae. While there, they were given a little red wagon with which to play.

About one-half block down the street was a scrap iron business, a vacant lot, and the home of the scrap iron business owners. Bobbi and Denny pulled their little red wagon to the alley in the back of the scrap iron business and picked up scraps of metal. They would pull the collection in the wagon around to the front, and sell it for a few cents to the owner. They did this several times. It was not until later in life when Bobbi learned that the adults knew what the two entrepreneuring children had been doing.

Bobbi's parents, George Everett Trout and Lola Denman, honeymooning in Colorado in 1905.

Zapporah Stevens (Bobbi's maternal grandmother): relatives included the Denmans, Doolittles, Wheelers, Bucks, Lyons, and many other renown families.

CREDIT: JERÉ CONZET

(lower right) Henry Gratiot Trout and Anna Frances Lyons Trout, (Bobbi's paternal grandparents married 9-6-1882), with their children George Everett Trout (born in 1886) and Gertrude Trout taken about 1988–1989 in Memphis, Tennessee.

Bank

Drug Store

Mercantile Store

MAIN STREET   GREENUP, ILL.

CREDIT: DENNY TROUT

Around 1900 the above buildings were owned by Grandfather Denman who gave the drugstore to Bobbi's parents as a wedding gift.

Family picture in 1904: (back row left to right) Nina Denman, Claude Robertson, Lola Denman, Daisy Denman Leggett (front row, left to right) Dr. William O. Denman, May Robertson Denman, Irene Denman, Edna Denman, Joe Leggett.

Bobbi's mother, Lola, age 19

George and Lola shortly after their marriage.

Report of a Birth to County Clerk

COUNTY OF CUMBERLAND
STATE OF ILLINOIS

1. Full Name of Child *Evelyn Trout*
2. Sex *Female*   Race of Color (if not of the white race)
3. Number of Child of this Mother *1st*
4. Date of this Birth *Jan 7th 1906*
5. Place of Birth *Greenup*   City / Village
6. Residence of Mother   "   Town
7. Town, State or Country.
   a. Father, Place of Birth *Ill*   Age *2.8* Years
   b. Mother, Place of Birth *Ill*   Age *2.6* Years
8. Full Name of Mother *Lola Trout*
9. Maiden Name of Mother *Denman*
10. Full Name of Father *Geo. E. Trout*
11. Occupation of Father *Druggist*
12. Name and Address of Nurse or Attendant, (if any)

Reported by *L. A. Fisher*   M. D.
Residence *Greenup Ill*   Midwife
Date *Jan 12   1906*   *J. L. Carr. Clerk*

COUNTY OF CUMBERLAND
STATE OF ILLINOIS

I, *W. E. Catey* County Clerk in and for the County and State aforesaid, and keeper of the files and records of the reports of Births and Deaths, do hereby certify the above and foregoing to be a full and complete copy of the report of birth of *Evelyn Trout* as the same appears from the files and records in my office remaining.

IN WITNESS WHEREOF, I have hereunto set my hand and affixed the seal of my office at Toledo, Cumberland County, Illinois, this *9th* day of *June* A. D. 19 *39*

W. E. Catey County Clerk.

Bobbi's birth certificate,
January 7, 1906

Bobbi, one year old

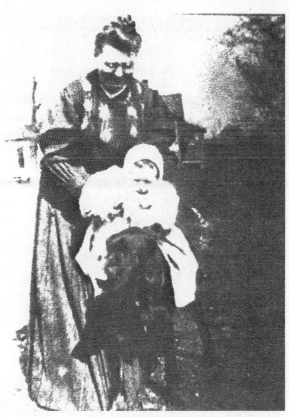

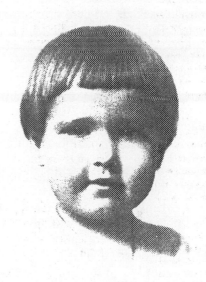

Bobbi at age 3, Greely, Colorado

One year old Bobbi under the watchful eye of her step grandmother, Mae Denman

4 year old Bobbi and 2 year old brother Denny in Manderson, Wyoming. Bobbi is wearing her "teddy bear suit" given to her by dear friend's Mack and Mary McDonagh, Greenup, Illinois.

During Bobbi's earliest school days, about 1911 in Greenup, her uncle, dentist Dr. John Paul Jones, filled one of her front teeth with gold. In those days, a gold tooth was a mark of prestige. The minute Bobbi met new kids, she was invariably asked, "Where did you get your gold tooth?" Bobbi only had the gold tooth for two or three years, until her baby teeth came out. It was very unusual for children to have a gold tooth—only adults had them. An obvious advantage of having a dentist in the family.

One afternoon in 1915, Bobbi and Denny were playing in the house when they again heard the sound of their parents arguing. Their mother had become more and more concerned about Bobbi's father, who continued to uproot the family time after time in search of some ephemeral dream. She for the most part had gone uncomplainingly along with him, but now she felt their children's education would suffer. They finally decided that Bobbi and Denny would stay with relatives: Bobbi went to her mother's sister, Irene, and Denny went to his father's sister, Gertrude Trout Conzet.

And so began a two-year period, from 1916 to 1918, when Bobbi and Denny spent the school years with relatives. Bobbi spent her fifth-grade year with Aunt Irene and Uncle Earl Hyett, in Seattle, Washington, while Denny stayed in Fort Collins, Colorado, with Aunt Gertie, cousin Jeré, and Uncle Duke Conzet.

Seattle with Aunt Irene and Uncle Earl was like being in Utopia after freezing through the very cold winters and toasting in the hot summers of the east and Rocky Mountain states. Uncle Earl built Bobbi a chinning bar for exercise, and bought her a BB-gun for target practice.

The United States entered the World War in 1917, and Bobbi learned the *Manual of Arms* from a neighbor who was an ROTC student at the University of Washington. They would practice shooting at targets in Bobbi's back yard. At age eleven, Bobbi was dreaming of the day she could be an ambulance driver and help out with the World War. From an early age she felt drawn toward service work.

Bobbi was always a truthful child. In the summer of 1916, Bobbi and her school friend, Edward Cannon, practiced shooting Bobbi's new BB-gun. Instead of target practice, they decided to shoot at objects in the nearby lots. Their first idea was taking aim at chickens in a neighbor's back yard. Accidentally, they killed one. It almost caused a lawsuit between feuding neighbors until Bobbi's Aunt Irene asked Bobbi if she shot at their neighbors' prize rooster. Bobbi hesitatingly admitted shooting at the chickens, but did not realize that they killed one—only that one chicken acted very strange.

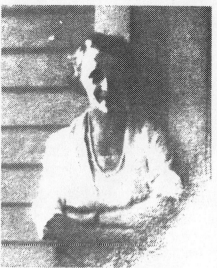

CREDIT: DENNY TROUT

Bobbi visited her aunt, Irene Denman Hyett in 1916, pictured here in Seattle, Washington.

1914 Bobbi's uncle, Dr. John Paul Jones, who gave her a gold tooth when she was a child.

Duke Conzet and Bobbi's Aunt Gertrude Conzet in 1916, Ft. Collins, Colorado.

George Trout took his family to Deleplane, Arkansas in 1914 and tried farming on acreage owned by Dr. W.O. Denman. Family: George, Lola, Bobbi and Denny.

Grandfather and Aunt Nina Denman Jones visit the family on the Arkansas farm in 1915. (Bobbi and Denny in foreground)

During the summer of 1917, Bobbi journeyed to Hamilton, a lovely city in Ontario, Canada, to live with her cousin Billy, Aunt Edna, and Uncle William O. Stevenson. Her uncle was a general M.D., one of the seven doctors who held the highest medical degrees in the Dominion of Canada. She traveled there on the new electrically powered Chicago, Milwaukee, St. Paul, and Pacific Railroad, which was the longest electrically powered railroad, six hundred sixty miles of it, at that time. Her new family spent many hours trying to make a lady out of her. She loved them dearly, but could not get over her need to do things that the boys always did.

12 year old Bobbi and cousin Billy in Canada.

Aunt Edna Denman and cousin Billy Stevenson in Hamilton, Ontario, Canada, 1915.

On a spring afternoon in 1918, while returning from school, Bobbi heard the unusual sound of an engine roaring overhead. The noise grew louder and louder, and she gazed upward, shading her eyes with one mittened hand. "An aeroplane!" she yelled excitedly. She stood in amazement while she gazed at the machine until it disappeared behind the trees. She ran home fast to deliver the news of her first sighting of an airplane to her Aunt Edna.

Bobbi rushed into the house and called for Aunt Edna, who was in the basement getting fruits and vegetables for dinner out of the sand bins, where they were buried for winter preservation. Aunt Edna rushed upstairs to see why Bobbi was so exuberant and excited because she had been worried at Bobbi's recent loneliness for her family. Bobbi longed for her mother and for her home. Aunt Edna smiled and hugged Bobbi, asking why she was so excited.

"Some day I'll be up there," Bobbi vowed. "Someday I'm going to fly an aeroplane." Aunt Edna agreed they were wonderful, but reminded her that young ladies of good families do not fly airplanes. Not wishing to dampen her high spirits at this point, Aunt Edna let it go. Changing the subject, she gave Bobbi a letter that arrived earlier that day. It was from Bobbi's mother. Tearing open the flap, she began to read the pages:

> Darling, I know this news will please you very much. You know how very much I have missed you and Denny. Your father is in California and has a very good position with the telephone company and is close to Grandfather and Grandmother Trout. I am not going to go with him this time. I plan to stay here in St. Louis and manage Aunt Daisy's millinery shop on Cass Avenue. I want you and Denny to come and live with me and to attend school here, so I am hoping Edna and Will may be able to drive you here this summer. Anxiously awaiting your return home. All my love, Mother.

"Mother says she wants me to come home," Bobbi told her aunt. Aunt Edna seemed saddened by the prospect of Bobbi returning to her mother. She understood how much Bobbi missed her mother though, and naturally wanted to see her happy. Bobbi left the room to finish her milk and cookies and to practice her piano lessons. She knew how much her mother wanted her to play the piano, and before long she would have the opportunity to play for her mother at home.

Aunt Edna, Uncle Will, and Billy drove Bobbi to St. Louis in the summer of 1918 to reunite her with her mother and Denny. She learned while eavesdropping on the adults' conversation that her father had made the acquaintance of a man named Lambert who owned an airplane. They had gone up in Lambert's airplane and were forced down on the Mississippi River. Luckily, neither one of them was hurt. Bobbi was very intrigued by her father's experience.

Bobbi remained silent and decided that this was definitely not the time to mention her plans to become a pilot when she grew up. After a few days, Aunt Edna, Uncle Will, and cousin Billy returned to Canada. They knew they left Bobbi where she belonged, with her mother and brother. Little did Bobbi know that this was the last time they would see Aunt Edna. She died in childbirth a few months later.

Lola's father, Dr. Denman, had tried to talk his daughter into moving back with Bobbi and Denny to Greenup, but her independent mother said she would rather make it on her own. Lola Trout was determined to stay in St. Louis to manage her sister's millinery shop.

The hot summer passed swiftly for Bobbi and Denny. Soon they were again making preparations to enroll in another school. By the first day at her new school in 1918, Bobbi had acquired a gang of friends who accepted her leadership in the neighborhood. When the students reached the play area after the first recess bell rang, Bobbi became surrounded by her classmates. They tried to keep her talking just to hear her Canadian accent. Her accent made her stand out as different and made her most popular.

Bobbi and a girl named Betty quickly became good friends and were soon inseparable. Denny was always a welcome third. One winter afternoon, the three walked along the street toward the movie theater, discussing their futures. They were on their way to see an early World War epic.

"I'm going to be an airplane pilot when I grow up." Bobbi stated. She explained that she read about Blanche Stuart Scott, who on September 2, 1910, was technically the first American woman to solo a powered airplane. Scott was also one of the first women to wear pants while flying. That is exactly what Bobbi wanted to do.

CREDIT: DENNY TROUT

Home of Dr. William and Edna Stevenson on King Street, Ontario, Canada, where Bobbi lived one year, 1917–1918.

As the war story on the screen unfolded, the scene shifted to a dogfight between a Fokker and a Nieuport. Bobbi was electrified. Trying desperately to see around a taller person in front of her, she stood and climbed up on her seat to get a better view. She then became so engrossed in the spectacle on the screen that she was oblivious to the unhappy cries of "down in front" echoing through the theater.

Within six months of Bobbi's return to St. Louis, the Armistice was signed, ending the World War. Bobbi, her mother, and friends celebrated with the mob, leaving Denny home to run his paper route. The women crunched through the snow in downtown St. Louis. Everybody was shaking hands with one another, blowing noisemakers, and waving flags. It was a really festive occasion.

In the next few months, reports of the dangers of Spanish influenza began to fill the newspapers. The disease spread with alarming speed across the United States, soon becoming an epidemic. Headlines in the papers were giving the daily death rates. Thousands lost their lives. Doctors frantically searched for a cure while the disease spread like wildfire. The death rate in St. Louis and the whole country continued to rise.

Bobbi's mother's worst fears were realized when Denny came home from school with a mild cough, fever, and a headache. She immediately put him to bed, hoping it was just a cold. Denny was always the first to catch whatever was going around school; he always brought it home to the rest of the family. By the next morning his fever was alarmingly high, and when the doctor arrived, he diagnosed his illness as the deadly Spanish influenza. By that evening both Bobbi and her mother had come down with it also, and for several days it was questionable whether any of them would survive. Finally, one by one, their fevers began to break, and they slowly began to recover. Fortunately, the Trouts did not become part of the thousands who died from the flu epidemic.

After months of recuperating, the family was again examined by the doctor. He said that Denny's lungs sounded fine, but Bobbi's were impaired. The doctor told Bobbi's mother that she needed to get Bobbi to a warmer climate.

Bobbi's mother was not about to take any more chances with her children's health after the scare they had just lived through. By the spring of 1920, Bobbi's mother tearfully said goodbye to her children when they boarded the train for California. It took three days and nights to get to Los Angeles. Their father met them at the Los Angeles depot, and they rode the Pacific Electric Big Red Car to Huntington Beach. Not long afterward, Bobbi and Denny were settled in their new home with Grandmother and Grandfather Trout. Once again, Bobbi was separated from her mother and prepared for a new school.

CREDIT: DENNY TROUT

Denny retreats from a strong left hook while he and Bobbi spar in Grandmother's Trout's backyard in Huntington Beach.

Bobbi playing the ukulele in Chula Vista, California in 1921.

Bobbi and her steel guitar harmonize with three residents of Grandmother Trout's boardinghouse.

Across the street was an inoperative oil derrick, which was wonderful for Bobbi and Denny to climb when they were not playing at the beach. Shortly after Bobbi and Denny's arrival, Grandmother Trout decided to move the family to San Diego where Grandfather Trout was in business. Bobbi and Denny enrolled in another school. After a very short stay in San Diego, Grandmother Trout rented a large house in Chula Vista, remodeled it, and turned it into a large boardinghouse. She brought Bobbi and Denny with her, enrolling them in Chula Vista Elementary School. Soon the house was filled with boarders who worked in the lemon groves surrounding the town. After school, Bobbi and Denny often took walks along the dusty roads between lemon groves. They would spend hours peeling and eating lemons.

The two children soon found new ways of entertaining themselves. Commandeering their grandmother's boarders for a captive audience, Bobbi and Denny performed song and dance routines for hours. Bobbi sang and played either the steel guitar or her ukulele. On weekends, they and some of the boarders would occasionally hike out into the surrounding land and hunt rattlesnakes with their borrowed .22 rifles. Bobbi enjoyed spending time with the boarders, but she still missed her mother very much.

By spring of 1921, Bobbi's lungs had healed completely. She wanted to return to St. Louis and made several subtle and some not so subtle, requests to her father for her and Denny to return to St. Louis. He was not enthusiastic about the idea.

After graduating from Chula Vista Elementary School in June 1921, Bobbi did not look forward to the long summer ahead. The year away from her mother seemed very long, and homesickness plagued her. One evening she sat on the porch steps thinking about the future. Her father had an idea of what she was thinking about. He then surprised Bobbi and handed her an envelope with train tickets in it for St. Louis. "They're not for you to just go back to St. Louis," he said. "They're for you to go to St. Louis and talk your mother into coming back with you. Okay?"

A few days later she arrived at the station in

St. Louis and Bobbi's mother rushed up to hug her. Tears of joy streamed down her mother's cheeks. Within days Bobbi had exhausted her supply of arguments to convince her mother to return with her to California. Gazing out of the window at the drab scene and dirty, old-fashioned buildings in front of her, she turned to her mother and continued to tell her how she must come to California, live in the year-round beautiful weather, and make their family whole again.

Bobbi's mother finally looked at Bobbi and said that if she was down to touting the weather that much, she must be desperate. Her mother finally relented. Within a few days, Bobbi and her mother were on their way back to California together.

Graduation Day from Chula Vista Elementary School, June 1921.

Chaptor Two

Working Toward A Dream

THE family was once again united. Bobbi's father held a good position at the local telephone company and moved the family to East Fourth Street, Los Angeles, to be close to his work. In September 1921, when Bobbi was fifteen, she enrolled in Lincoln High School and was soon struggling with the intricacies of verbs and sentence structures of beginning Spanish. She hated it.

Thumbing through the *Los Angeles Evening Herald*, Bobbi came upon an article about two young women running a service station. "I could do that!" she said, not realizing she had spoken out loud.

Her father read the headline over her shoulder, then ruffled her hair and said, "I bet you could, Bobbi."

That night at the dinner table, Bobbi brought up the idea of quitting school and running a service station. Bobbi's mother was definitely against it. Bobbi, with her father's support, convinced her mother that it would be good practical experience to work for a while.

Bobbi's mother reluctantly agreed to finance the project. A short time later, she and Bobbi opened a gasoline station called Radio Service. They selected this name because broadcasting and sales of radio receivers had just begun. The Trouts were one of the first to buy a radio and share it with their neighbors and customers who crowded the station lot in the evening.

"Trout's Radio Service Station" at 4th and Soto Sts., Los Angeles, Ca., 1922. The house to the right is where the Trout family lived.

CREDIT: DENNY TROUT

This job gave Bobbi the opportunity to wear slacks, which few women then wore. Bobbi always tried to be practical and thought women's clothes such as corsets, high heels, long hair, and buttons on the back of blouses, were silly. She also wanted to demonstrate that women could do most anything a man could.

The Trouts quickly acquired a reputation for good service with a smile, and their business prospered. Her father and Denny helped run the business whenever possible, but the main responsibility fell upon Bobbi and her mother. Within a few months they found the business growing so rapidly that her father gave up his position with the telephone company to give all his time to running the gasoline station. This ended Bobbi's hiatus from scholarly pursuits; however, she found herself once again struggling to learn Spanish.

Bobbi helped at the station after school and on weekends. She took all the jobs that no one else in the family wanted. She even became the first licensed female headlight adjuster. Her zeal had a purpose now, for she had made a firm pact with herself to become a pilot eventually. Her devotion to work faltered only when an airplane engine roared overhead, prompting her eyes upward. She would gaze at the airplane flying over with envious eyes, wishing she were the pilot at the controls.

Bobbi transferred to Roosevelt High School when it opened in 1924. To her amazement and disappointment, her first class was Spanish. Her last class of the day was music appreciation with Miss Olga Sutherland. Bobbi never forgot her because later there were times when Bobbi would fall asleep in class and Miss Sutherland would rib her about it. Bobbi needed protein— slow-burning fuel—to function properly. While practicing to be a vegetarian, her diet lacked protein and she would doze off in class. This protein imbalance persisted until 1944.

CREDIT: DENNY TROUT

Denny and Bobbi take a break in front of their home next door to the service station.

While working at the service station in 1922, she confided her dream to become an aviator to a friendly customer, W.E. "Tommy" Thomas. They discussed flying quite often. Tommy, along with Ross Hadley and Palmer Nichols, formed the Pacific Aeromotive Corporation, still in business today. With a grin, Tommy told her he owned a Curtiss Jenny, powered with a Curtiss OX5 engine. This biplane was used to train World War pilots, and Tommy asked Bobbi if she would like to go up for a ride. Would she!

CREDIT: DENNY TROUT

A view of the service station from Soto St.

SAM BALTER
Basket-ball Captain, 24, '25
Sport Editor of Round-Up
Managing Editor of Rough
  Rider, S'25
Treasurer of Senior Class, S'25
Aldebaran Society, S'25

Bobbi performs in a Roosevelt High School play, 1925, with Sam Balter (left), who later became a prominent radio sports announcer.

Fairfax Ave.

Rogers Airport

HOBBS

Wilshire Blvd.

DeMille Field No. 2

Bobbi took her first airplane ride with Tommy Thomas in an OX5 Jenny at Rogers Field, which was the same site that Amelia Earhart took her first airplane ride.

As a member of the Lincoln High Winchester Junior Rifle Corps, Bobbi (5th from the left) earned a "sharp shooter" award——the highest possible. Below is her diploma.

CREDIT: DENNY TROUT

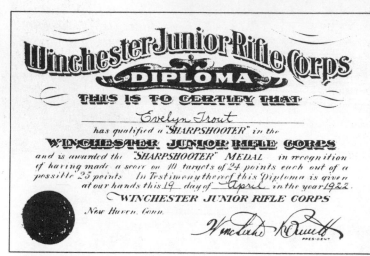

CREDIT: ED LUND

Tommy Thomas

On the morning of December 27, 1922, Bobbi awoke with a feeling of intense excitement. At last the long-awaited day had arrived. She was going to find out what it felt like to fly. Donning brown trousers and a white shirt, she hastily combed her hair and half heartedly tried to eat breakfast. Tension knotted her stomach. She pushed the breakfast plate away and rushed out into the clear, beautiful morning.

Tommy was waiting for her at Rogers Airport, at the corner of Wilshire Boulevard and Fairfax Avenue in Los Angeles: this was out in the country in 1922. He proudly escorted her to where his Jenny was parked and watched her eyes light up. It was the most beautiful thing Bobbi had ever seen. It even had chromed exhaust pipes.

Tommy began his pre-flight inspection and explained the need for making it each time. Bobbi watched his every movement and took her place in the cockpit. He warmed up the engine, taxied the Jenny to the airstrip, paused, and made a ninety-degree turn into the wind. He turned in his seat, smiled, and gave her a thumbs-up signal. She returned the signal, and they moved down the bumpy dirt runway. Bobbi could not believe she really was about to fly.

Bobbi expected to feel a lift on takeoff, imagining it would feel something like an express elevator going up. When she didn't experience that sensation, she began to wonder why. The ride suddenly smoothed out and she glanced over the side. They were airborne.

Delight charged through her, and a huge smile spread across her face. Peering down she felt like a spider—swinging safely from its web while the world beneath moved leisurely by. Even the engine's roar seemed muted and distant.

Tommy circled around Los Angeles, while Bobbi gazed at the landscape, trying to recognize some landmarks. The barren fields and oil derricks offered much to see. The sight from above was like looking at a map in detail.

Tommy brought the plane in to land at the old dirt airstrip, while Bobbi memorized every sensation in order to bring them out again later and relive every second of this wonderful flight.

Tommy taxied to the parking spot and shut off the engine. Bobbi began to ask question after question. Without pausing to give him a chance to answer, she asked more questions than Tommy could handle at once. He held up his hand to stem the tide and grinned at her exuberant enthusiasm. "Give me a chance." he said. He understood how interested Bobbi was in learning to fly. At last he told her, "Young lady, you just hang on to that feeling. Some day you'll be a pilot."

Bobbi turned for a last look at the beautiful Jenny. Tommy understood how entranced Bobbi was and told her that if she would climb back into the cockpit and don her helmet, he would take her picture. Afterwards, they had a nickel glass of Coke, and he tried to answer her questions.

From that moment on, all her energies were directed toward becoming an aviator. She spent every free moment either working for the cash to finance her dream or reliving the experience in daydreams. While her girlfriends were finagling dates for Saturday night, Bobbi schemed how to earn extra money.

CREDIT: DENNY TROUT

Bobbi after her first aeroplane ride.

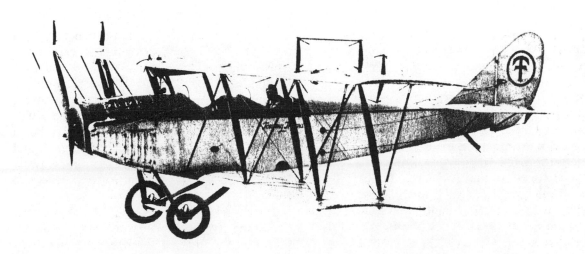

CREDIT: D.D. HATFIELD AVIATION COLLECTION

Tommy Thomas in his OX5 Jenny. Tommy co-founded the Pacific Aeromotive Corp.

Principal---Thomas H. Elson

*Roosevelt High School principal
Thomas Elson in 1924.
He frequently patronized
Radio Service Station.*

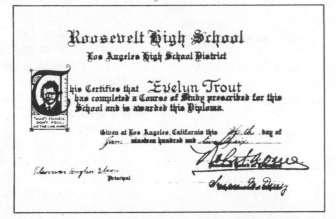

The 1926 winter graduating class. Bobbi is to the right of principal Elson, center.

After graduation from Roosevelt High School, in January 1926, her plans suffered a setback. At her mother's insistence, she registered for the architecture course at the University of Southern California. Reluctantly, she handed over two hundred dollars of her savings for tuition and entrance fees. She rationalized that maybe she could become a flying architect.

Frank Olney, Bobbi's architecture teacher at Roosevelt High School, where Bobbi was his "right-hand-man."

ROOSEVELT HIGH SCHOOL,
LOS ANGELES, CALIFORNIA,
JUNE 19, 1924.

TO WHOM IT MAY CONCERN:

EVELYN TROUT HAS BEEN A MEMBER OF MY ARCHITECTURAL DRAWING CLASS THIS SPRING AND HAS DONE SUCH EXCEPTIONAL WORK THAT I AM VERY GLAD TO RECOMMEND HER FOR ARCHITECTURAL DRAFTING.

HER WORK IS UNUSUALLY NEAT AND ACCURATE, HER LETTERING IS ARTISTIC, AND I HAVE FOUND HER VERY QUICK TO UNDERSTAND AND CARRY OUT INSTRUCTIONS.

VERY TRULY

Frank D. Troe
INSTRUCTOR,
ARCHITECTURAL DRAWING.

U.S.C. W' 1926		Shoes etc	4.25
Tuition	$146.-	Dep. on L. Key	.75
F. B.	2.60	Smock	2.-
Draw. Material	3.90	Light Bulb	.45
D.M.	7.85	Syllabus + paper	.65
Draw Set	14.50	Eraser etc	.50
Lock	.50	English book	2.60
Gym Suit	4.-	Shadows + Light	5.15
			$195.70

Bobbi's first semester's expenses at USC

She certainly enjoyed it—she had been the assistant to her architecture teacher, Mr. Frank D. Olney, all through Roosevelt High School.

It was about this time that stage and screen star Irene Castle decided to have her hair bobbed. Vernon and Irene Castle were the trendsetters of their time, until Vernon died in February 1918, in an airplane crash. The new hairstyle immediately became the rage, and Bobbi decided to have her own dark, fine locks sheared. The practicality and freedom of short, straight hair fit Bobbi's idea of a perfect hairdo. When her family and friends teased her about her new look, she quipped, "Just call me Bobbi." The nickname stuck, and soon everyone in her circle used it instead of Evelyn—which she did little to deter because she liked the breezy, modern sobriquet. Subsequently, Evelyn adopted Bobbi as her given name.

A few months later Bobbi came home to discover her mother with tear-reddened eyes and puffy eyelids. Her parents had again decided to separate. Bobbi shared her mother's pain in the days that followed. She was forced to drop her studies at University of Southern California and shoulder the responsibility of keeping the family business afloat. Since Denny was still in high school, it was obvious that the major portion of work should fall on Bobbi and the hired help. Often during the night, she would hear the sound of her mother's crying. Bobbi resolved never to let herself be caught in the trap of marriage.

Her parents decided to split the profits from the service station. Bobbi's mother paid her father for his half out of her own savings, whereupon he left for Kentucky.

At the close of 1926, time passed slowly for Bobbi and she grew restless. She continued to set aside a portion of her earnings for her dream, but her responsibilities offered very little free time, and the time she had was spent around airports.

It was in May 1927, that Bobbi celebrated with the rest of the world when a shy young man made the first solo flight across the Atlantic. She felt almost as though she had been a part of Charles Lindbergh's great and fantastic achievement. By now she identified with aviation.

Meanwhile, her father had lost all his money from the family service station at the race tracks in Kentucky. He returned to California and went to live with his mother in Anaheim. Grandmother Trout operated the Anaheim Union High School Cafeteria. It always seemed she was cooking in a business of her own, even while she leased the high school business. Bobbi's father bought a second service station, on credit. It was located at the corner of Chartress and Lemon Streets in Anaheim. The area was surrounded by orange groves, and all the growers had their own gas tanks. They sold gas to their friends at a much lower price than the competing service station. It seemed customers frequented his station for little more than to get air in their tires or for water. He laughingly referred to them as "airdales."

Bobbi had sacrificed her education in order to shoulder the responsibilities that should have fallen on her father; still, he decided to give her

Regular customer service at Bobbi's Anaheim Service Station in 1927. Service included checking the water, adding oil and putting air in the tires.

Bobbi made sure her Moon roadster received excellent care.

his Anaheim service station and all its debts. "You'll have to work very hard to make a profit at that station," her father warned Bobbi when he handed over the keys. For a few months Bobbi's parents maintained their separate residences, then reconciled, after her father turned on his personality and salesmanship.

One of Bobbi's first customers in Anaheim came into the station to put air in his tires. Bobbi took the valve cap off to put air in the tire when the customer very seriously and excitedly yelled, "Stop. You have to let the old air out before you put in the new air, or the tire will explode!" Bobbi stifled a laugh and calmed the customer down, explaining about inflating tires. Such were the strange experiences of running a gas station. There were also days when men would come in to have their oil changed, and many were afraid to drive their car up on the grease rack. It was no effort for Bobbi to drive cars up onto the grease rack—she had

Bobbi advertises for Lightning Gasoline.

Ask "Bobbie"--She Knows

"Bobbie" Trout is the young manager of a station in Anaheim selling a large quantity of Lightning every day. Bobbie is a fair young lady, popular with all the folks in Anaheim and all way stations between there and the big city.

Ask Bobbie anything about your motor, gasoline or lubricants, for Bobbie "knows her oil."

Miss Trout is earning funds with which to complete a college course. She deserves tremendous credit for the way she has taken hold and developed business, and Lightning Dealer hereby predicts a happy and successful future for her.

plenty of experience, until Trouts' Radio Service purchased and installed the second hydraulic lift in town. In later years Bobbi discovered the salesman for the lift was the father of famous test pilot Tony LeVier.

After several months of limited income from the Anaheim station, with only a small rise in both customers and profits, Bobbi had to concede her father was right. She put the Anaheim station up for sale.

After the sale was finalized, she took a long trip with her good friend, Vi Grant, and Vi's mother. Vi's father, Hugh Grant, discovered oil in Huntington Beach, and was vice-president of Julian Oil Company. Because of his responsibilities, he did not go on the trip. Bobbi returned from Vancouver, Canada, where she and the Grants had driven. She again took up her duties at the Radio Service station in Los Angeles, helping out and doing her utmost to save all money possible. She even added a body and repair shop.

With a profit of almost two thousand dollars cash from the sale of the Anaheim station, the opportunity to make her dream of flying a reality was finally at hand. She was not going to put it off one day longer. Her father was all for it. He encouraged Bobbi in her desire to learn how to fly.

Bobbi's savings had slowly grown until she had accumulated a tidy sum of about twenty five hundred dollars. She had discovered that Burdett Fuller, who owned an airport on South Western Avenue in Los Angeles, would teach a person to fly, from first flight through solo, for two hundred fifty dollars.

Almost daily, the newspapers were filled with the exploits of an aviator having performed a daring deed. Bobbi had just recently read about her distant cousin, Jimmy Doolittle, setting out on his South American tour. Each news article only increased her impatience to begin her own aviation career. It was now time to become an aviator.

Bobbi and Vi Grant riding along the beach in Santa Barbara before they returned to Los Angeles from their trip to Canada.

Mrs. Hugh Grant and Bobbi toured Buchart Gardens, Vancouver, B.C., in 1927. They stopped every few miles at the orange juice stands to cool off.

Chapter Three

Learning To Fly

THE next morning Bobbi parked her classy maroon "bug" automobile outside Burdett Air Lines, Inc., School of Aviation, South Western Avenue. Burdett's office building was next to Jack Fry's Aero Corporation flying school. She paused to enjoy the moment, inhaling the strange mixture of dust, gasoline, oil and other odors that permeate airports. She felt a sense of sureness in place.

She entered the small office and walked over to a large, tidy desk. She waited until the seated man, who appeared to be a pilot, finished totaling up a line of figures in a ledger. She took the opportunity to study her instructor-to-be.

Introducing herself to the man behind the desk, she stated her purpose. He stood up and returned the greeting. "You've come to the right place," Burdett said. "When do you want to start?" With an exchange of smiles and a handshake, he motioned for her to take a seat.

Bobbi emphatically said that she was ready to begin her lessons that day. She reached into her pocket, withdrew her checkbook, and looked at him expectantly, her pen poised above the check.

Burdett laughed. That sounded good to him, but first he wanted to explain that the instruction would be two hundred fifty dollars. Burdett said he would teach her everything she needed to know to solo. After her solo, she would have to put in ten hours of solo flight time to receive a private license. The cost of renting the airplane, after the solo, would be extra.

Bobbi stands beside her maroon "bug" in 1926.

While he explained, Bobbi made out the two hundred and fifty dollar check. When he finished, she ripped the check from her book, handed it to him, and commented, "It's a deal." Still smiling, Burdett accepted the check and asked her if she had any questions. "Just one," Bobbi said. "Can you explain to me what makes an airplane fly?"

Burdett took out a pencil and paper. He began to rapidly sketch, explaining the theory of flight. He explained that when the wind hit the front edge of a wing and flowed over the top curved part, it caused a partial vacuum. The propeller, as it screwed itself through the air, pulled the plane forward and caused the flow of air over the wings to move faster, increasing the vacuum. The wing, trying to fill the vacuum, is forced upward by the air beneath the wing. That is how Burdett explained lift.

Nick Galloway, Bobbi, and Burdett Fuller.

Burdett Field, 1927. Bobbi learned to fly from Burdett Fuller and Al Hobart, his partner.

He told her how aviator John Joseph Montgomery glided around Otay Mesa in San Diego between 1883 and 1889. Montgomery had rediscovered that the curve, or camber of an airplane wing, was the same curve that God gave to birds. Bobbi understood and they talked about it for a while.

He then told Bobbi that before they began she would have to see Dr. Theodore Lyster and get a physical examination. Then he wanted her to go see Dr. Isaac Jones for an eye examination.

Bobbi left Burdett's office and went immediately to Hollywood for her physical exam. Next she went to visit Dr. Jones to get her eyes checked. Before long she held a physical exam certificate for a transport pilot's license—the highest license at that time. By the time she returned to the airport it was late in the afternoon, and Burdett told her they would have to wait until the following day for her first lesson.

Bobbi's first day of ground school included Burdett's drawing of how an airplane flies, a medical certificate, and an introduction to Al Hobart, (top left) who helped teach her to fly, Dec. 1927.

BURDETT AIR LINES, Inc.
SCHOOL OF AVIATION
9401 SO. WESTERN AVE.
Los Angeles, Calif.

ALBERT HOBART

TRANSPORT PILOT
LICENSE NO. 1983

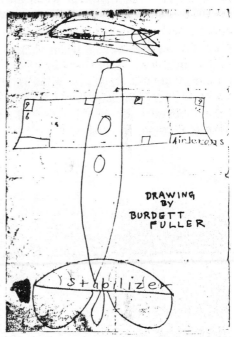

DRAWING
BY
BURDETT
FULLER

Date 12. 29. 27

This certifies that I have, this date, physically examined

Evelyn Trout

and subject to the approval of the Department of Commerce, have found him physically _____ qualified for *Transport pilot*

Theodore E. Lyster

Authorized Medical examiner
for the Department of Commerce.

On New Year's Day 1928, Bobbi was up at first light. Excited and eager, she made her way back to Burdett's airport and startled her instructor, who was about to have a cup of coffee. Her enthusiasm impressed him.

Quickly downing the last swallow of coffee, he led her out to one of his five Jennies. Being a cautious and conscientious instructor, Burdett paused before allowing her to climb aboard. He told her he wanted to make sure she understood some of the fundamentals before they started. "You may not live to a ripe old age," he told her, "if you disregard any of my instructions, even for a moment." Burdett told her to take notes and keep them in what he called a "Flier's Bible." He said a good pilot first inspects the airplane and then immediately after takeoff, checks the instruments and looks constantly for places to make an unexpected forced landing. If the engine were to conk out, she wouldn't have time to look. The plane glides like a stream-lined-brick without a running engine. If she were to lose power, Burdett told her, she must nose down immediately.

He also cautioned Bobbi to always be alert for high-tension lines, be able to glide to a landing field without engine power, and never depend on the engine to respond to the throttle. That could be the time it would surely die. "Okay," he said, "now if I haven't scared you away, let's go flying!"

Burdett had Bobbi sit in the back cockpit. He stepped up alongside Bobbi and reached for the belt to cinch her in tightly. Burdett continued to explain the controls to her and Bobbi placed her hands on them in the correct manner—left hand on the stick and right hand on the throttle. Trying to stifle a quick thrill of excitement, she glanced up at him and smiled.

"Pay attention!" he admonished her. "This may save your life, and someone else's."

Bobbi was all attention. Burdett continued his ground school, explaining that at times mechanics get the control wires mixed when working on a plane. This causes pilots to be killed because the wire controls become reversed. He paused and reemphasized the importance of going through the control movements, watching to see that the ailerons moved up and down in coordination with the stick. In

Bobbi before a lesson in Burdett's Jenny.

Bobbi in 1928 during her flight training.

flight, the ailerons in the downward position cause a greater curve and thus give more lift on that side and less on the other.

Bobbi listened to his words and watched every movement. She told him she could understand why Orville and Wilbur Wright warped the wings to make turns.

Bobbi learned how Glenn Curtiss got the idea of the hinged ailerons. She then put her feet on the bar in front of her and pushed it back and forth. She turned around and looked at the tail of the plane, seeing how the rudder moved when she pushed the rudder bar back and forth. "Oh, yes, Pop," she said as she began to understand. "Burdett," or sometimes "Pop," were the names Bobbi called Burdett Fuller from the time she first started her lessons with him. Bobbi then learned why a plane banks in a turn. It is the same reason an auto race track has turns banked highly—to keep cars from slipping away from the curve. So simple, she thought, comparing this to Ascot Speedway in Los Angeles where she enjoyed watching the auto races.

Bobbi was so busy looking and trying the controls that she stopped asking questions. Thinking and getting these bits of information well placed was going to be her every thought, twenty-four hours a day, for a long time. Finally, she noticed the flat, small part of the tail in front of the rudder and Burdett told her that it was called the fin, and that it was offset from center a bit to help take care of the airplane's torque from the propeller as it turns.

Burdett decided the controls had been explained enough for now and crawled up into the front cockpit where Bobbi could see his hands gesture that he was ready to start the engine.

A helper approached to swing the wooden prop, "Switch off!"

Bobbi, June Smith, and 2 friends at an air show in Banning, California.

Burdett answered, "Switch off."

The prop was turned several times. The assistant then called for the switch to be turned on.

"Switch on," Burdett answered. The assistant turned the prop and the engine took hold. After a little warm-up, the chocks were pulled away from the wheels and Burdett gave it full throttle. After much bumping they were airborne and smoothly gaining altitude. She was crazy about becoming a pilot, *Just Plane Crazy*.

As soon as they were airborne, Bobbi could no longer maintain her solemn façade. She was enjoying the thrill of flying too much. An exhilarating sense of freedom filled her while she lightly held the stick in her left hand. Gaining altitude, Burdett banked the plane to the right. He must have sensed her emotions for, turning in his seat, he motioned her to look downward. Below them was Inglewood Cemetery. Bobbi got the message!

On that first lesson he let her have the controls for only a short time, but Bobbi was lightly feeling the controls all the time. She had assumed control with a confidence that surprised him. They took off going west and right after the landing field were other miscellaneous fenced-in fields. To their right was the longest and best field if one had to make a forced landing.

Burdett landed at his airport. They walked back to the hangar and he continued to instruct her. "Always remember," he emphasized, "when you are flying, at any altitude, if the engine conks out—put the nose down immediately." He explained that if the nose isn't lowered, the Jenny would immediately go into a spin.

Burdett grinned and told her that he couldn't afford to lose either a student or a plane—they were too few and far between. He continued to tell her that if she were at a low altitude and the engine conked out, she should never try to make more than a quarter turn before landing. He told Bobbi it would be better to hit a barn or a fence than to try it. "Just remember the Jenny was not designed to make a full two hundred seventy-degree turn at low altitude without power—so don't try it!" Bobbi nodded seriously in agreement and made note of it in her journal. Burdett finished his lesson for the day.

During the days that followed, Bobbi was a daily visitor to the airport. She did not make it into the air every day though. It was rare that more than two of Burdett's Jennies were flyable at the same time. Burdett's partner, Al Hobart, gave her instruction too. Most of the free time, the students and licensed pilots gathered in the hangar to help repair airplanes, or to talk about the latest exploits of their fellow fliers in what was commonly called "hangar flying."

Nick Galloway (l),
(center unidentified)
and
Jim Granger (r)
in front of
Burdett's
office.

Bobbi soon gained an understanding of what flying was all about. Burdett and Al were both meticulous taskmasters, making sure Bobbi understood each phase before going on to the next. To teach them how to get into the air properly, Burdett forbade his students to use a windshield. He wanted them to feel the slipstream against their cheeks, so that they could tell whether to use more or less rudder. Since it was impossible to converse while in the air, he would bang on the top of his head—meaning "use your head." Hand gestures made up all communication because vocal instruction could not be heard over the engine noise.

There were very few instruments in the Jenny, usually just an altimeter. Some of them had oil gauges and tachometers, but never compasses. For direction they utilized the railroad tracks—calling them the "iron compass." If an airplane happened to be equipped with a compass in those days, it was called an instrument airplane. These were the days when intrepid airmen and "ladybirds" really flew by the seat of their pants. During the time Bobbi was taking lessons, a number of women enrolled at Burdett's school.

Some airplanes crashed. This did not dampen Bobbi's spirit, though. After all the years she had to wait to get the chance to fly, a few little crashes were not going to affect her decision. She expected to make a career of flying.

Bobbi, decked out in her breeches and boots, poses in front of a Waco 10.

No 5987

This is to certify that the signer of the release bearing the duplicate number of this ticket has taken an aerial sightseeing trip in one of the airplanes owned or operated by

BURDETT AIR LINES, Inc.

9401 S. Western Ave.
Los Angeles, Cal.

Pilot

A $5.00 ticket for one airplane ride.

Shortly thereafter, Bobbi enrolled in meteorology and a navigation course at the University School of Aeronautics. Bobbi was hoping that she could find a salaried flying position.

Several years later, in the middle of the Depression, Bobbi took the government examination for meteorologists. It was the first time in ten years the government had given the examination. She never dreamed she would not pass. All went well until she reached the part of the test that required the use of algebra.

Bobbi sighed in exasperation. It had been so long since she had used algebraic equations. It was impossible to solve the equations when x + y always = airplane. Bobbi did not think she was the type for an office job; she wanted to be in the air.

Chapter Four

The Big Crash

BOBBI noticed the calendar on Burdett's wall. March 15, 1928: "The Ides of March." She remembered how Miss Bessie Reaves in English Literature had drummed the date into her students' heads. Bobbi had no idea that the date would become anything other than the anniversary of Caesar's downfall.

Dale Page was an assistant instructor at the field and assigned to teach Bobbi the technique of forced landings, which in the early days were common. Gasoline tanks were typically small, and engines were far from reliable. Pilots during the '20s and '30s accepted the ill fortunes of equipment failures associated with flying as a normal, and even an expected occurrence. Still, it did not scare Bobbi away from aviation. Her friends would often work on their planes all week to fly twenty to thirty minutes on Sunday.

Bobbi pulled her helmet and goggles on and followed her instructor, Dale, out to the Jenny. She climbed into the rear seat, fastened her seat belt, and positioned herself to start the airplane.

Bobbi verified proper aileron, elevator, and rudder movement. Satisfied that the airplane was ready, Dale prepared to pull the prop through. He checked that chocks were in place and shouted out, "Switch off."

Bobbi checked to be sure the switch was off and yelled so back. Dale pulled the prop through a couple of times to prime the engine; it was standard operating procedure for starting most of the early airplanes. This was a dangerous procedure for the person swinging the prop; one mistake could cost him his life. Satisfied that the engine was primed and ready to start, Dale called to turn the switch on.

Bobbi called back, "Switch on," and turned the switch to "On." Dale pulled the prop through once more and watched carefully that the plane was being held by the chocks. The engine chugged, spit, coughed, then took hold.

While the engine idled, Dale pulled the chocks and then climbed into the front seat. He fastened his seat belt and signaled Bobbi that they were now ready to go.

She taxied down the runway to takeoff position. Checking the sky to be sure all was clear, Bobbi moved the plane into the wind and pushed forward on the throttle with her right hand, keeping her left hand on the stick to keep the wings level. Her feet operated the rudder, guiding the plane straight as it became airborne.

Bobbi and Dale slowly gained some altitude. When they were about one hundred twenty-five feet high, just past the end of the field, Dale cut the throttle.

Bobbi immediately put the nose down and started making a quarter turn to the right to come down in the largest adjacent field. She resisted her desire to make a three-quarter turn to the left in order to have the whole field on which to land. But Burdett's words on her first lesson echoed in her head: "Don't ever try to make more than a quarter turn at low altitude."

The moment she began a right turn, Dale advanced the throttle and took her back to the airstrip to land. After he turned off the engine, he turned to Bobbi and asked why she didn't make a two hundred seventy-degree turn to the left so as to have the whole field available.

Bobbi knew better. She explained Burdett's first lesson, but he thought Bobbi had misunderstood Burdett. Dale told Bobbi he would take her up again and show her the proper procedure.

Bobbi maintained that she understood Burdett, but Dale insisted that he would have to prove it to her. They restarted the airplane and took off again. Reaching the same position as before, Dale cut the throttle. Turning to the left he quickly realized that he was too low. Because he forgot to nose down, the airplane immediately entered a spin and out of control.

In the few seemingly endless seconds before impact, Bobbi's mind screamed: "You can't do it. I told you so." She had time only to draw a swift breath and brace herself for the imminent crash.

Hours later she slowly awoke. The first thing she saw was a policeman who was standing by her in a room at Inglewood Hospital.

The policeman told her that she spun in and she had a few stitches where her goggles cut into her eye area and she received a slight concussion. All in all, he said, she was a pretty lucky girl.

Concerned about Dale, Bobbi immediately asked what happened to him. The policeman assured Bobbi that he was fine. Dale had been knocked unconscious for a few minutes, but was all right. Burdett had someone take him back to the airfield, to go up again before he lost his nerve.

The policeman then chuckled. Bobbi frowned and thought there was nothing funny about the situation. Although silent, her expression must have spoken volumes because the policeman immediately stopped and began to explain.

He was thinking about the expression on two little kids' faces who saw Bobbi and Dale spin

NARROW ESCAPE— Was experienced yesterday by Evelyn Trout, 22, aviatrix, and Dale Page, 20, when plane he was attempting to land crashed from 100 feet. Above, Burdett airport attaches examining wrecked craft. Below, rear fuselage and tail, with number and identification stripped.

WHEN AN INSTRUCTOR MISCALCULATES————

L. A. Aviatrix, Pilot Escape Death as Plane Falls 100 Ft.

A 22-year-old woman student aviator and a pilot crashed 100 feet to the earth in an airplane shortly after noon today at Fifth avenue and Ninety-Fourth street.

The student, Miss Bobby Trout, of 418 South Soto street, received a gash over her left eye, for which she was treated at the Inglewood hospital. Dale Page of Arcadia, the pilot, was uninjured.

The "Jenny" plane "cracked up" as Page made a landing on an emergency field. The plane failed to make altitude after rising 100 feet in the takeoff from Burdett Air Lines field at 9401 South Western avenue, Page said, so he attempted the landing.

Bobbi first big splash in the news!

in. The kids ran out to the airplane and were first on the scene. When the policeman arrived, Bobbi and Dale were both slumped over as if they were dead. Dale then gave a low moan and sat up, kind of like a dead man rising out of his coffin. As the policeman put it, the two kids yelled and scampered off like a couple of scalded cats. Bobbi and the policeman both grinned, and she grimaced with pain. Her bandage pulled at her forehead and left eyelid. While Bobbi was being treated, her mother was at home, reading the evening edition of the Los Angeles Times. Her face suddenly paled when she read Bobbi's name under the headline, *GIRL FLYER CRASHES*.

Throwing the paper aside, she rushed down to the hospital. At Bobbi's bedside she ran her fingertips lightly over Bobbi's head to reassure herself of Bobbi's survival. Her mother was somewhat relieved to hear the doctor inform her of Bobbi's superficial injuries.

"You might have been killed!" Bobbi's mother admonished.

"Maybe," Bobbi responded, "but in that case, I'd never have known the difference —would I?"

Aviatrix Hurt in Plane Crash During Lesson

Student Suffers Concussion of Brain While Pilot Escapes Unharmed

Evelyn Trout
—Examiner photo

MISS EVELYN TROUT, 22, 412 South Soto street, student aviatrix, suffered concussion of the brain, cuts and bruises about the face yesterday when a plane from Burdett Airport, in which she was receiving instruction from Dale Page, crashed a short distance to the ground after its motor stalled.

The injured girl was hurried to the Inglewood Emergency Hospital and treated for a deep cut over the eye and later taken to her home. Page was unhurt. The plane came to earth near Fifth and Manchester streets, Inglewood.

Miss Trout's father had accompanied his daughter to the flying field with the intention of buying her a plane, it was said.

And Yet Both Live to Tell About It

What They Found After Thrilling Air Crash
N. B. Gregory and Jack E. Martin of Burdette Airport examining wrecked plane.

LUCK RIDES WITH PAIR IN AIR FALL

Pilot and Girl Student Escape Critical Injury as Plunge Wrecks Plane

Two occupants of an airplane which fell from a height of between 300 and 400 feet yesterday into a vacant lot at Fifth avenue and Arbor Vitae street, Inglewood, escaped critical injury, although the plane was demolished.

Dale Page, 20-year-old pilot employed by the Burdette Airport, 9401 South Western avenue, was teaching Miss Bobbie Trout, 418 South Soto street, the intricacies of flying when the accident occurred.

He refused medical attention, and his pupil was treated at the Inglewood Hospital for concussion of the brain and lacerations.

As the shock began to fade, Bobbi's mother remembered how she had learned of the accident. Anger surged through her as she turned toward the policeman, asking why she had not been informed in person. It did seem an oversight on the part of his department, but having her daughter alive, and in relatively good shape, considering the circumstances, quieted her accusations.

Bobbi's mother tried to convince her that her flying days were over. Bobbi, however, insisted that she was still determined to earn her license and continue to fly. If Bobbi insisted on flying, then her mother thought she was going to have a more modern airplane. Remembering how Bobbi told her that the Jenny glides like a streamlined brick and that they were used in 1917-1918 to train pilots for the World War, Bobbi's mother intended to get Bobbi out of the Jennies.

Burdett came into Bobbi's hospital room later, and Bobbi's mother talked to him about helping her find a more modern machine. Burdett owned an International Aircraft Corporation biplane, the International, which was powered by a Curtiss K-6 engine and it was for sale.

Bobbi had seen the International K-6 in the hangar and admired it. She knew Burdett made good money when he flew newsmen over the Saint Francis Dam after it broke. It was a four-place airplane, and Bobbi's head filled with business possibilities. She lay back quietly and watched her mother continue to debate with Burdett about the Jenny's safety.

A short while after Bobbi's visitors had to leave, a red-headed, lanky young man appeared around the edge of the door. Bobbi recognized the familiar face; it was June Smith.

June Smith, a good friend to Bobbi, who watched over her during her flight training days.

She got to know him during the many afternoons at the airfield. He was a good friend and pilot who also had at one time experienced a bad accident. June was very watchful and protective of Bobbi.

June would later grow romantically attracted to Bobbi, though she resisted involvement with him and other men friends. After her parents' turbulent relationship, Bobbi chose to immerse herself in aviation and avoid romantic relationships.

She liked June a lot, but for her, friendship with him was more important. June knew Bobbi was a good pilot and wondered why they had spun in. Bobbi told him that Dale decided the Jenny could make a complete two hundred seventy-degree turn at one hundred feet. It

surely was a hard way to be proven wrong. June and Bobbi discussed the Jenny some more before the nurse came in and told June he would have to leave. Bobbi's begging for June to stay did no good.

The next morning Bobbi's mother returned, bringing the previous day's evening paper. She pointed out the article about Bobbi's crash: *GIRL FLYER HURT AS PLANE FALLS.* "Wouldn't you know it?" Bobbi thought. "They never get anything right. Always blaming the woman."

Bobbi's mother had brought the paper hoping it would convince her daughter that an airplane was no place for a woman. Instead, Bobbi now seemed more determined than ever to be an aviatrix.

Bobbi's solo certificate; a dream come true.

June Smith and Bobbi on their way to a Banning Air Meet.

Bobbi felt her depth perception was impaired, and with one eye bandaged, did not attempt to fly or even drive her "bug" automobile. For two weeks while her cuts were healing, she worked around the service station. When the bandages were off, she resumed her normal schedule of flying whenever there was a Jenny available.

Six weeks later, on April 30, 1928, Burdett instructed Bobbi to taxi to the hangar. He jumped out and turned to her, "Okay, Bobbi, take her up."

A wide grin split her face. Taxiing back to the strip, she took off. She made a short ten minute flight around the field and then a perfect landing. A feeling of complete joy filled her as she hopped down from the cockpit, knowing she had done it at last—she had flown by herself. She was now a pilot. The time was 6:55 p.m., April 30, 1928.

Bobbi completed her after-flight logbook entries and gazed fondly at the Jenny for a moment. She turned, watching Burdett and June Smith walk up to her.

June congratulated her with a big bear hug. Bobbi was all smiles. Burdett also congratulated her, then reminded her that she still had to complete ten hours of flying time before she could take her private pilot's license test.

Within a two-week period of time she had logged the ten hours and then made a flight around the field with a government examiner, who gave her the official okay. She was now a full-fledged pilot. He issued Bobbi private pilot license number 2613. This was a very low number compared to today's huge numbers.

The first page of Bobbi's logbook.

Chapter Five

The International K-6

BODDI'S mother purchased Burdett's International K-6 for her in the spring of 1928. About this same time, Amelia Earhart became the first woman to make a transatlantic flight when she, Wilmer Stultz, and Lou Gordon flew from Newfoundland to Wales on June 17.

Bobbi's first flight in the International K-6 was on June 21, and it lasted only thirty minutes. The K-6 was much larger than the Jennies and Bobbi knew becoming accustomed to it would take practice. She often took her friends for rides. One of her special friends, Dick Costello, comptroller of Wurlitzer Music Company in Los Angeles, often flew with her. He often took Bobbi to dinner.

Bobbi diligently continued to perfect her skills in the International K-6, flying out of Burdett's field on the hot summer days. She watched, along with the rest of the aviation cadre, while a barley field, known as Mines Field, was converted within two months into an airfield with three seven thousand-foot paved runways and a grandstand. The site, which is now Los Angeles International Airport, had to be completed in time for the National Air Races, which were scheduled to run from September 8 through 16 of 1928.

Advance publicity promoted the fact that both Charles Lindbergh and Amelia Earhart were scheduled to appear, along with other notable aviators. This event was the first big air show organized by Bobbi's friend and aviation promoter, Cliff Henderson.

1928 National Air Races Program

Bobbi had high hopes of meeting both Lindbergh and Amelia. She did manage to get an introduction to Lindbergh before he led the three musketeers, The Blue Angels of that era, in fantastic maneuvers during the meet. She was not so lucky however, in her efforts to meet Amelia. That day would come later.

Not long after the air show, Bobbi felt quite comfortable at the controls of the International K-6, and began to look for business ventures to help fund the airplane's expenses. She was contacted by a representative from the May Company department store. They wanted to display her airplane in an aviation exhibit. The K-6 was hoisted onto the Los Angeles department store's roof, and the airplane quickly became the most popular of the entire show, mainly because it was owned by a woman.

The exposure at the display created opportunities for more sponsorships. Sunset Oil Company, which had been the vendor used at the family service station, offered Bobbi aircraft fuel and oil in exchange for permission to paint its logo on the side of her International K-6. She accepted the offer.

GIRL FLIER HONORED

Miss Bobby Trout, said to be the youngest girl flyer on the Pacific coast, who was one of the honor guests at a dinner party last week given by Mr. and Mrs. Emery Kann, of 448 Rialto avenue, Venice, for the officials of the Masters Aircraft Corporation of Los Angeles. Others present were Mr. and Mrs. Jeff Warren, Mr. and Mrs. "Bon" McDougal, Mr. and Mrs. "Burdette" Fuller and Nixon Galloway. Miss Trout has entered her K-6 International plane in the races at Mines Field this week.

An early recognition given to Bobbi in 1928.

Bobbi's first airplane, a four-place International K-6

MAY CO. TO HOLD AIRPLANE EXHIBIT

Dick Costello learned to fly along with Bobbi at Burdett's flight school.

Photo shows Miss Bobby Trout, owner and pilot of the International, one of planes to be exhibited on the roof of The May Co. next week. This plane is entered in the national air races to be held at Mines field.

What is declared to be the first store exhibit of airplanes and airplane equipment ever held on the Pacific coast will open next week, beginning Tuesday, on the roof garden at the May company.

Every care is being taken to turn the roof garden into an authentic air field. Airport beacons and lighting equipment are now being installed to add to the atmosphere.

Six racing ships, all of which are entered in the national air races, are included in the exhibit, as are many interesting war and post-war trophies.

The uncovered Nieuport fuselage of the ship used by Captain Nungesser on his American tour, a German silk parachute used during the war and a relief model of Mines field, where the national air races are to be held, will be included in the exhibit.

According to Wilbur May, under whose direction the exhibit is being conducted and who is himself a licensed pilot and plane owner, it is the endeavor of the May company to pioneer in the linking of mercantile commerce with the progress of aviation in Los Angeles.

"The time is not far off," he said, "when planes will, in reality, be 'taking-off' and 'landing' on the specially arranged roofs of downtown stores.

"This exhibit is being held in the interest of one of the world's rapidly growing industries and shows the infinite possibilities in the immediate future of using the plane as a common carrier."

SIS
LOVE
DICK

Bobbi and her K-6, advertising for the May Company.

Race Entrant

Miss "Bobby" Trout competitor in the international air races here, will be on hand to answer questions at the May Company's airplane exhibit opening Tuesday. She is shown in the latest in fashion as worn by the smart aviatrix.

AIRPLANES EXHIBIT TO BE OPENED

Local Store Plans One of First Shows of Kind to Start Tuesday

One of the first store exhibits on the western coast showing actual airplanes and airplane equipment is

Miss "Bobby" Trout and her plane, the International, who will attend May Company exhibit attired in fashionable clothes for aviation.

AVIATRIX IN SMART 'TOGS OF AIR' TO ATTEND MAY CO. PLANE SHOW

Articles on the May Company exhibit.

now being arranged to take place next week, beginning Tuesday, on the Roof Garden at the May Company where six racing ships, entries in the national air races, will be on display.

According to Wilbur May, who is himself a licensed pilot and plane owner, it is an endeavor on the part of the May Company to pioneer in the linking of mercantile commerce with the steady progress of aviation in Los Angeles.

Among the race planes on exhibit will be the International, owned and piloted by Miss "Bobby" Trout. Miss Trout will be on hand during the week to answer questions.

Other planes on exhibit will be a Thunderbird, three-place biplane, made in Glendale, a three-place biplane Swallow and a three-place monoplane Simplex Red-Arrow. Airplane motors, parts and accessories will also be shown. Airport beacon and lighting equipment is installed by the General Electric Corporation.

Many interesting war and postwar trophies will be included in the exhibit.

Six Racing Machines to Be Exhibited on Roof of Large Downtown Department Store

Six racing airplanes, all of them entries in the national air races to be held at Mines field here next month, will be exhibited in one of the first store shows of its kind on the roof of the May Company all of next week, it was announced today by Wilbur May, who is himself a pilot and plane owner, and director of the show.

The project is an endeavor upon the part of the May Company to pioneer in the linking of commerce with the steady progress of aviation in Los Angeles, May said.

"The time will soon come," he said, "when airplanes will be taking off and landing on specially constructed roofs of metropolitan stores. This exhibition will show the possibilities of using the airplane as a common carrier in speeding up fashions, store news and special orders."

Among the planes to be shown is the International, owned and piloted by Miss "Bobby" Trout, well known aviatrix. Miss Trout will also be seen "in the latest thing for the smart aviatrix."

Others to be shown are the Thunderbird, three-place biplane, built in Glendale; the three-place Swallow, a three-place Simplex Red Arrow, and a full assortment of equipment, both new and old.

Included in the exposition will be German silk parachutes used during the war, the uncovered Nieuport fuselage of the ship used by Captain Nungesser on his American tour and a relief map of Mines field.

To complete the aeronautical atmosphere, the General Electric Corporation is installing airport beacon and lighting equipment.

THOUSANDS VIEW MAY'S AIR EXHIBIT

Small boys gazed in awe at a slim youth in white riding breeches today who stood by an orange biplane. It was on the roof of the May company and one of the principal features of the store's aviation exhibit on the roof now.

Then the youth smiled and turned out to be a "she"—namely one Miss Bobbie Trout, owner and pilot of the plane.

Miss Trout is 22, diminutive and pretty and knows her air groceries.

She took to the air the first of the year. She holds a private pilot's license and is now waiting for her commercial license.

She plans to fly in the national air races September 8 to 16 at Mines' field.

Bobbie is intensely enthusiastic about flying. She knows more about engines than most flappers know about parties.

The May company exhibit is a preliminary to the Mines' field affair. Thousands are viewing it daily. There are six planes on the roof which probably will enter the national races.

Anything you want to know about air trips ask it there. How do you climb into a cockpit? Will you get dizzy? What's the most graceful way to fall out of a plane? What do they keep in air pockets?

There are pilots to explain everything you don't know about planes. Lieutenant H. H. Ogden, round-the-world flier, is on hand ready to answer multitudinous questions about his trip.

All the latest modes in what's what for the air in planes are on exhibit.

There's a Simplex Red Arrow, a Thunderbird, a Steerman, the Swallow and a Monocoupe besides the Miss Bobbie Trout.

There are two engines identical to the one used by Lindbergh in his Atlantic flight. There are goggles, helmets and medals and trophies of all kinds in the display.

Advertising for the May Company.

CREDIT: DICK COSTELLO

Bobbi in her suede flying suit, 1928/1929

Bobbi's first letter home (3 page letter) during her Golden Eagle demonstration tour.

Central Hotel — Palm Springs
5:30 P.M.

Dearest Mother & family, —

still here - I expected to fly to Calexico this afternoon but one Mag was giving trouble and I came back while I could. I shall start in the A.M. tho — Mr. Gray says that I should do some good there.

I phoned Mr. Bone a while ago and he said to come back Sat. nite.

Gee, Mother but I surely do miss home - this dirty hotel business is the bunk — I guess I am too particular but I am always so skeptical of the public places. Tell Dad he should come

I rode a beautiful horse a little while this morning.

How is baby? Dad, how are the toes? Oh, by the way, I certainly ran a beautiful cactus into my foot while riding this morning — the horse ran by the cactus and about 6 of the needles ran thru my boot and into my foot - I had to take my boot off and Mr. Brown (owner of the horses) pulled them out of my foot 'cause they were in so tight I couldn't — I'm all right now tho so don't get excited.

Well, Dears, see you Sat. nite and do hope you're not having too many pitched battles while I'm left out. Lots of love
Bob

here and stay at the Desert Inn. It is the largest Inn in the world. Cottages from $8.50 to $360. a nite is all - a regular Bradstreet & Dunn where one can play the board of trade and everything. The lady who owns it owns nearly the whole town including the Mountain back of us.

I have several people interested in my plane but no sure buyers yet. Mr. Bowling left for Kingman Arizona this morning with two passengers and won't be back 'till tomorrow, I guess.

How is Grandmother? Is Jess' there? Tell her 'hello' if she is.

Dearest all; —

I have said all I know on the other paper but I will say that you must not worry about a thing. See?

I looked for you when I circled back over the field this afternoon but could not see you.

I started to bed this evening and the sheets hadn't been changed so I had to have them remake my bed.

Lots of love,
Bob

Bobbi's letter home on her second night of the tour.

The recognition also brought an even greater opportunity. After a contracted ferry flight, she parked the airplane and finished her after-landing logbook entries. She noticed a wiry looking middle-aged man walking toward her. He smiled, lifted his hat politely, and extended his hand in greeting. He introduced himself as R.O. Bone, builder of the Golden Eagle monoplane, at the R.O. Bone Company, in Inglewood.

Bobbi had seen his little red and gold monoplane flying over the area and had wanted to take a closer look. Bobbi was excited and overjoyed when Bone told her that was precisely why he had come over to meet her. He said he needed a good pilot to show the Golden Eagle around the country and was sure Bobbi was the one to do it. He offered to pay her thirty dollars a week and all expenses.

When asked how soon she could start, Bobbi remembers that she grinned mischievously and replied, "Would today be soon enough?" She was talking Bone's kind of language and immediately accepted the job. To her, it was a dream come true.

Her first job, though, was to spend several weeks at the factory learning about laminated spars, ribs, types of wing curve, bays, stations and all the other intricacies of manufacturing the Golden Eagle. Her service station experience and perseverance of staying in the all-boys wood shop classes in grammar schools was now paying off. Bobbi quickly learned the concepts and procedures used in the factory, and she soon was performing flying demonstrations of the little high-winged monoplane.

Bobbi flew the Golden Eagle in the official dedication of the Los Angeles Metropolitan Airport, which is now Van Nuys Airport. She flew the Golden Eagle to a first-place finish in the race that December 14.

Bobbi remembers a clear and sunny day in 1928, when she flew the Golden Eagle to Palm Springs. After showing off the plane she flew over the desert near the Salton Sea, when she noticed deep tire tracks in the sand next to the water's edge below leading to a downed aircraft. She decided to offer help—and brought her little Golden Eagle to earth, taxiing up beside the huge, high-wing monoplane,

R.O.Bone, owner and builder of the Golden Eagle, with Bobbi, his new demonstration pilot.

called the Albatross. Suddenly she saw a man with a shotgun emerge from around the tail of the aircraft. Bobbi's hands went up in the universal sign of peace, until she recognized who it was.

Joe Nikrent laughed heartily. He told her he was only guarding the ship and looking for ducks until the air cooled off. The plane was under-powered and they could not fly in that air. John Guglielmetti and Charles Bocheville, the pilots, would be there to fly the Albatross home and give up their endurance flight. Bobbi's help was not needed, so she turned her little aircraft to the south and took off.

The man she had just left was the official timer for the Fédération Aéronautique Internationale (F.A.I.). He installed the barograph,

Bobbi with 60-hp Golden Eagle at Metropolitan Airport at Van Nuys, in December, 1928. Picture taken after Bobbi won the women's race at the official opening.

Early 1928—Employees at the Golden Eagle factory, Industrial Street, Inglewood, Ca. From left: R.O. Bone, unidentified, Bobbi, unidentified, Roy Russell, Joe Harrison, and tall designer Mark Campbell, is ninth from left.

Golden Eagle experimental model with a 60-hp Le Blond engine.

a machine which records the elevations the airplane has been flying, and whether or not the airplane had made any landings. It was required in all aircraft attempting record-breaking flights. Any plane attempting to break a record, had to land at the same airport it took off from, in order for the flight to be declared official.

Bobbi enjoyed flying the Golden Eagle, and she became very knowledgeable about its construction. She was an enthusiastic and convincing ambassador for Bone and the Golden Eagle. Weeks began to pass with uneventful regularity, broken only by meetings of the fledgling women pilots' groups. Her days were spent flying the Golden Eagle on demonstration trips or, when such flights were unscheduled, putting on a pair of coveralls and going to work in the factory. She became an accomplished mechanic, doing everything from covering the wings with linen, to putting the substance they called "dope" on the linen to coat and harden it.

Between her various trips to demonstrate the aircraft and her work at the factory, when not flying, Bobbi's International K-6 sat unused at the Walter M. Murphy Aircraft Airfield at Atlantic Boulevard and Telegraph Road in Los Angeles, not far from her home and the family service station.

Bobbi considered selling the International K-6, but it was not until Glen Bolling phoned to ask about purchasing the airplane that she gave it serious consideration. Bobbi sold the K-6 to Bolling that day.

A few weeks later she read in the newspaper that Bolling had crashed the International K-6. He had apparently taken some friends on a gold mine hunt in the Arizona desert and had overloaded the K-6 with promising samples. He tried to take off in the hot air, but the overloaded aircraft could not clear the high-tension lines at the end of the field. No one was seriously hurt; however, the K-6, a plywood airplane, was totaled.

Aviation in L.A. Area During 1920's

HOW THE USED AIRCRAFT PARTS BUSINESS STARTED

The following historical data and reproductions were compiled by D.D. Hatfield and are in the book titled "Los Angeles Aeronautics 1920 - 1929" published by Northrop University Press.

In September, 1925, a lone "Jenny" heading south over the Tehachapi mountains was struggling for altitude attempting to clear the summit before continuing the relatively easy remaining trip to Clover Field, Santa Monica, California. The pilot, Arrigo Balboni, was thinking of the $100.00 he would receive for bringing his airplane to the air meet to be held on September 27, 1925, for the first annual anniversary of the first Around-the-World flight by the U.S. Army fliers in 1924.

His pleasant thoughts were cut short by a sudden silence as the engine sputtered and quit. Having little altitude above the mountainous terrain he had no choice but to set it down in the nearest open space which he did with little damage to the plane but in a position impossible to fly out of if he could repair the damage.

Having no money and his only airplane cracked up on a mountain top dampened his spirits considerably, but as events later proved, the wreck was to be the direct cause of the start of a large and profitable business.

Balboni hitch-hiked to Santa Monica and told his sad tale to all pilots who would listen but the best offer he had was from Al Wilson who offered him $50.00 for the wreck provided he would deliver it to Wilson at Santa Monica. Borrowing enough money to rent a truck he brought the dismantled plane to town but before delivering it to Al Wilson he decided to try for a better offer. Knowing many airplane owners needed various parts, he sold the entire plane part by part and found he had collected $900.00. As the Jenny had cost him $350.00 originally the large profit convinced him there were excellent prospects in selling used airplane parts. He immediately bought another wrecked plane for $50.00 and had no trouble in selling $150.00 worth of parts in a short time and he was in business.

Requiring a space from which to operate and store his stock

ARRIGO BALBONI
......*The flying junk man*

he settled in a vacant space of the Los Angeles River bed at 1543 Riverside Drive in Los Angeles where he intended to stay until asked to move or until he had enough money to buy a location. However, he was to remain there for many years. He built a warehouse with an open-air penthouse on top for living quarters.

A visitor was always welcome to the yard and was usually greeted with a glass of wine and a request to sign the "Gold Book" a guest book which eventually contained the names of most of the famous pilots of that time. Balboni's attire was usually "Plus Fours" golf knickers, no socks, sleeveless undershirt and a wristwatch worn above his elbow.

Balboni, known to his many friends in the flying fraternity as the "Flying Junkman", was born in Renazzo, Italy, August 20, 1893. He came to America with his parents at the age of 12. He learned to fly from Silas Christofferson at Redwood City, California in 1916 and served with the Army Air Corps during the first World War. In 1919 he purchased a Jenny and barnstormed through the west. In 1921 he was employed by the U. S. Treasury Department as a prohibition agent from which he

resigned in 1923 to resume the less hazardous occupation of barnstormer.

News of his collection soon spread far and wide resulting in orders for airplane parts from all over the United States and many foreign countries. He sold fuel tanks to Brazil, propellers and motors to the northern states to be used on snow sleds, complete wrecked airplanes to motion picture companies for movie sets and many airplane parts to individuals to be used for mementos. Up to 1930 Balboni had bought more than 200 abandoned planes.

All was not serene on the river bed as at one time a fire destroyed most of his stock and at another time the Los Angeles River flooded and washed away many wings and fuselages.

He later moved everything to a location near Corona, California, but a short time afterwards he was killed in an automobile accident and was buried at Sawtelle by the Aviator's Post of the American Legion whom he had served for many years as Sergeant at Arms.

He had never had a bank account having paid all his transactions with cash and after his death no assets were found. Neither has the Gold Book ever been found.

The "Flying Junkman" – Arrigo Balboni, examines a part of his inventory of used airplane parts. Balboni turned what could have been financial disaster for him into a profitable parts business by selling the parts of his wrecked Jenny at a large profit after he crashed the aircraft in September, 1925.

Aviation hi-lights in the 1920's

Bobbi later heard about her old International K-6 from an eccentric junk dealer named Arrigo Balboni. Known as "The Flying Junk Man," Balboni greeted visitors to his junkyard with a glass of wine and a request to sign his "Gold Book," a guest book that eventually contained the names of most of the famous pilots of that time.

In his usual attire of golf knickers, no socks, sleeveless undershirt and a wristwatch worn above his left elbow, Balboni told Bobbi that he had acquired the wreckage of the International K-6 from Bolling. It had been sold for parts.

Bobbi after a flight, 1929.

Bobbi in front of Lindbergh's Ryan Brougham in Long Beach, California, 1928.

Chapter Six

Shattering and Setting World Records

WHEN Bobbi drove past Murphy Airfield, she looked for her International K-6, even though she knew it would not be there. She felt sad about the International K-6's fate. Between her flying and the service station, Bobbi had little time for anything else.

Christmas of 1928 was near. Bone came over to Bobbi in the factory and asked if she could keep this airplane aloft long enough to beat Viola Gentry's eight-hour endurance record. Positive she could, Bobbi enthusiastically replied, "Give me the plane, gas, and oil, and I'll stay up as long as it will let me!" Bone laughed and commented how glad he was Bobbi was working for him instead of one of his competitors. Wanting to retain the record, Bobbi asked him if she could have other tries at regaining the record if someone else bettered it. He agreed and they sealed the bargain with a handshake.

Bone, however, had some second thoughts about asking Bobbi to take the risk. The next day, while additional gas tanks were being fitted to the plane's forward section, he came up to her with a worried expression on his face. He told her that he had been thinking about the flight, and it seemed to him that twelve hours was a long time to be up in a plane by herself. Bobbi assured Bone not to worry. "Once I make up my mind to do something," she said, "I do it, or know the reason why." This was an opportunity for both of them to benefit from making a new record. The advertising would be great. Bobbi was going to give it her all.

Soon after Bobbi had become Bone's demonstration and test pilot, she wore a black leather jacket, heavy wool sweater, a tight pair of warm wool breeches, and her boots.

On January 2, 1929, before the sun came up and the morning chill had been broken, Bobbi Trout took off from Van Nuys Airport on a flight that would not end until it was dark again. The start was six twenty-five in the morning and she did not land until twelve hours and eleven minutes later.

The crew had been very secretive about this flight until after Bobbi was in the air. When she took off, only factory personnel, Joe Nikrent, the official timer, and Bobbi's family were present.

After a long takeoff run in the dark, the plane was airborne. It felt sluggish and harder than usual for Bobbi to control. The weight from the extra gasoline demanded an extremely sensitive touch at the controls. As the day wore on, and the fuel level dropped with usage, she was able to gain altitude. If she relaxed even for a minute, the aircraft would venture any direction except straight ahead.

Prominently Speaking

By J. E. P.

BOBBIE TROUT, W'26

SHE took a hair cut in 1924 and since then it's been "Bobbie". No doubt "Evelyn" was a good name, but it didn't mix well with her course in auto-mechanics and architecture. The change was made in spite of the fact, that, adding the suffix "dy" to the last three letters of her christened signature would produce a resemblance to her flying inspiration, the former "Lone Eagle."

Bobbie has been "up in the air" since the first day she wore overalls to kindergarden. When the school principal told her she could not take "woodshop" for the third period, she flew into a tailspin and broke the dishes in the "cooking" class, demolished four sewing machines in "dressmaking," and put glue on the typewriter keys. By the time the police arrived, she had graduated.

The writer was shown early pages of the "scrap" book from which Bobbie reconstructed the above incidents and property.

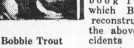

Bobbie Trout

Students of Roosevelt who knew her when she attended high school will recall that she was the first and only member of her class to receive the Girls' A. C. emblem. The felt stars, which showed the number of hours overtime spent in a given sport, had to be ordered in dozen lots, so Bobbie cooperated with the purchasing department and entered every athletic contest in the arena. In 1926, she hopped into a red, gold, and blue bathing suit and joined the swimming team. For bringing up more oysters, goldfish, tin-cans, and peanut shells from Lincoln Park lake than any other R.H.S. mermaid, she was elected president of the organization and thus became the original neptune's daughter."

Bobbie Trout's final term at high school found her Vice-president of the Senior class. Graduation came in February 1926, and the recorders' Alumni book is not yet settled as to whether the class contained 74 or 75 boys.

Operating a service station is quite a job especially when there is a war on and you haven't a gas mask, so Bobbie enrolled in the architectural school at U. S. C. where her mind was undecided as to pursuing the building trade or refueling planes.

After a year of squares and drawing boards, she exchanged the University for a landing field and became one of the greatest flyers of her sex.

Bobbie's air experiences date back to 1922 when she took her first ride with both feet off the ground. Following that trip, her parents had a difficult time keeping her from jumping off of downtown buildings with an umbrella for a parachute.

After four months of instructions, she soloed for ten hours and received her private license, "which showed that she could keep silent for that length of time without even alking to herself.

In 1928, Bobbie obtained a commercial license while piloting her own ship and was soon connected with a large air-plane constructions corporation, serving as their demonstrator. Prospective buyers were at first skeptical about taking a trip with a girl-pilot, but when her ability was once established, the firm couldn't produce the planes rapidly enough.

A transport license, one of the few issued to women, was awarded Bobbie in 1929, and in November of that year, she and Eleanor Smith got into a huddle and established the women's

(Continued on page 3, column 1)

Bobbie Trout Visits

Miss Bobbie Trout (below) phenomenal 19-year-old girl flier, stopped last night in the Biltmore to visit Mr. and Mrs. R. Skofield while making a flight from Los Angeles to San Francisco in a Golden Eagle monoplane. Miss Trout holds the world record for sustained flight for women, which is 12 hours and 11 minutes. She will continue her journey this morning, stopping in Santa Maria and San Luis Obispo.

BOBBIE TROUT
(Continued from page two)

with a total of 42 hours away from "terra firma." They were forced to land when the lettuce dropped out of a cheese sandwich which was being sent up to them.

When Bobbie is not riding through the air, she is talking on it. A local radio station recently broadcasted her flying advise over the microphone—which fact reminds us that she also has a Radio operator's License.

Bobbie says her life work will be devoted to refueling records, establishing a box-lunch factory for endurance flyers, and abolishing all dressmaking firms.

Nothing provokes her daughter more, Mrs. Trout told the writer, than recieving gifts of a feminine nature and Bobbie herself adds that her friends should consider the trouble connected with exchanging ear-rings, beaded bags, and necklaces, for bow-ties, flashlights, and collar-buttons when her birthday comes around.

Some publicity on Bobbi's endurance flight.

Bobbi fought through the lonely hours, never easing up on the plane's controls, which increased her fatigue. As sunset approached she continued to circle over the San Fernando Valley, knowing that she had long ago passed Viola Gentry's eight-hour record. She had to be sure to stay close to the Van Nuys Airport. In order to make her endurance record official, she had to land at the same field from which she had taken off.

After twelve hours in the air, Bobbi knew there wasn't much gasoline left in the wing tanks. Night was upon her and she didn't want to make a dead stick landing in the dark. On the field below were just enough lights to make out the landing strip, and Bobbi brought the little aircraft in for a smooth landing. She had set a new solo endurance record for women, topping Viola Gentry's record by four hours, and made her first night landing.

A crowd of raucous, excited, and noisy people converged on her. Her brother, Denny, was among the first to reach her and enveloped her in a bear hug, and yelled excitedly, "You did it! You did it! Even without the help of your kid brother."

The congratulatory yells and hugs of family, friends, and strangers alike crowded around her vanished her fatigue. Flash bulbs began to pop and Bone, with the aid of Joe Harrison, the company's mechanic, began to exert some control on the frenzied crowd, making way for news reporters and photographers. Bobbi stood patiently for over an hour answering questions fired at her by the newsmen. After an hour, Bobbi laughed tiredly. She gestured at the starlit heavens and pressed her fingertips into the tense muscles in her neck.

The crowd then escorted Bobbi into the Airport Cafe, not far away from the landing strip. The autographing kept her so busy she had time to eat very little.

Denny then invited friends to their house for another party. They all climbed into automobiles and made the hour-long trek back to Los Angeles. At the Trouts' home they were joined by neighbors—a party was soon in full swing. It was hours before the last well-wishers left and Bobbi was finally able to crawl into bed.

As she slept, the early morning editions of the Los Angeles papers went on the stands. *AVIATRIX BREAKS WOMEN'S ENDURANCE FLIGHT MARK*, the headlines read. Further down the front page, another headline read, *QUESTION MARK STILL UP IN THE AIR*. The United States Army Air Service flew a Fokker Tri-Motor named the *QUESTION MARK* at the same time Bobbi was up. The U.S. Army Air Service was making the longest successful military refueling endurance record of the time. When Major Carl Spatz, the commander in charge of the *QUESTION MARK*'s crew learned of Bobbi's record, he wrote a note to Bobbi while the Fokker circled the Van Nuys Airport.

CREDIT: R. O. BONE

Bobbi took off in the dark at the start of her first solo endurance flight. It was also her first night landing.

Remains Aloft Over 12 Hours

Breaks Women's Mark— Miss Bobbie Trout, 18, landed her tiny Golden Eagle monoplane at Metropolitan airport last night after remaining in air 12 hours, 11 minutes. Exclusive photos show Miss Trout at controls and as plane appeared in flight.

L. A. Girl Flyer, 18, Breaks Endurance Flight Records

Setting a new world's record for sustained flight by a woman, Miss Bobby Trout, 18-year-old Los Angeles aviatrix, remained in the air for 12 hours and 11 minutes yesterday.

The flight, from dawn to dark, started at the Metropolitan airport, near Van Nuys, at 6:25:03 a.m. The girl made a perfect landing in the dark at 6:36:03 p.m. A piercing beacon light guided her onto the field. She did not appear greatly tired, and stood in the cockpit of her Golden Eagle plane to wave to the large crowd that had gathered.

"I kept waiting for the gasoline to run out," Miss Trout said. "I knew it would at any time, but when it didn't I came down."

LITTLE GAS LEFT

Only a few gallons of fuel remained in the plane's tanks and the diminishing supply would not have sustained her for the intended flight of 15 hours.

over the airport.

The former unofficial record of 9 hours and 6 minutes, set by Viola Gentry at Mitchel Field, N. Y., was equaled during the afternoon. The Los Angeles aviatrix was assured of a new mark when she stayed up the required one hour longer, which ended at 4:31:03 p.m.

LICENSED PILOT

The aviatrix, a firm-jawed, pleasant young woman, had 101 hours flying before starting her endurance test. She is a licensed pilot and has a limited license which permits commercial flying within 10 miles of the field from which she takes off.

She attended the University of Southern California for two years, studying architecture, before deciding to take up aviation. She learned to fly in a Jenny, in which she crashed from a height of 2. She had eight stitches taken above her eye after the drop.

MESSAGE FROM 'Q'

Army flyers in the plane Question Mark, making a sustained flight over Southern California, dropped a congratulatory message for Miss Trout, to be relayed here from San Diego.

The note, written before she landed, read:

"The crew of the Question Mark sends warmest regards to the woman endurance flyer and hopes she will set a high record for others to aim at."

More newspaper articles on Bobbi's endurance flight.

U. S. ARMY AIR SERVICE REFUELLING MISSION

PERSONNEL
Major Carl Spatz
Capt. Ira C. Eaker
Lieut. H. A. Halverson
Lieut. Elwood Quesada
Sergt. Roy W. Hooe

Tri-motored Fokker *"QUESTION MARK"*

On board the *"Question Mark"*
over Southern California

January _____ 1929

_____ day of flight

Crew of Q.M. sends warmest congratulation... women endurance fliers. We ... ship the Q.M. ... she will set a high record for others to climb for

Carl Spatz

A congratulatory letter from Major Carl Spatz, organizer and Commander of the miltary refueling endurance flight, named the "? mark."

Miss Bobby Trout, 19, with her mother and brother at Los Angeles after she broke world's endurance record for women, flying over 12 hours.

The Golden Eagle and Bobbi Trout became familiar sights to the public and coverage of her feat spread throughout the world via newsreels and newspapers. She discovered there was an adverse side to being a celebrity when requests for her presence at banquets, lectures, and other such functions became so frequent that they interfered with her work schedule. She enjoyed the small taste of fame, however, and carried on with her life.

She and Bone sat in his office sifting through the stacks of congratulatory messages a few days later. Bone told Bobbi how he had received several requests for more information about the Golden Eagle. Bone was excited and knew he would be receiving additional orders. He was so delighted that he told Bobbi of his plans to begin work on a new model. He wanted to get a new engineering designer from Douglas Aircraft to redesign the airplane.

All the planes Bone first built were experimental and not licensed to sell. Bone engaged the services of F.M. Smith, Ed Heinemann,

and two other men from Douglas to redesign the Golden Eagle. Bobbi would never forget the evening in the spring of 1929, when she dropped by the R.O. Bone Company factory and met a man named Ed. Little did she know that young Ed Heinemann would one day become one of the most famous aircraft designers in aeronautical history, designing attack aircraft for Donald Douglas.

Douglas had gained a reputation as a top-flight aircraft designer in September 1924, when a team of Americans in matching Douglas World Cruisers successfully completed the first round-the-world flight. Bobbi smiled at Bone. Bone's reference to Douglas had brought to mind the pilots on that famous flight. One of them had been Lowell Smith, a fellow Californian who had, shortly before the round-the-world flight, been the first of two military pilots to be refueled in mid-air. With the aid of a refueling device, Smith and John Richter remained aloft more than thirty-seven hours in August 1923.

A congratulatory telegram from Viola Gentry, the first woman to hold a flight endurance record.

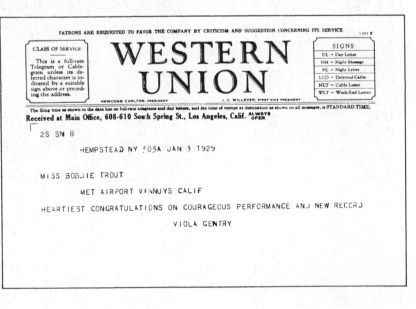

Aviatrix Finds Gift 'Timely' in Record Flight

BOBBIE TROUT
Wearing Her New Wrist Watch

BOBBIE TROUT, record breaking aviatrix, took no chances on landing before she had established a new mark for sustained flight for feminine flyers.

She revealed this yesterday in exhibiting a new wrist watch, a Bulova, presented by Dave Peach, general manager of Hart's Jewelry Company. The watch was handed the aviatrix just a few minutes before she took off and is similar to those worn by Colonel Lindbergh, Amelia Earhart and Ruth Elder. The presentation was made by girl in person.

"The watch made doubly effective checking of the time in the air." Miss Trout said. "I could not have a more timely gift. The only thing I was worried about was accurate checking of my time in the and with the new watch and the abilities I already possessed there was no danger of landing too soon."

CREDIT: R.O. BONE

Flying Flapper Sets Record

The world's endurance flight record for women is now held by Bobbie Trout, 19, Los Angeles' "flying flapper," who remained aloft for 12 hours and 11 minutes, shattering the former womens' record of 8 hours and 6 minutes. Here she is just after she brought her plane to earth at the Los Angeles airport as her mother (shown in picture) greeted her. Inset is a closeup of Miss Trout.

Newspaper reviews of Bobbi's record flight.

DARING AVIATRIX VISITOR TODAY AT LOCAL AIR FIELD

Salinas American Legion airport was honored last night when Miss Bobby Trout, holder of the international endurance air record for women, dropped down at the landing field just at dusk and came into town to be a guest at a leading hostelry over night. Miss Trout flew up from the south yesterday in her tiny Golden Eagle monoplane. This morning, the daring young and pretty aviatrix and her beautiful plane were an added attraction at the airport, with a large crowd gathered to see her take the air in continuation of her flight.

Miss Trout nears the distinction of having been the first aviatrix to land at Legion airport. She continued her trip toward the bay city shortly after the breaking of the fog cap this morning.

(lower right) The N.A.A. official report acknowledging Bobbi's endurance flight.

DEPARTMENT OF COMMERCE
————
BUREAU OF STANDARDS
Report
on
Endurance Flight
made by
Miss Evelyn "Bobbie" Trout
in a
Golden Eagle Landplane
with a
LeBlonde Air-cooled 60 h.p. motor
at
Los Angeles Metropolitan Airport
Los Angeles, California
on
January 2, 1929
requested by
National Aeronautic Association
Washington, D. C.
on
January 30, 1929.

Data and Instruments.

The barograph and data relative to an endurance flight made by Miss Evelyn "Bobby" Trout in a Golden Eagle landplane on January 2, 1929 were submitted in order to verify the duration flight time which was given by the official observer as 12 hours and 11 minutes, and also to determine whether or not an intermediate landing was made.

The instrument was a Richard barograph, B.S.Serial No. 3163, Ident. No. 83599. Its range was 10,000 feet and the recording drum makes approximately one revolution in 6 hours.

The instrument was received at the Bureau of Standards with the seal unbroken. The trace was made on a smoked chart.

TESTS.

The smoked chart was "fixed" by immersion in a solution of collodion and Duco solvent. After drying, the chart was replaced on the barograph drum. The time scale of the instrument B.S.Serial No. 3163 was then carefully checked against a standard time piece. The duration of the flight as recorded by this barograph was 12 hours and 6 minutes. The barograph trace indicates that no landing was made between the start and finish of the flight.

George K. Burgess, Director.

Washington, D. C.
February 6, 1929.

Official flight timer, Joe Nikrent, shows Bobbi the barograph used to record and prove her record.

LOS ANGELES AVIATRIX SETS NEW WORLD'S RECORD

Publicity from Bobbi's first endurance flight.

- Photos by Hollywood News.

Upper left: Bobby Trout, 18-year-old Los Angeles aviatrix, stepping out of her tiny monoplane after breaking two world's records at the Metropolitan airport in San Fernando valley last evening.

Lower left: Close-up of the new record holder, who piloted her plane over San Fernando valley yesterday for 12 hours and 11 minutes, breaking the world's endurance flight record for women, and also for a plane powered with a 60-horsepower motor.

Center: In front of her plane with Joe Nikrent, official timer, who sealed the barograph they are holding in the plane yesterday morning.

Lower right: Miss Trout, right, with her mother, Mrs. L. O. Trout, standing in front of the plane at the end of the flight.

Upper right: Miss Trout signing the official record books at the Metropolitan airport, which also contains the autographed signatures of the crew of the army plane Question Mark, on a special page. Her mother is standing back of her, while on the left is Miss Lois Ritchey, and on the right is Mrs. Eddie Anderson. Photograph taken in Beacon cafe at the airport.

Bobbi to participate in Harmon Field dedication, San Jacinto, January, 1929.

FAMOUS AVIATION FIGURES PRESENT

Cliff Henderson, Speaker of the Day, Praises Sponsors of Project for Air-Mindedness; 'Round-the-World Pilot Introduced

Twenty-one airplanes and 3500 people participated in the dedication of Harmon Field, San Jacinto's municipal airport last Saturday. The success of the event exceeded the fondest hopes of San Jacinto's city council and chamber of commerce, the two organizations responsible for the arrangements. The visiting aviators were enthusiastic in expressing appreciation of the hospitality extended them. The spectators were thrilled and satisfied.

Notables of the aviation world who piloted planes to San Jacinto for the dedication were:

Major Millard F. Harmon, commandant of March Field and the man for whom the San Jacinto airport was named.

Lieutenant Ogden, one of the army's famous 'round-the-world flyers.

Miss Bobbie Troutt, holder of the world's endurance record (12 hours, 11 minutes) for women.

Cliff Henderson, director of municipal airports for the city of Los Angeles and general manager of the recent National Air Races held at Mines Field.

Major Harmon led a group of nine army planes from March Field. Five commercial planes came from Los Angeles, one of them a three-motored cabin ship piloted by Lt. Ogden. Other commercial planes arrived from Long Beach, Santa Ana, Riverside, Banning and Palm Springs. At one time 14 planes were in the air over the field.

Program Is Brief

Spectators began arriving before 10 o'clock. When the dedication program began at 11:30 it was esti-

Aviatrix Louise Thaden, who was a sales representative for Travel Air Company.

CREDIT: BERTE PORTER

January 28, 1929—Bobbi visits Oakland Airport.

FAMOUS AVIATRIX VISITS ALAMEDA

Bobbie Trout, Winner of World's Endurance Record, Guest at Hotel

Because Hotel Alameda's strategic position in regard to Oakland and Alameda airports has made it the favorite of visiting aviators, Alameda entertained last night a noted aviatrix, Bobbie Trout, and her friend, Bertie Porter. The two young women flew to Alameda for a short visit at Oakland airport.

Miss Trout is demonstrating a new monoplane. She is the holder of the women's endurance record in the air. At the Oakland airport she met Mrs. Louise Thaden, holder of the women's altitude record.

WATCHES RACE

With her companion, Miss Porter, Miss Trout made a flight from Oakland airport, soaring to height the two young women observed a race between Mrs. Thaden and Denny Wright. Miss Trout expressed her disappointment that her fellow woman aviatrix lost the race but observed sagely: "Women can't always expect to win, I guess."

Miss Trout praised highly the Oakland field and the staff and aviators she met during her visit. The general activity, good fellowship and co-operation between field staff and pilots made a noteworthy impression.

UNANNOUNCED

Miss Porter, an attache of the airport, said that Miss Trout appeared at the airport unannounced Saturday morning, breaking through the clouds into sudden sight in her monoplane. She was immediately taken in charge by the airport management and the pilots and was generally congratulated on her recent capturing of the world's endurance record for women. She said that the Oakland airport undoubtedly is one of the finest flying fields in the United States.

The special certificate issued by the Fédération Aéronautique Internationale to record-breaking pilots as part of the official flight documentation.

In January 1929, Bobbi left on another demonstration trip. This time her itinerary included various airports on the way up the Pacific Coast to Sacramento, California, but she only made it as far as Oakland. At each stop she was treated royally. Her itinerary included landings at Carpinteria, where she first met Pancho Barnes; Santa Barbara, Santa Maria, Salinas, and smaller towns along the way. She ended the northward trek in Oakland, and on her return trip made stops at Stockton, Modesto, and several other places, because of engine trouble.

As she climbed from her airplane at the Modesto Airport, a reporter greeted her with the news that Elinor Smith, a New Yorker, had bettered her endurance record by one hour on January 31. The Modesto city officials wanted to discuss the possibility of having her next endurance flight over Modesto, and were ready to offer her almost anything if it could be arranged.

Bobbi called Bone to get his okay, but Bone had already made arrangements to have the flight start from Mines Field. She was to return immediately to Los Angeles.

About an hour after takeoff from Modesto, and just before reaching Madera, Bobbi's engine sounded as if it were about to disintegrate. She set the airplane down in a cow pasture and took out a broken connecting rod and metal pieces from inside the engine, and she carefully checked everything for further problems. Thumbing a ride to town, she called the factory for the necessary replacement parts.

The next morning, when she checked out of her hotel room, Bobbi discovered a storm moving into the area. After picking up the parts at Fresno, she was driven back to the airplane. She spent a miserably cold, rainy afternoon cleaning additional broken pieces out of the crankcase and replacing the parts.

By evening, the engine was fixed and ready to go except for a lost flange stud off the cylinder. She hoped it would get her home. The next day she discovered that the cylinder was too loose. The loss of the stud caused the cylinder to crack, and she had to send for another and install it before she could get underway.

Bobbi left Fresno in a heavy downpour, flying the Golden Eagle through dark, wind-lashed rain. The clouds above were illuminated in alarming frequency by lurid flashes of lightning. The storm had not let up when she set down in Visalia.

She took off before daylight next morning, and not long afterward, was gassing up at Bakersfield Airport. After topping off the tanks she tried to restart her engine, only to discover she had fouled spark plugs. The mechanic at the field took all the plugs out and cleaned them for her while she tried to get warm again in the small hangar at the field before starting her last leg back to Los Angeles under large, dark clouds.

It was raining over the Ridge Route. Undaunted, she headed for Mines Field and the challenge of breaking another record. Her thoughts were once again interrupted when the engine sputtered and quit. She made another forced landing among many rocks, which she carefully dodged. There was an old piece of canvas in the cockpit and she used it to cover herself as she walked through the rocky field.

Looking up and down the road, she saw a man in a pickup truck coming her way and signaled for him to stop. Bobbi explained what had happened to her, and got the impression the man felt honored to give her a lift to the R.O. Bone Company airplane factory.

The next day Bobbi and Harrison, the mechanic, drove back up the curvy two-lane Ridge Route to the plane, located high in the Tehachapi Mountains—a good distance from the factory. After getting the engine started, Bobbi took off between the rocks, but the engine still did not work right. She made another rock-dodging landing.

Disappointed, Bobbi and Harrison removed the wing from the plane and persuaded the driver of an empty flatbed truck to help them by hauling the wing to the factory. They hooked the plane up to Harrison's Ford and towed the Golden Eagle to the factory where it was repaired.

A few days later Bone and Bobbi looked over the Golden Eagle, which was being readied for her second attempt at a record-breaking solo endurance flight. Larger gasoline tanks were being installed, and the engine was being tuned to perfection. Nothing must go wrong.

Her friend and official F.A.I. timer, Joe Nikrent, had installed a barograph in her sixty-horsepower Golden Eagle. He had to literally stand on his head within the cockpit, his feet sticking into the air, to properly install the barograph before her takeoff. The barograph made a graphic record of the flight from which officials could determine if the plane had remained aloft the hours claimed. For the record to be official, the machine must be aboard.

For Bobbi's second attempt at the record, there was much publicity. The press, movie stars, and spectators contributed a great deal of commotion. Rufus Pilcher of Richfield Oil Company offered to furnish all the fuel and oil if Bobbi would advertise the company's logo on her plane.

At five-ten in the afternoon of February 10, Bobbi took off from Mines Field, for her second try at the solo endurance record for women. She was aware that she only needed to beat Elinor Smith's record by one hour to regain the title, but Bobbi was determined to extend the time by four hours, as she had with Viola Gentry's record.

CREDIT: R.O. BONE

R.O.Bone (left) discusses the second endurance flight with Bobbi.

CREDIT: R.O. BONE

Prior to take-off for second endurance flight at Mines Field, Los Angeles.

R.O. Bone gives Bobbi some last minute advice.

Bobbi ready for take-off.

Bobbi taxing for take-off, second endurance flight.

*Christmas card from"
Richfield Red" (right) a
dear friend who always kept
Bobbi's gasoline tanks
topped off.*

Bobbi in 1929.

Bobbi just airborne.

Joe Nikrent's foot sticks up, behind Bobbi, as he installs the barograph in her airplane. Bobbi's friend, Lois Richie, wishes her luck.

Girl Makes 3 Records For Flying

MISS BOBBY TROUT

'Tomboy' Stays in Air 17 Hours to Avoid Washing Dishes

United Press

LOS ANGELES, Feb. 11.—Miss Bobby Trout, an 18-year-old "Tomboy" who took up flying to avoid dishwashing, broke three world's aviation records here today.

She established a women's endurance mark of 17 hours, 5 minutes and 37 seconds. In doing so she completed more hours of continuous night flying than any woman before her. The third record was smashed when she drove a 60 horse-power heavier-than-air craft on a longer sustained trip than any man or woman.

The distance Miss Trout traveled could not be announced officially for some time but it was to be certain that she broke the previous 932-mile mark for a 60 horse-power plane.

The aviatrix appeared in good condition despite the long grind of the flight.

"I was pretty tired last night," she said after she landed, "I guess it was a good thing it was cold as the devil at 5,000 feet or I'd probably have gone to sleep."

"Gosh, I hate to take the record away from Elinor Smith, but I had to do it. I just loaned it to her for a couple of weeks."

Elinor Smith, the New York "Flapper Flier," shattered Miss Trout's mark a few weeks ago with a record of 13 hours and 16 min

CREDIT: INTERNATIONAL NEWSREEL

Bobbi tail up on take-off of second solo endurance.

Bobbi wore a woolen sweater and breeches, boots, gloves, and a newly-tailored, sheep's wool-lined leather jacket for the cold night ahead. Bobbi, carrying Sunkist oranges and Coca-Cola to help her remain awake, began the grueling flight. During the night that followed, she started to nod, and even dozed a little. Each time she did, however, the sound of the engine racing faster and the slipstream getting colder awoke her. The Golden Eagle would begin to dive, but Bobbi somehow managed to right the aircraft without a mishap. She maintained her course around the designated checkpoints.

In an effort to stay awake, Bobbi went through her entire repertoire of songs that she used in her vocal lessons, which she had been taking in her spare time. She expected to land at ten thirty in the morning on February 11, which was when she calculated her supply of gasoline would be exhausted. At 10:00 a.m., she watched her trusty Bulova's hands creep through the minutes as she circled the field, knowing the ordeal was almost over. At 10:05 a.m. her engine started cutting out, starved of fuel, and she gunned it several times before it died completely.

She was never ground shy, a phenomenon that sometimes gripped pilots who have spent many hours in the air. Bobbi remained calm as the Golden Eagle glided downward. She sideslipped to control her descent, bringing the airplane in for a perfect landing at 10:16 a.m.

It had been a long and arduous night, but when Bobbi looked at the list of records she had broken, she felt that all the hours of discomfort and weariness had been worth every minute.

Bobbi's new records included: a takeoff with more load per horsepower and wing area than any sixty-horsepower engine up to that time; a course with the most miles in a circumference; the most miles covered by a sixty-horsepower engine; the first all-night flight by a woman; and a new seventeen hours, twenty-four minutes solo endurance record for women.

There were newspapermen from local papers, national syndicates, and Fox Movietone newsreel. Movie stars and even humorist Will Rogers came out to greet Bobbi. Headlines beamed across the United States. The Los Angeles Record had an "Extra" edition that read *SKY GIRL SETS MARK: Flies for 17 Hours.* Another paper read, *"Tomboy" Stays in Air 17 Hours to Avoid Washing Dishes.* After the flight, telegrams and letters arrived from Amelia Earhart, Aviation Editor of Cosmopolitan magazine, the Women's Aeronautic Association of California, and the National Aeronautic Association.

GIRL SHATTERS

VERY LATEST NEWS

Adds Four Hours to Old Flight Time

VOL. XXIX, NO. 186—P. M.   CHICAGO, MONDAY, F

"Bobbie" Trout, 23-year-old girl flyer, who today shattered Elinor Smith's endurance flight record at Mines Field, Los Angeles. Miss Trout is shown with a friend. (R.O. BONE)

International Newsreel photo.

EAST SIDE ACCLAIMS BOBBIE TROUT AFTER RECORD AIR FLIGHT

YOUNG LOCAL AVIATRIX SETS THREE NEW RECORDS FOR WOMEN FLIERS; TELLS OF HAZARDOUS 17-HOUR FLIGHT IN SPARKLING INTERVIEW.

By SYLVIA BERKE.

Just a wisp of a girl piloting a wisp of a Golden Eagle airplane, alighted at Mines field in Inglewood Monday morning, still smiling, though worn, to receive the acclaim

BOBBIE TROUT
Courtesy Illustrated Daily News.

of thousands after having broken three world records for women fliers.

Unassumingly and with becoming grace, the 23-year-old aviatrix, Bobbie Trout, modestly accepted the hearty praise of the entire world for her courageous, undaunted feat.

AIR MARKS

AMERICAN FINAL Peach

FEBRUARY 11, 1929   Registered Office.   PRICE THREE CENTS
U. S. Patent

GIRL SETS FIVE FLYER RECORDS

When the wheels of Miss Bobby Trout's little 60-horsepower Golden Eagle touched Mother Earth last Monday morning at 10:15:22 a. m., the daring aviatrix had hung up a quintet of records for feminine flyers—some brand new and some raising—old world's records.

The chief of these was the endurance record. Next in importance, perhaps, was the fact that this was the first time that a lone girl flyer ever had accomplished an all-night flight.

With the exception, of course, of the proud makers of the Le Blond motored "job" which had performed so beautifully for over seventeen hours in the air, none was more jubilant over the record than officials of the Richfield Oil Company, it is declared.

The jubilation of the latter arose, it might be explained, from the fact that Miss Trout's ship used Richfield gasoline, was lubricated with Richlube motor oil, even greased with Richlube grease.

"Miss Trout chose Richfield products," explained Dudley Steele, head of the Richfield aviation division, "on the reputation they have scored in the air in similar endurance tests. She knew that Richfield gasoline had carried Captain

Giving Fuel a 'Big Hand'

B OBBY TROUT, record aviatrix; Rufus Pilcher of Richfield Oil Co., and Miss Trout's endurance plane Golden Eagle after its epochal flight Monday.

Wilkins over the North Pole and Art Goebel in his Yankee Doodle non-stop flight from coast to coast. She knew, too, that three out of five winners of the National Air Races were Richfield users; that it was Richfield which was used in the record-setting Question Mark."

The Record

A Scripps-Canfield Newspaper

Two Cents   HOME   LOS ANGELES, MONDAY, FEBRUARY 11, 1929   Number 10610

SKY GIRL SETS MARK

FLIES FOR 17 HOURS

Miss Bobby Trout, an 18-year-old "tom-boy," who took up flying to avoid dishwashing, broke three world's aviation records here today.

She established a new women's endurance mark of 17 hours, 5 minutes and 37 seconds and in doing so completed more hours of continuous night flying than any woman before her and drove a 60-horsepowered, heavier-than-air craft on a longer sustained trip than any man or woman.

The aviatrix landed her Golden Eagle monoplane at Mines field at 10:16:22 a. m. today having piloted it over a triangular course since 5:10:45 p. m. yesterday.

Twelve hours of the time she was in the air she was flying in darkness. The best previous night-flying time was eight hours.

The distance Miss Trout traveled could not be announced officially for some time but it was said to be certain that she broke the previous 982-mile mark for a 60 horse-power plane.

The aviatrix apeared in good condition despite the long grind of the flight.

"I was pretty tired last night," she said after she landed, "I guess it was a good thing it was cold as the devil at 5000 feet or I'd probably gone to sleep."

Miss Trout made an expert although almost a dead stick landing when she touched Mines field. The 80 gallons of gasoline she carried on the jaunt had been almost entirely consumed.

Mrs. Lola Trout, mother of the girl, embraced Miss Trout and called her a "wonderful baby." Mrs. Trout remained at the field throughout the night.

"You'd think I'd been flying instead of Bobby," she said. "I'm all played out and I'm colder than she is."

It was possible that Miss Trout also broke the distance record for planes motored by engines of 60 horsepower.

In her flight which started at Mines field last night, Miss Trout also established a new night sustained flight record for women. She drove her plane through darkness for a period of 12 hours. The best previous night flying mark for women was eight hours.

Oleson lighting equipment gave this endurance record-breaking young lady assurance of safety and helped her to carry on.

We take to the air With thunderous applause the public are taking their aerial jaunts with the same nonchalance used on trains and autos. But their safety has to be considered just as it has been in other modes of travel.

Recently Bobbie Trout established an endurance record for women at Mines field airport in order to make safe for a possible forced landing at night the Otto K. Oleson Company, pioneers of lighting equipment for the past 17 years in this section equipped the airport with flood lights that illuminated the entire field. "This," says Bobbie Trout, "gave me an assurance of safety that enabled me to carry on through till the break of day and a new record of endurance for women."

Otto K. Olesen maintains a technical and mechanical staff on flood lighting and furnish the many necessary details to our numerous airports on their night lighting, thus enabling the fliers to have safe landing fields at night as well as in the daytime. This firm has the unique distinction of installing their equipment and shipping to all parts of the world where flood lights and lighting is necessary.

The engineering department now covers all of the Southern California and Arizona fields, this they are expanding to cover the entire western part of the United States and will soon be invading the Eastern territory, according to Otto K. Olesen, who has recently returned from a business trip to Chicago and other eastern cities. "Western airport is the most modern fields west of New York, is entirely illuminated with flood lights furnished by the Olesen Company, as well as the

BOBBY TROUT

Bobbi makes the headlines as she flys through the kleig light.

Joe Nikrent shows Bobbi and Will Rogers the official flight records.

Mat. Div. A. C. 312-Wright Field 4-1 20M

**WAR DEPARTMENT
AIR CORPS**
MATERIEL DIVISION
OFFICE OF THE CHIEF OF DIVISION

SPM:rec

WRIGHT FIELD, DAYTON, OHIO
February 12, 1929

Miss Bobbie Trout,
418 South Soto Street,
Los Angeles, California.

Dear Miss Trout:

     We also would like very much to have an airplane which is
capable of making an official altitude of 40,000 feet. Our present
interest in altitude work is that of developing suitable apparatus,
camera, oxygen equipment and so on, which would be necessary in the
event that future military requirements necessitated flight at these
altitudes.

     The airplane we are using at the particular time in our
experiments is known as the XCO-5, a biplane which more nearly
resembles the observation type of airplane than any other in service.
The fuselage of this airplane is built of steel tubing containing
two cockpits and one Liberty water-cooled engine. This plane is
equipped with a high lift wing section known as the Joukowski
S.T.A$_\theta$ 27a. This section has been used for much previous altitude
work, notably, Lieutenants Macready, Bleakley and Doolittle and
Captains Streett and Stevens . In this machine the pilot's cockpit
has been completely lined for his protection against the cold.
Temperatures as low as 70° below zero have been recorded and temperatures of 40° to 60° are quite common, necessitating considerable
protection.

     A standard 400 horsepower Liberty engine is used, equipped
with a high altitude supercharged. A Liberty engine unsupercharged
will develop about 400 horsepower at the ground, approximately 200
horsepower at 20,000 feet and only about 60 horsepower at 35,000
feet. This tremendous decrease in power is due, of course, to the
rarified air encountered, a cubic foot of air at 20,000 feet being
worth only about as much as one-half a foot of cubic of air at sea
level for carburetion purposes. The supercharger on this engine,
while adding about 140 pounds weight in addition to the weight of
the increased load of gasoline necessary, permits the engine to
retain its normal horsepower to altitudes approximately 28,000 to
30,000 feet, from which point its power wanes.

     The propeller used in connection with this particular
plane is a two-bladed adjustable pitch propeller with steel hub
and duralumin blade. The adjustment of this propeller is made on

*Three page letter from the
War Department to Bobbi's
inquiry about high altitude
flying.*

. . continued from previous page

Official report of the second solo endurance flight.

GIRL SETS 5

SPECIAL EXTRA NIGHT

THE CHICAGO

THIRTY-NINTH YEAR— OFFICIAL NEWSPAPER OF CITY OF CHICAGO   * MONDAY, FEBR

CREDIT: R.O. BONE

R.O.Bone congratulates Bobbi after her record flight.

NEW AIR RECORDS

EVENING POST

SPECIAL EXTRA NIGHT

UARY 11, 1929. *   THIS ISSUE CONSISTS OF TWO PARTS   PART I—*PRICE THREE CENTS*

The Grand Central Airport opening in Glendale where Margaret Perry, Pancho Barnes, and Bobbi flew pylon race.

The next big event was the official opening of Grand Central Airport on February 22, 1929, which included the first women's pylon race of record. Bobbi flew her sixty-horsepower LeBlond Golden Eagle monoplane against Pancho Barnes in her two hundred twenty-five–horsepower J-5 Travel Air biplane and Margaret Perry in her Siemens-Halske one hundred fifteen–horsepower Spartan Aircraft Company biplane. Bobbi came in third behind Barnes and Perry. It stands to reason that Bobbi's sixty-horsepower engine was no match for the huskies, but she enjoyed racing.

At this opening, there were over two hundred celebrities, practically all of Los Angeles' politicians and stars from Hollywood including Jean Harlow, Gary Cooper, and Wallace Beery flying his new Travel Air.

Little did Bobbi realize how aviation would affect her life when Bone, owner of the R.O. Bone Company, came to her that day six months earlier and asked her to be his demonstration and test pilot. Bobbi loved it all.

AIR RECORD IS SET BY L.A. GIRL

Los Angeles' 23-year-old aviatrix, Bobby Trout, today brought back to this city the world's women's endurance airplane record when she landed her ship at Mines field at 10:16:22 a. m. today, after 17 hours 6 minutes in the air.

She beat the previous record of 13 hours 16 minutes, set by Elinor Smith, 17-year-old flapper flier of New York, by nearly four hours.

She made the record flight in a 60-horsepower Golden Eagle plane carrying only 90 gallons of Richfield gasoline.

Four world reco   were set by the daring woman in her flight, Dudley Steele, contest chairman of the National Aeronautical association, officially announced.

In addition to the endurance record, she set a record of flying 860 miles without a stop with a 60-horsepower engine, and another record of having made a sustained flight at an average speed of 50.29 miles per hour. The fourth attributed to her was the new night flying record which she shattered by four hours.

The records were hung up after an all night grind that started immediately after Marvel Crossan, San Diego girl, had attained a height of 20,000 feet in an attempt to establish an altitude record with her Travelair plane at Clover field.

THOUSANDS CHEER

Thousands of cheering spectators crowded around Miss Trout's ship as it settled down on Mines field.

Smiling and happy, Miss Trout stepped down into the arms of her mother, Mrs. L. D. Trout, who had remained up all night to watch her daughter's flight.

"I'm not tired at all," the girl said. "I could have stayed up hours longer if I had had more gasoline.

"Tell Elinor Smith I hated to take the record from her, but it just had to come back to California. I only lent it to her for a couple of weeks."

Miss Smith established her record of 13 hours 16 minutes about two weeks ago, lowering the previous record set by Miss Trout.

Immediately after the greeting between mother and daughter, the two were hurried away in the car of R. M. Bone, designer and builder of the plane used in the flight.

Miss Trout took off from Mines field at 5:10 p. m. yesterday and at 6:26 a. m. today had equaled Miss Smith's record with her plane still functioning perfectly.

Shortly after daylight Pilot W. E. Mead took the air with messages of cheer to the flier, painted on the sides of his ship.

On one side of the plane was painted:

"You're a plucky kid."

On the other side:

"Good morning, Bobby.—Mother."

Half an hour before the flight ended, Mrs. Trout and Lois Ritchey went up with Pilot Eddie Burke and signaled Miss Trout to come down, but she waved them away.

The landing was made with the gasoline tank of the plane almost ~~~

Miss Trout spoke in high praise of her plane, declaring it had winged its way through the long hours without any trouble developing. It was lubricated with Richlube oil.

Miss Trout took off at 5:10 p. m. yesterday and throughout the night her plane droned its way between Mines field and the Aero Corporation of California field.

Carrying a load of nearly 1500 pounds, the little plane took a run of 2000 feet before lifting into the air, just as the wheels sank into a muddy spot on the field.

Joe Nikrent, official timer at Mines field, held the watch on the flight, and Fred Framm, stationed at the Aero corporation's field, kept the time at that end of the course.

Flood lights were kept on throughout the night as the little whip soared back and forth through the darkness.

Miss Trout wore a fur-lined flying suit and carried a lunch of sandwiches and coffee.

Miss Crossan, who attempted the altitude record, was in the air only 2 hours and 30 minutes, but in that brief time soared approximately 20,000 feet, in spite of engine trouble that developed early in her flight.

AIR-MINDED

Bobby Trout, record breaking aviatrix, is air-minded in more ways than one. She will take to the air via the microphone, this time on Manhattan Beach program at 7 tonight in KHJ's intercity radio contest.

"Hard on the Feet" Says Bobby Trout After Long Flight

LOS ANGELES, Feb. 12—(A)—It tires one's feet to fly and smash air records.

The authority for that paradoxical statement is Miss Bobby Trout, 22-year-old aviatrix who regained her women's endurance flight record here yesterday with a continued flight of 17 hours, 5 minutes and 37 seconds and also broke the women's night flying and distance records.

"The most tired parts of me are my feet," Miss Trout said just before she retired for a needed rest. "During the night I replaced my heavy boots with moccasins to keep my feet warm. And constantly working those rudder pedals was simply 'murder.' First I used my toes, then my insteps and then my heels. Next time I think I'll take a chance of frozen toes and and keep my boots on."

Bobbi advertised the Golden Eagle on the spare tire cover of her car. 1929. This picture taken in front of the Golden Eagle plant by 15 year old, Boardman Reed.

180 NAILS
...and still
no punctures
That's *news!*

These Albertina Rasch girls each drove thirty ten-penny nails into an inflated tire.

A revolutionary development • • • the **Goodrich Air Container** seals punctures as they occur

Bobby Trout, famous aviatrix, holder of women's altitude and endurance records, official starter of the race, awarded a cup to the winner of the contest.

More than half of all motor accidents are traceable to tire collapse. The Air Container seals punctures, increases tire mileage, and makes motoring safer.

WATCH FOR THIS AMAZING TEST ON THE SCREEN!!
At your FOX WEST COAST THEATRE

PACIFIC GOODRICH RUBBER COMPANY ⬧ LOS ANGELES, CALIFORNIA

Bobbi advertised for Goodrich (left) and Richfield (above).

The opening of Grand Central Airport. (left to right) Marvel Crosson, Bobbi, Al Wilson, Louise Thaden.

L IEUT. D. W. Tomlinson, former navy stunt flier and leader of the "Three Sea Hawks," was given a signal to taxi forward by some self-appointed "official." He was unable to see to the rear, and when he gave the motors gas, the horizontal stabilizer on the tail section caught the party amidships, knocking several persons to the ground.

Miss Sullivan and Miss Hamilton were slightly injured and recovered shortly. Miss Mayo turned her ankle and the mayor broke his glasses in the confusion.

Interest in the flying centered on a race between Miss Bobby Trout, holder of the women's flight endurance record; Mrs. Florence Barnes, Pasadena aviatrix, and Miss Margaret Perry, of Beverly Hills.

Mrs. Barnes won the event, which consisted of two laps from the Glendale field to Metropolitan airport, in Van Nuys, and return. Her ship was a Travelair with a Wright Whirlwind motor, and she made the 40-mile distance in 24.6 minutes.

Miss Perry, in a Sparton with a Siemans-Halske 115-horsepower motor, placed second, and Miss Trout, in her Golden Eagle monoplane, with a 60-horsepower LeBlond motor, took last, although it was her challenge that started the race.

The dedication of Gov. C. C. Young was an impressive tribute to the science and skill embodied in the new field. He termed it one of the greatest in the United States.

Alexander R. Heron, state director of finance, made the formal dedication address in behalf of the governor and the people of California.

Mayor Cryer spoke the appreciation of Los Angeles for the forward step in the development of aeronautics.

An article on the events of the airport opening.

AIRGIRLS HELP START AIRPORT

GRAND Central Air Terminal in Glendale began its actual operation as a union air station today, with hundreds of congratulations being sent to C. C. Spicer, director of the project, for his initiative in constructing the finest field in Southern California.

Thousands crowded the field yesterday to watch the dedicatory exercises, participated in by state, county and city officials and countless celebrities.

A slight mishap furnished the biggest thrill of the day without resulting in any serious injuries.

A tri-motored Ford cabin plane taxied to the front of the reviewing stand to discharge its cargo of famous personages. The party disembarked and stood by the tail of the giant ship to pose for photographers.

The party included Mayor George Cryer, Ruth Elder, Art Goebel, Peggy Hamilton, Virginia Sullivan, W. B. Mayo, chief engineer of the Ford company, and his daughter Olive.

* * *

Spectators at the opening of Grand Central air terminal saw some high-powered flying by the three girls in the upper photo, when they staged a race. Left to right: Margaret Perry, Mrs. Florence Barnes, who won the event, and Bobby Trout, holder of the women's endurance flight record. Below is Governor C. C. Young addressing the assembly in his dedication of the airport. Col. Art Goebel, famous trans-Pacific flier, is on the left.

Courage Like That of Pioneer Ancestors
Helped Bobby Trout Set Air Record

When Bobby Trout broke the record for sustained flight by a woman February 11, it was her own courage that helped her to make that record, but the intrepid spirit of a long line of American ancestors went into the making of that courage.

Bobby Trout isn't the first member of her family to stand an endurance test, even though she is the first to do it in modern fashion in a plane. Generations ago her forebears were performing valorous deeds that took strength and stability and bravery, meeting the severe tests of those pioneer days with a dauntlessness equal to Bobby's own.

Lincoln is especially interested in the 20-year-old California aviatrix, as her cousins, Misses Etta L. and Marhyann E. Dodds reside in the city at 2717 Everett street. She is to fly to Kansas City in the near future, and will visit them while in the middle west, landing on the South Fourteenth street field.

Broke Two Records.

When she landed at Mines field in Los Angeles at 10:16:23 February 11, Bobby Trout had shattered two world's air records for women and established two new American flying marks. She took back to California the world's endurance record for women of 17 hours, 5 minutes, and 37 seconds, beating by more than 3 hours and 48 minutes another recent record. In addition, she broke the night flying record for women, established an American distance record over a closed course of 860 miles for her particular type of ship, a Golden Eagle monoplane, with a record-breaking average speed of 50.292 miles per hour.

In regaining her title lost to Miss Eleanor Smith of Freeport, N. Y., Miss Trout in her plane with its sixty horse power motor, looped the same course taken by the Question Mark. She took off at 5:10:45 in order to make a night flying mark at the same time as her endurance record, while crowds stayed on the field all night to wait for the end of her lonely spin, and to greet her as she got out of the cockpit, cramped, but not especially weary.

Her monoplane carried 80 gallons of gasoline, said to be the heaviest load ever taken aloft by so small a ship. When she alighted, little more than four gallons remained. She had planned to remain in the air until 10:30 o'clock, and descend voluntarily. However, just before she landed, the five-cylinder motor sputtered and died, and the young aviatrix glided to earth with a dead stick. The motor fired before reaching earth, but she did not attempt to regain her altitude. Shortage of gas was diagnosed as the cause.

In those long night hours, she had a little tea and a few sandwiches. And an orange or two—a California girl would have to eat oranges.

Latest photograph of Miss Bobbie Trout, who recently broke the record for sustained flight for women, in Los Angeles. Lincoln cousins of Miss Trout received the picture Thursday, and with it, word that she is planning to visit Lincoln within a short time.

An article on Bobbi and her ancestry.

Licensed Last June.

Bobby Trout—whose official name is Evelyn—was born in Greeley, Colo., late in the fall of 1908. She was educated in the schools of Los Angeles and of St. Louis, and at the University of California.

She was granted her air pilot's license last June, the first girl in southern California to be granted a commercial flying license. At that time, she had had in excess of 200 hours in the air. Her future plans are indefinite, but they are definite to the point that flying will form a part of them.

Bobby Trout is a light little thing, weighing 110 pounds. She is dark, and of medium height, about five feet four.

If Miss Trout had not decided to be an aviatrix, she might have been an architect with equal ease. And not always might have been at that.

In Los Angeles, she was awarded a prize of $500 for her design for a school building. The structure was built from the plans she submitted. At that time, she was only a girl in her mid-teens.

While attending school in St. Louis, she was enrolled in a drafting class attended only by boys. She has always had a mechanical mind, and has been more interested in the classes ordinarily chosen by boys—although she has little time for any social life in their company.

Visited In Lincoln.

Miss Trout visited her cousins when she was just a child, and they are anticipating her visit when she flies over to see them. They saw her about five years ago in St. Louis, but at that time she apparently had no flying ambitions, or at least concealed them. Her family does not mind her choice of occupation, feeling that is what she should do, if flying is her choice.

Her ancestors made many original records in America, and it is probably the blood of pioneers which urges the young Los Angeles girl to her air feats. Those men and women of an earlier day might have been surprised at the exploits of their descendant, but they could not but be pleased that she, too, dares, in a strictly up to date fashion.

Colonel Ephriam Doolittle, son of one great great great great grandfather, secured the charter for the colony of Vermont, the first colony founded after the original thirteen. Three great great great grandfathers were numbered among the first Green Mountain boys in the capture of Ticonderoga. The three, Abel Stevens, Issac Buck, and Obediah Gilbert, had gone into Vermont with Colonel Ephriam Doolittle, and were prominent in the founding of the colony. Abel Stevens later was the first surveyor of the Thousand Isles, and his hardy experiences are history with Great Britain and the United States.

The Wheelers and the Becks, also numbered among her ancestors, were prominent in the early Colonia history of Maryland. The Rev. Richard Buck of Virginia, who assisted at the marriage of Pocahantas, and June 10, 1610 preached the first sermon in Jamestown, the first ever given in a church in America, and opened by prayer the first House of Burgesses at Jamestown, was also on her family tree.

Miss Trout's great grandfather, Dr. Stephen Stevens, who first practiced in Cyrethiana, Ky., and later became a noted pioneer doctor in southern Illinois, made many calls in the wilderness, when it took him as long to make a fifteen-mile trip and return as it did Bobby Trout to make her endurance flight of more than 900 miles. Isaac Wheeler, another ancestor, was in one of the first caravans to cross the country from Maryland to California in 1848, and was prominent in the gold history of Marysville, Cal.

One of several cartoons depicting Bobbi and her flying activities.

Chapter Seven

Spring of '29

DURING the early days of aviation, any record-breaking flight garnered so much publicity that enterprising large companies soon realized the advertising advantages of having their company logo painted on the side of potential record-breaking aircraft. Bobbi was approached by several companies.

Bobbi used Richfield gasoline and oil on her second solo endurance flight, and after that successful flight a Richfield representative offered to give Bobbi one thousand dollars and all the gasoline and oil she would need on future flights if she would advertise Richfield on the side of her airplane. She accepted the offer and endorsed their products in advertisements. Bobbi used the money from Richfield to purchase a brand new Nash automobile, with the help of Cliff Henderson. Cliff convinced his brother, owner of a Nash agency, to reduce the price of a new Nash and sell it to Bobbi. It was Bobbi's first brand new car.

Bobbi was in demand for many other events including the inaugural celebration of Pickwick Airways. Pickwick Stages Systems operated a bus line between Los Angeles, San Francisco and San Diego. In the early days, the Civil Aeronautics Administration (C.A.A.) franchised certain routes for airline companies to fly. Transcontinental Air Transport, Maddux Airlines, and Western Airlines, had the franchise to fly from Los Angeles to San Francisco.

On March 29, Pickwick Airways, Incorporated, inaugurated airline service between Grand Central Air Terminal and San Diego.

ORANGES ACCOMPANY AVIATRIX

Bobby Trout, Los Angeles aviatrix, is not only air minded but Sunkist minded. She recently set a new world's women's endurance record by remaining in the air 17 hours, 5 minutes.

Sunkist oranges are among the principal food items in all her flights, according to Miss Trout.

Miss Bobbie Trout, holder of the world's endurance record for women flyers, is here shown with the tiny record-breaking Golden Eagle monoplane she piloted to fame twice this year, and her recently purchased Nash Standard Six two-passenger coupe.

Famous Girl Flyer Joins Ranks of Nash Owners

On the morning of February 11th, at 10:15:22 a.m., Miss Bobbie Trout brought her tiny 60-horsepower Le Blond motored Golden Eagle monoplane back to earth at the Los Angeles Municipal Airport at Mines Field (near Inglewood) after remaining in the air 17 hours, 5 minutes and 37 seconds, thereby regaining the world's endurance record for women which she lost to Elinor Smith of New York late in January.

The previous record established by Miss Trout (on January 2nd of this year) was 12 hours and 11 minutes, while the New York aviatrix boosted the mark up to 13 hours, 16 minutes and 45 seconds. It will be seen, therefore, that when the California girl (she is only eighteen) raised the mark she did a thorough job, for she stayed up very nearly four hours longer. And not

only that, but she established four other records, principal among these latter being the first time in history a lone girl flyer has made an all-night flight.

Then, on February 16th, the youthful feminine record holder took delivery of a Nash Standard Six "400" two-passenger coupe, which she purchased through Phil Henderson of the Henderson Nash Co., a metropolitan Nash dealer in Los Angeles City. To say that she is delighted with the performance and comfort of this dashing Nash model is, of course, unnecessary.

Like Col. Arthur C. Goebel, famed Dole Flight hero and transcontinental flyer, who owns a Nash "400" Advanced Six 7-passenger sedan, Miss Trout plans many future conquests of the air. Nash owners everywhere will wish this daring miss a full measure of success.

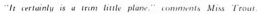

"It certainly is a trim little plane," comments Miss Trout.

"And my new Nash coupe is surely a beautiful motor car."

Bobbi and her Nash coupe.

Hearst's International
combined with
Cosmopolitan

INTERNATIONAL MAGAZINE BUILDING
FIFTY-SEVENTH STREET AT EIGHTH AVENUE
NEW YORK CITY

February thirteen
1 9 2 9

New Altitude Record Set; Other Records

With additional records made, one long-distance flight completed and the failure of another attempted long-distance hop, this week has been fairly active.

Navy flier Apollo Soucek is reported to have set a new world's altitude record for planes of all types in his recent flight at Anacostia Field (Washington, D. C.). Calibration of his barography by the Bureau of Standards shows that the navy flier attained a height of 43,166 feet. Previous record was held by Willie Nuenhofen (Germany) at 41,794 feet. Lieut. Soucek also holds seaplane altitude record at 38,000 feet which he made a year ago from the same flying field.

Mexican aviator Roberto (Col.) Fierro arrives at Curtiss Valley Stream Airport (Long Island) in his Lockheed Vega (Detroit Aircraft) in good-will flight from Mexico City. He is preparing ship, putting plane through motor and altitude tests and expects to start a non-stop flight from New York to Mexico City. He has hopes of making the trip in 15 hours.

Bobby Trout believes she has bettered the women's altitude record for cabin monoplanes after a two-hour altitude test at Los Angeles last week. She said her altimeter registered 15,200 feet which would be about 2,000 feet above the cabin monoplane record for women. The Men's record for this type ship is approximately 19,200 feet. She is awaiting reports of the Bureau of Standards which is inspecting her barograph.

William Brock and Edward Schlee attempt Rockwell Field (San Diego) to Jacksonville (Florida) hop in attempt to smash the transcontinental speed record now held by Lieutenant James H. Doolittle and Major Theodore Macauley. Record is 21 hours, 20 minutes (2,079 miles). Eastbound is 19 hours, 10 minutes.

Alexander Magyar, Hungarian pilot, who is scheduled to attempt a non-stop Detroit-Budapest flight, confers with officials or backers of flight to make final arrangements for the purchase of a Lockheed-Sirius (Detroit Aircraft). Trip will be made with Captain George Endress (Hungary) as co-pilot.

Roger Q. Williams, one-time conqueror of the Atlantic, plans to make it two-in-a-row. Williams is believed preparing for a flight to Paris over Lindbergh's route. The plane which he has been working on recently was fitted with a special glass roof to facilitate navigation. It is the Colombia with Clarence Chamberlin once flew to Germany.

Jean Mermoz is having his hydroplane repaired at the Natal (Brazil) base before his attempt to fly the South Atlantic from West to East. He has already successfully crossed from St. Louis (Senegal) to Natal on the first of a series of experimental flights. Capt. Charles E. Kingsford-Smith is awaiting favorable weather at Dublin and the Southern Cross is being held in readiness for his westward crossing of the North Atlantic.

Dear Miss Trout:

May I add my congratulations for your endurance mark, seventeen hours? I am, of course, very much interested in what women are doing in the air.

As you know, I have been advocating separate records for women, so that their accomplishments may be officially recognized. I think the type of thing you are doing will help to give them a standing, and will also be an aid to the industry as a whole.

Sincerely yours,

Amelia Earhart

Amelia Earhart

Miss Evelyn Trout
418 South Soto Street
Los Angeles, California

ae.na

Amelia Earhart sent Bobbi a congratulatory letter after her endurance flight.

CREDIT: NORM GRANGER

March 28, 1929—Bobbi, bottle in hand, christens the airplane, with Ruth Elder looking on.

PICKWICK AIRWAYS, Inc.
ISSUED ON AUTHORITY OF

Tickets are NON-TRANSFERABLE and if presented by any person other than original purchaser, this ticket will be void and may be confiscated by any agent of the Pickwick Airways, Inc.

Stopovers will be permitted at the option of the Company, but resumption of the trip is subject to previous reservations of other passengers.

The passenger agrees with the Company, that if, in the judgment of the Company, it is not deemed safe to proceed after landing at any point, that the Company may cancel the balance of the trip and refund the part of fare equal to the unused portion of this ticket.

The company reserves the right to cancel any schedule, if in its opinion, weather or other conditions will not permit safe flying.

The Company assumes no responsibility for delay due to any cause whatsoever.

Passenger *Bobbie Trout*

Agent

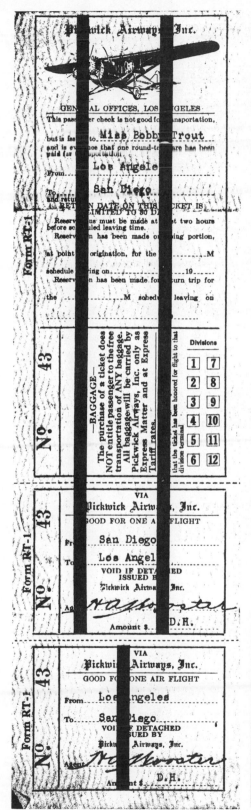

The inaugural dedication of Pickwick Airways flight contract.

Girl Flyers Help Start New Sky Route

Bobby Trout and Ruth Elder
They assisted in ceremonies at Grand Central Air Terminal when Pickwick System put first Bach ship into service.

STAGE LINE SPROUTS WINGS

Pickwick System Inaugurates Daily Air Service from Los Angeles to San Diego

Land transportation sprouted another full-fledged set of wings yesterday with the inauguration of the Pickwick Airways, a creation of the Pickwick Stages System, at the Grand Central Air Terminal in Glendale. The initial flight marked the beginning of regular service between Los Angeles and San Diego, with a schedule of three round trips daily.

Passengers arriving on the plane from San Diego could transfer to a Pickwick Nite Coach sleeper bus and arrive in San Francisco at nine o'clock the following morning after a night's rest. For this celebration Bobbi and Ruth Elder were on hand. Bobbi broke a bottle of vintage champagne against one of the propellers of the Bach Tri-Motor in the traditional christening ceremony. Bobbi attended all of the air shows and airport openings in Southern California to demonstrate the Golden Eagle Chief, in addition to working at the R.O. Bone Company factory. She was a busy aviator.

She knew her Golden Eagle was a fast little airplane and was capable of helping her set additional endurance records. Bobbi was sure that the only way she could create a new endurance record now was to be refueled in flight—and Bone adamantly refused to let her do this. Instead, she went after a record for which he would give his approval.

Bobby Trout, Up 15,200 Feet, Sets World's Record

Setting what is said to be a world's altitude record for women in a plane equipped with a 90-horsepower motor, Bobby Trout yesterday climbed to 15,200 feet above Grand Central air terminal. The old record was 12,747 feet.

Thousands who had come to watch the Curtiss - Wright flying service air demonstrations saw Miss Trout climb into her tiny plane and ascend until the ship was a mere speck.

Miss Trout's barograph will be sent to Washington to be calibrated. Her altimeter showed 15,200, but to make the record official, the barograph must be inspected, it was stated.

Leading Woman Flier Rides Motorcycle to Field

CREDIT: CARL MUTER VIA ANN PELLEGRENO

A MOTORCYCLE is ridden to the Los Angeles Airport each day by Bobby Trout, one of the outstanding women fliers in America, who is shown astride her motorcycle beside her plane. Friends expect her to win the air race.

Four months after her second endurance flight, on June 16, Bobbi strapped herself into the cockpit of the new ninety-horsepower Golden Eagle Chief. The Richfield logo, painted on the golden fuselage, stood out in the early morning sunlight. She was out to shatter an altitude record for light class aircraft.

Bobbi made a thumbs-up for the photographers and reporters and took off. The Kinner engine whined as she spiraled upward. She continued to climb, thirteen thousand feet, fourteen thousand feet, and still upward. The air was thin and very cold at fifteen thousand feet. Bobbi sensed that the Golden Eagle Chief had reached the limit of its capability, but still continued to climb. At fifteen thousand two hundred feet she could not coax any more out of the altimeter and decided to head for home. She had broken the record!

Her name and the Golden Eagle Chief again made the news with the story syndicated worldwide. Bobbi enjoyed a few more weeks of being lauded at parties and banquets while the publicity continued.

A few days after her altitude record flight, Bobbi and Jack Helm, distributor of the Golden Eagle Chief in Southern California, flew up the coast to the opening of the Santa Rosa Airport to show the plane. En route they stopped at the Oakland Airport. At Oakland, Bobbi met Louise Thaden, another girl flier, and D.C. Warren, a dealer for Travel Air aircraft who supplied Louise's airplane.

Louise was a soft-spoken, easygoing woman from Arkansas who turned into a tiger when it came to competition flying. She set an international altitude record of twenty thousand feet in 1928 in the Travel Air biplane, a heavy class of engine and airplane. In addition, she had just set a one hundred fifty-six miles per hour speed record in the weight class of her Travel Air.

Bobbi poses with two aviation buffs, in front of the tent Bone set up, to advertise general aviation: especially the Golden Eagle. Bobbi also gave demo rides during these promotions.

Jack Helm, distributor of the Golden Eagle monoplane.

OAKLAND BRANCH
FRUITVALE 6177

SAN FRANCISCO
GRAYSTONE 8779

D. C. WARREN COMPANY
1125 POST STREET, SAN FRANCISCO, CALIF.
PACIFIC COAST DISTRIBUTORS

April 8, 1929

Dear Bobbie:

Darned late with this. Been North for a week, and just got back. Told
Hamilton to write you, and guess he did, but where have you been ?

Took my written on Transport yesterday, and will get flying off tomorrow, rained like H -- today.

When are you going up for endurance again ? All kinds of luck, think
you can have it -- too much work.

Have gotten the vice-president of Travel Air all interested in this re
fueling flight -- he is back at the Detroit show, and is seeing about
getting a J-6 for us to put in one of the new Travel Air 4 place
cabin monoplanes.

Have you worked out anything with the airports there in L.A. ? These
up here do not seem to be so interested at the present time, but maybe
after we get the plane and start on experimental work, they will get
more interested, especially if they think we are going to L. A. with
it. That Grand Central bunch look pretty hot, and would suggest that
you see what you can do there, if not already. We should get a few
thousand out of some airport, and especially from that one, as they
seem anxious to get their field known.

Believe I have the plane etc all arranged for, and we can provably
run the thing off in July -- now its up to you to get the airport to
put up some money.

Going back East this week, write me 1326 Oliver Bldg., Pittsburgh, Pa.
Mrs. Herbert V. Thaden.

Lots of luck old girl, wish I could have seen you more in l.a. but
you know how it is.

Louise

WOMEN FLYERS TO TRY
FOR ENDURANCE MARK

Miss Bobbie Trout and Mrs. Louise Thaden, aviatrixes who pioneered in women's solo endurance flights, yesterday announced that they will start a refueling flight here in an effort to take the endurance record away from the men, Jackson and O'Brine, with their mark of 420h. 21½m. The starting date will be some time between September 10 and 20, next, depending on fogs and other climatic conditions. The take-off will be from Metropolitan Airport.

A Sunbeam biplane, a cabin ship, is being prepared especially for this attempt by the Commercial Aircraft Company, Van Nuys. Jack Sherrill and S. George Ullman, Associated, are promoting the women's endurance refueling flight.

Bobbie Trout set two endurance marks for women in solo, the second and longest being 17h. 24m., February 10 and 11, last. Mrs. Thaden stretched this to 22h. She also established an altitude record for women, a trifle under 20,000 feet. Both are competing in the coming National Air Derby for women, another reason for their delaying the start of their refueling endurance attempt.

*Louise Thaden
writes Bobbi about a
refueling endurance
flight.*

*Pre-publicity about
Bobbi's refueling
endurance record
attempt.*

RIVALS PLAN JOINT FLIGHT

Will Go After Refueling Record

Left to Right, Mrs. Louise McPhetridge Thaden and Bobbie Trout

BOBBIE TROUT of Los Angeles and Mrs. Louise McPhetridge Thaden of San Francisco, aviatrixes who have competed during the past two months for the women's air endurance record, have decided to call off their mutual challenge and co-operate in setting a refueling record, Miss Trout admitted last night.

The California women flyers are planning to take off as copilots as

Bobbi and Louise pre-publicity for a proposed flight.

Women to Seek Refueling Record

Two famous aviatrices, Bob. Trout and Louise McPheteridg Thaden, will attempt to set a new refueling endurance record.

It will be the first flight of like character in which women act as pilots.

This was the announcement yesterday by S. George Ullman and Jack Sherill, backers, who declared the pair will take off from Metropolitan Airport between September 10 and 20.

Kansas Reached by Bobby Trout

Miss Bobby Trout, Los Angeles girl flyer who is holder of the women's endurance record for sustained flight, arrived late yesterday at Fairfax Field, Kansas City, Mo., after a flight from Los Angeles, according to a dispatch from the Middle West city last night.

The youthful flyer is accompanied in her Golden Eagle monoplane by W. G. Mead, test pilot for the Golden Eagle company. The pair left here last Monday on a trip which is expected to last two weeks.

Warren invited Helm and Bobbi to join them for the evening at a local nightclub. Bobbi, dressed in practical flying attire of breeches and riding boots, was very reluctant. She had not brought any dress clothes along; there was no room in the Golden Eagle.

Warren told her they were only going to a little Italian restaurant and not to worry about her dress. Bobbi had her doubts, but agreed to the arrangement. However, when Warren picked them up at the hotel that evening, he and Louise were dressed nicely. Warren and Louise tried to put their guests at ease during the meal at a very posh Italian restaurant. Soon Bobbi's feeling of concern abated and she regained her composure.

When the dancing began, Warren took Bobbi's hand and led her onto the floor. Helm followed with Louise, and the other diners looked a bit startled at first. Bobbi's group was having so much fun by this time, their good humor soon infected the other diners. The orchestra changed to a lively tune, and the staid atmosphere of the club disappeared.

Bobbi had no idea at the time that she was establishing a reputation as the "pants-wearing female." It soon became a part of her personal distinctiveness. This really made Bobbi happy because she always hated dresses, high heels, and elegant clothes. Slacks were the only sensible attire any way she figured it, especially around airplanes.

That evening Bobbi and Louise discussed the idea of joining forces in an attempt to establish the first women's refueling endurance record. Louise planned to talk it over with Warren and her company and let Bobbi know.

Early the next morning, May 19, the two couples made their separate ways to Santa Rosa. They enjoyed the airport opening and air races, and Bobbi showed off the Golden Eagle Chief. Bidding goodbye to their new friends, Bobbi and Helm climbed in the Golden Eagle Chief and Bobbi steered for home.

Low-hanging clouds forced them to take off earlier than they planned, and the fog was so low over Berkeley and Oakland that Bobbi was forced to fly just above the rooftops. She worried about where she would land if the Golden Eagle Chief developed engine trouble. The little engine purred right along without missing a beat, however, and soon they were out of the fog and homeward bound.

CREDIT: ROY RUSSELL

The first Golden Eagle Chief Monoplane to roll out of the factory: this plane was powered with a 90 hp Kinner engine.

Bobbi and the Golden Eagle Chief monoplane.

FROM LADY HEATH
A. R. C. Sc. I. M. R. Ae. S. F. R. G. S.
100 CENTRAL PARK SOUTH
NEW YORK

July 14ᵗʰ 23

Dear Bobbie

How good of you to write to Mr Henderson
I am sure it will help a lot.

I would love to enter for the Derby, but
honestly I'm not too keen on it unless I could
take a good mechanic from the factory along
— a pilot is supposed to be a pilot, & not
a garage hand. I think it is <u>undignifying</u>
the profession to force the person who
corresponds to the Captain of a Ship to
be also the Coal heaver!

Of course in a pinch
to do these thi...
in that...

The first and last parts of a long letter from Lady Mary Heath, who believed that women pilots should not be mechanics. Bobbi disagreed.

I am afraid I feel a "Superiority
complex" as far as the average mechanic
is concerned, & feel that a non-pilot man
on the machine — but one who has an intimate
knowledge of my motor would be a great
asset as a passenger.

Best wishes — & the very best of
luck to you. You deserve to win

Yours
Mary Heath

CREDIT: R.O. BONE

1929—Bobbi as the Golden Eagle test pilot in her sheepskin flying jacket.

A day or so after her return to Los Angeles, Bobbi received a letter from Louise. Louise said that she had talked the idea of a refueling endurance flight in the Travel Air over with Warren, and he was willing to let them try. Bobbi and Louise discussed the idea and both agreed that refueling was the only answer to a new record.

Sure that Bone would give his okay now that she was going to be using a larger airplane, Bobbi approached him with her plans. She told Bone that Louise could get a Travel Air plane and how they would like to try for the first women's refueling endurance record. He did not react the way Bobbi had predicted.

Bone would not allow Bobbi to try. She was surprised when her usually easygoing boss lost his temper. The smile left his face, and he immediately told Bobbi, "Are you crazy? I don't want you killed." Since he felt so strongly about it, she was willing to drop the subject. Bone felt that this was a very foolhardy idea, and thought he was protecting her from herself.

That evening Bobbi called Louise to tell her the flight was a "no go." She told Louise that she could not jeopardize her job with Bone, and

that is what would happen if she persisted in making this flight. Louise was a little upset but agreed that the price was a little too high for Bobbi.

About two months later, Bobbi met a man named Jack Sherrill, who was a publicity agent for Ullman Associates. They were the firm who had managed Rudolph Valentino and many other celebrities. After Valentino's death they were looking for a promotional venture and Sherrill had come up with an idea of managing and promoting the first women's refueling endurance flight. He thought Bobbi, with her experience in solo endurance flights and achievements, would be perfect as one of the pilots.

During the weeks since Bone had refused to let her try for the record, Bobbi had regretted letting the opportunity pass her by. She resolved that she would not lose a similar chance in the future. She accepted Sherrill's offer with the provision that he wait until after the first Women's Transcontinental Air Derby, which was scheduled for August 1929. Bobbi didn't want to jeopardize the opportunity to fly the new Golden Eagle Chief for Bone.

Pacific Aeromotive Corp. employees. Ed Lund (4th from the left—kneeling), worked on Bobbi's J-5 Stearman plane. Tommy Thomas (eighth man from left standing) and Mr. Nichols (tenth man from left standing), Tommy's partner.

Chapter Eight

First "Powder Puff" Derby 1929

A T age twenty-three, Bobbi Trout had been flying almost a year as a demonstration and test pilot for Bone, builder of the Golden Eagle, high-wing monoplanes. She had set altitude records, and solo endurance records, was winner of several air races, and had even become the first woman to fly all night in an airplane. She was well qualified to enter the first Women's Transcontinental Air Derby.

Frank T. Copeland, managing director of the National Women's Air Derby; Mrs. (Beth) Ulysses Grant McQueen, president and founder of the Women's Aeronautical Association; L.C. Kronk, president of the California Exchange Clubs; and Cliff Henderson, promoter of the 1928 National Air Races held in Los Angeles helped to promote the Derby. For months they planned and publicized the event. Sunday, August 18, 1929, was set for the takeoff from Clover Field in Santa Monica. The Derby headed for Cleveland, Ohio, to help promote that big week's air show.

Will Rogers dubbed the race the "Powder Puff Derby," and news reporters quickly picked up the catchy phrase, adding more press coverage to the race. Any qualified female pilot who had a license and a plane could enter the race. The flight would be long and difficult.

The officials were sure that a pilot experienced in navigation and weather would be as successful as any man flying the same course. The course was planned to include the cities that paid the most money along the route to have the pilots land at their field.

Bone promised Bobbi that she could fly his just-completed and licensed Golden Eagle Chief for the race. It was originally built with a ninety horsepower engine. About two weeks before the Derby, however, the ninety horsepower was removed to install a new one hundred–horsepower Kinner engine. The plane would then be capable of speeds up to one hundred twenty miles per hour, which made it the fastest ship in the light plane class.

A week before the race, the second week of August 1929, Bobbi stopped by Clover Field to finalize her entry into the race. Clema Granger and her husband, Jim, one of the fixed-base operators at Clover Field, provided their hangar for the race committee as the sign-up location for race entrants. She recognized a lithe young woman striding toward her. A wide smile lit Bobbi's face when she recognized that the woman was Amelia Earhart.

The two exchanged greetings and Amelia told Bobbi she had just finished signing up and planned to fly a Lockheed Vega. Bobbi had

—Staff Photo

TREASURES EXPERIENCES — C. Lee Cronk, investment firm executive, says, "I wouldn't give a lot for my background and experiences." While state president of the Exchange Club, in which he remains active, he started what is now the aviation Powder Puff Derby. Cronk worked for the federal government during World War II.

People Who Helped Put Air Derby Over

The committees appointed by the Bay District Exchange club to look after the many requirements of the National Women's Air Derby cover a wide range of activity. They have not failed to perform with a readiness and enthusiasm which speaks volumes for the spirit of the club. These committees, working under Managing Director Frank T. Copeland, are enumerated hereunder:

Frank T. Copeland, managing director.

Aeronautical Committee—F. T. Copeland, chairman; Carl R. Henderson, Cecil S. Dickinson, D. D. S., Richard K. Gandy, Gordon Cornet, J. B. Daniell, Lloyd W. Keith and Al Pratt.

Reception Committee—George Greene, chairman (national president Exchange club).

Honorary Reception Committee—Hon. Herman Michel, mayor; F. A. Helton, commissioner of finance; John Morton, commissioner of public works; A. R. Pratt, president chamber of commerce; T. H. Dudley, president Ocean Park Business Men's association, Mrs. Lucy M. Pirotte, president Santa Monica Professional and Business Women's club; Elizabeth L. McQueen, Women's Aeronautical Association of California; Mrs. R. J. Morrison, Daughters of the British Empire; W. R. Alexander, president Santa Monica Realty Board; Russell Hart, president Rotary club; A. P. Rehwold, president Kiwanis club; Frank Pratt, president Lions club; Ira Miller, president Optimists club; Charles E. Hewing, president Bay District Clubs association.

General Committee—Frank T. Copeland, chairman; Clark Sammons, Cecil Dickinson and Gordon Cornet.

Contest Committee—Dudley Steele, chairman (National Aeronautical association, phone TRinity 2231.

Concessions Committee—Ralph Kreuger, chairman.

Grand Stand Committee—W. S. Hawthorne, chairman.

Parking Committee—Hugh Logan, chairman.

Traffic Committee—Carl Henderson, chairman; C. E. Webb, chief of police, Santa Monica; W. L. Hagenbaugh, captain, Sawtelle division, Los Angeles police department; W. H. Behrendt, captain, Venice division, Los Angeles police department; L. P. Rober, sergeant of police, Santa Monica.

Public Safety Committee—C. E. Webb, chairman, chief of police, Santa Monica; W. L. Hagenbaugh, captain of police, Sawtelle division, Los Angeles police department; W. H. Behrendt, captain of police, Venice division, Los Angeles police department; Ed E. Randall, lieutenant of police, Santa Monica.

Airport Committee—Duff Willson, chairman, manager Clover Field airport.

Finance Committee—John Stintin, chairman.

Sticker Sales Committee—Lloyd Keith, chairman; Ed Hammack, Al Pratt, Manley Danforth, Merrit Hull and Tom Neeley.

Publicity Committee—Al Dorris, chairman; J. B. Daniell.

Addressograph System—Don Forker, E. R. Carter.

Supply Committee—Ed Hammack, chairman.

Managing Director

Frank T. Copeland, managing director of the Women's National Air Derby, to who much of the credit for the success of the flight is due. Through his energy and enterprise and unfailing vigilance many of the difficulties which beset such an undertaking as this have been straightened out.

Breakfast Club Had Record Event When Fairest Fliers Fed

The National Women's Air Derby contestants prove to be one of the greatest drawing cards in the history of the justly celebrated Los Angeles Breakfast club, when, on Wednesday morning last, one of the largest gatherings of members and friends gathered to greet ten of the women flyers. In addition to the tremendous crowd of breakfastiers, numbering almost one thousand men and women, the feminine pilots attracted one of the largest aggregations of newspaper reporters, photographers and motion picture weeklies, ever assembled on the Pacific coast. The "bird women" faced at one time approximately fifty cameras.

Maurice De Mond, founder and president of the Breakfast club, whose hospitality was thoroughly enjoyed, said concerning his honored guests, "We have had presidents, members of royal families, great naval and military officers, and celebrities of all kinds, to breakfast at our club, and with full and due respect to all of them, there has never been a more enjoyable gathering than the breakfast that we shall all long remember as the women flyers' breakfast. It was splendid of so many of them to come and we wish all of them the greatest success."

earlier promised Jack Sherrill, the publicity agent with Ullman Associates, to look for another woman with whom to make a refueling flight. Bobbi asked if Amelia had time to make the flight with her. Amelia paused for a moment and told Bobbi that she would not be able to commit herself right away, but she thought the flight would be a terrific new type of record. Amelia had to check with George Putnam, her manager.

Amelia was interested to learn Bobbi's plan for staying in the air for a month. No other women had tried to refuel in the air. Both women agreed that it would be fun to do something so different. They chatted briefly about the Army's in-flight refueling plane, the *Question Mark*, which was up for about one hundred fifty hours, at the same time Bobbi was setting her first solo endurance record.

Amelia said she would talk to Putnam that night and let Bobbi know as soon as she could. Amelia commented however, since she flew the Atlantic a year previously, she had received so much publicity, she felt like she was only a sack of potatoes on that friendship flight. Now she really wanted to prove women would be known as good pilots.

Bobbi poses with hopeful derby entrants at Margaret Perry's Culver City Airport.

Mrs. Ulysses Grant McQueen, a staunch supporter of women fliers who helped organize the first Derby.
(left)
Derby contestants (Bobbi sitting) watch an acrobatic demonstration before the competition.

THE FIRST AIRPORT TO BE OPERAT-
ED BY A WOMAN.—A group of famous
feminine flyers at the dedication of the new
Culver City, Calif., airport, owned by Mrs.
Margaret Perry. Left to right: Patty Willis, Bobby Trout, Gladys O'Donnel, Margaret Perry, Vera Dawn Walker, Aline Miller
and Jean Stapf.   (*Internat'l*)

Margaret Perry's Culver City airport gathering.

Most of the derby contestants at the opening of Margaret Perry's Culver City airport.

35 Women Pilots to Race in 2,200-Mile Air Derby to Cleveland, Ohio

* * * * * * * * * * * * *

Men to Be Barred as the First Cross-Country Dash for Fair Sex Is Staged

LOS ANGELES, Cal.—(NEA)— The greatest sporting event for women ever held anywhere will get under way at the Santa Monica airport here on August 18, when 35 women pilots take off in a 2,200-mile aerial race to Cleveland.

This transcontinental air derby for women, the first of its kind ever staged, will be an eight-day affair, and will bring the women pilots into Cleveland on the second day of the National Air races there.

Its course will take the women over 10 states and through 19 cities.

Starting at Santa Monica's Clover Field, the race will follow a southern route through New Mexico, Arizona, Texas, Oklahoma, Kansas. Missouri, Illinois, Indiana and Ohio. There will be 18 stopping points, and cash prizes totaling between $6,000 and $10,000 are offered for the winners. In addition, the first woman pilot to reach the Cleveland airport will receive a trophy, the "Symbol of Flight."

Some of the most famous women fliers in the world will be among the contestants.

Lady Mary Heath, whose aviation feats amazed all of England, will be one of the racers. So will Amelia Earhart, only woman to cross the Atlantic by plane; Ruth Elder, who nearly beat Miss Earhart to it, but was balked by motor trouble in mid-Atlantic and rescued by a cargo steamer; Miss Marvel Crosson, who holds the women's altitude record; Miss Bobby Trout, who held the altitude record until Miss Crosson broke it—and many others of only slightly less prominence.

SPONSORED BY EXCHANGE

This race, incidentally, is being sponsored by the Santa Monica Bay District Exchange club, under the auspices of the National Exchange club and the National Aeronautic association; and the 18 control stops designated for the race are being planned, as far as possible, to fall in cities where there are Exchange clubs, which can thus partake in the race themselves. Every plane in the race will bear the Exchange club emblem.

An ingenious method of financing the race has been adopted by the Santa Monica club. Parking space for automobiles at Clover Field is being sold at one dollar per car to spectators desirous of seeing the start of the race, and accommodations for more than 2,000 cars have been arranged. It is expected that at least 100,000 spectators will see the race begin.

The race will be a real test of the skill and airmanship of the women pilots.

The crossing of the mountains in the southwest does not offer as many hazards as the more northerly routes, but it is no job for a novice. Under almost any conditions, 2,200 miles of cross-country flying can be considered a fairly stiff job for any but a professional aviator.

When the race was first proposed, the officials considered making a rule that each woman pilot be accompanied by a male mechanic, to take care of forced landings and the hazards of the trip over mountain ranges and desert wastes. The women, however, objected vociferously, and through Amelia Earhart, their spokesman, talked the officials out of it.

The rules now stand that the crew of each plane shall consist of a woman alone, or a woman pilot and not more than one woman mechanic or passenger. The woman riding as mechanic or passenger must be one who has never made a solo flight, and the use of dual controls will not be permitted.

Each of the woman contestants holds a department of commerce license and each has had at least 100 hours of flying experience, including 50 hours of cross-country flying.

According to present plans, the derby will be flown through the following cities:

Santa Monica, Calif.; San Bernardino, Calif.; Yuma, Phoenix and Tucson, Ariz.; Lordburg, N. M.; Paso, Pecos, Abilene and Fort Worth or Dallas, Tex.; Oklahoma City and Tulsa, Ok.; Wichita, Kansas City and St. Louis, Mo.; Terre Haute and Indianapolis, Ind., and Columbus and Cleveland, O.

Overnight stops are planned at Yuma, Phoenix, El Paso, Abilene, Fort Worth or Dallas, Wichita, St. Louis and Columbus.

More than 35 feminine pilots are expected to hop off from Los Angeles August 18 in a race for women fliers, terminating at Cleveland, Ohio, where the National Air Races will then be in progress. Seven of the best known women pilots now preparing for the race are pictured here: 1, Bobbie Trout; 2, Marvel Crosson; 3, Mrs. Louise Thaden; 4, Amelia Earhart; 5, Mrs. Florence Barnes; 6, Lady Mary Heath; 7, Ruth Elder. En route stops will be made at Yuma and Phoenix, Ariz., El Paso, Abilene and Fort Worth, Texas, Wichita, Kansas, St. Louis and Columbus.

Announcement of Derby contestants.

Most of these women pilots were in the derby and now deceased. From left: Louise Thaden (1979), Bobbi Trout (still breathing), Patty Willis, Marvel Crosson (August 19, 1929), Vera Dawn Walker (1978), Amelia Earhart (1937), Marjorie Crawford, Ruth Elder Camp (1977), and Pancho Barnes (1975).

Ready for Derby Day Take-off

WOMEN *aviators who will race from Clover Field to Cleveland, photographed at the Breakfast Club yesterday.*

AMELIA EARHART, *Bobbie Trout, Marvel Crosson and other noted flyers were included.*
—*(Examiner photo.)*

Left to right the women are: Louise Thaden, Bobbie Trout, Patty Willis, Marvel Crosson, Blanche Noyes, Vera Dawn Walker, Amelia Earhart, Marjorie Crawford, Ruth Elder and Florence Low Barnes.

CREDIT: R.R. MARTIN

The 90-hp Golden Eagle Chief that Bobbi flew in the Derby. This photo was taken just before R.O.Bone installed a new 100-hp Kinner engine, to make the plane the fastest in the small class.

METROPOL-GESELLSCHAFT

F Mathes & Co

Berlin paper, August 18, 1929—A picture of Bobbi that appeared in a German paper and was sent to Thea Rasche. Thea gave it to Bobbi.

Bobbi said how sure she was that Amelia would be the right choice. Amelia said she would get right in there and work, just like she had done all during her aviation career.

After talking with Amelia, Bobbi continued visiting with other aviators around the field. There was a great air of excitement at the field. Preparation was being made for the big event the next Sunday. Reporters and photographers from newspapers and the newsreel services roamed around the field and interviewed the pilots.

The next day Amelia met Bobbi at the airfield. Amelia told her that she just couldn't find the time in her hectic schedule and was sincerely sorry. If the refueling flight were only going to be for a day or two, Amelia could work it into her schedule, but Putnam had her schedule booked for the next several months. Amelia apologized for not being able to make the flight, and told Bobbi how she would love to spend a month over Los Angeles with her, making a new record.

Bobbi was extremely disappointed. There was so much activity going on in preparation for the race, however, that she dismissed her disappointment. The Derby was going to begin that weekend, and she still didn't have her airplane. The engine change was taking longer than anticipated.

The evening before the race, the Golden Eagle Chief, without being tested, was delivered to Clover Field. Early the next morning, Bobbi taxied it over to the "compass rose" to check the compass. She saw that something was radically wrong. The needle swerved wildly instead of remaining on north. Bobbi and Joe Harrison, the engine mechanic from the factory, began to troubleshoot the problem. They discovered that the compass had been mounted on a piece of bent iron, which caused the aberration. After finding and installing a non-magnetic material on which to mount the compass, they reinstalled it.

Bobbi compensated the compass and taxied to her takeoff position. She was now ready to load the airplane. Bobbi's luggage included evening wear for the end-of-race banquet and a change of clothes for flying. She loaded the suitcase, bottled water and food, in case she had a forced landing. She then supervised the fueling of her airplane, making sure that the gas tanks were completely full. Kendall oil products were used because Bobbi liked their quality. Not only that, they offered to supply it for free.

On the morning of August 18, 1929, excitement reigned supreme on the airfield. Bobbi and the nineteen other contenders waited anxiously in line to take off. The Golden Eagle Chief was now ready. Bobbi had applied the Exchange Club logo to the ship's fuselage and did all her last-minute checks. She relaxed for a moment before climbing into the cockpit and watched the spectators milling around the planes. She said goodbye to her mother, father, and Denny. After it was time for family and friends to leave the field, Bobbi talked over a few last-minute details about the new engine and its performance with Harrison and Bone. Satisfied that she was fully prepared for the race, Bobbi strapped herself in and waited her turn to be flagged off.

CLOVER FIELD STARTING POINT OF WOMEN'S AIR DERBY
Five widely known women flyers who will participate in the race are shown above. In the center is Clover Field as it appears today and below is the Union Oil automobile service station operated at the field by J. E. Granger. In the oval from left to right— E. R. Carter, special Union agent in Santa Monica; Mayor Herman Michel and Duff Wilson, manager of the airport.

Clover Field where the Derby began.

20 Women Fliers to Race

'Queens of Air' Start Race to Ohio Tomorrow

Map shows route of National Women's Air Derby from Santa Monica, Calif. to Cleveland, Ohio

All-feminine Air Derby starts from Clover Field, Santa Monica, at 2:00 p.m. tomorrow

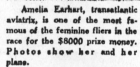

"Queens of the air" will take off from Santa Monica tomorrow afternoon in history's first all-feminine air derby, a race to Cleveland, Ohio.

Amelia Earhart, transatlantic aviatrix, is one of the most famous of the feminine fliers in the race for the $8000 prize money. Photos show her and her plane.

Many of the "flying queens" are "queens of beauty" as well. Marvel Crosson, who holds the world's altitude record, will be the first to take off.

Among the Southern California contestants in the race of the nation's finest feminine fliers are Bobbie Trout, at left, and Margaret Perry, at right, friendly rivals. Miss Trout is the former endurance champion and she and Miss Perry are listed among the favorites.

At top is Gladys O'Donnell, Long Beach beauty. In center is Louise Thaden, prominent aviatrix of Pittsburg and California. Lower photo shows Florence Lowe Barnes, San Marino society woman and flier.

Edith Foltz

Miss Neva Paris

Mae Haizlip

Twenty women who flew the first Women's Transcontinental Air Derby.

Ruth Elder, first woman to attempt to fly the Atlantic, is one of the reasons that flight is called the "race of winged beauties."

Phoebe Fairgrave Omlie

Claire Fahy, pretty wife of Lieut. Herbert Fahy, famous test pilot, hopes to bring additional laurels to the "flying family" by winning the national race.

Miss Vera Dawn Walker

Here are three more aviatrices in the derby. Reading from top, Thea Rasche, Germany's premier woman flier; Ruth Nichols, Detroit society aviatrix, and Blanche Noyes, whose husband holds the men's endurance flying record.

Mrs. Keith Miller

Women in Aviation

Mrs. Florence
Lowe Barnes

Bobby Trout

Mrs. Louise Thaden

National Women's Air Derby

Considerable attention is being focussed on the forthcoming Santa Monica-Cleveland Women's Air Derby to be staged in conjunction with the 1928 National Air Races to be held in Cleveland August 24th to September 2nd.

This colorful classic derby is sponsored by the Santa Monica Bay district Exchange Club, under the auspices of the National Exchange Club and the National Aeronautical Association.

Prizes amounting between $8,000 and $10,000 will be divided on an equitable basis between the two classes of contestants. Liberal lap prizes are provided for; eight overnight stops are placed in route.

Marvel Crosson

The following is a partial list of entries, many of whom either now hold or have held many world's records for endurance, altitude and speed:

Lady Mary Heath of London.

Mrs. Nova Finlay Paris of Great Neck, N. Y.

Mrs. Keith Miller of New York City.

Mrs. Gladys O'Donnell of Long Beach, Calif.

Miss Marcella Huyette of Pomona, California.

Miss Amelia Earhart of New York City.

Miss Cousello Williard of Los Angeles, California.

Mrs. Louise M. Thaden of Pittsburg, Pennsylvania.

Miss Ruth Elder of Beverly Hills, California.

Miss Marvel Crosson of San Diego, California.

Miss Bobby Trout, Los Angeles, Calif.

Mrs. Florence Lowe Barnes of San Marino, Calif.

Miss Peggy Hall of Santa Ana, Calif. Mrs. Margaret Perry of Beverly Hills, Calif. Mrs. Sarah Warrender of Venice, Calif. Miss Ruth Nicols of New York City. Miss Dorothy L. Stocker of Houston, Texas. Mrs. Annette G. Verner of Charlotte, N. C.

Sunday August 18, 1929- —Spectators at Santa Monica airport waiting to see the start of the first Woman's Transcontinental Air Derby.

Bobbi applies an Exchange Club emblem on to her Golden Eagle Chief, just before take-off—August 18, 1929.

The crowd eagerly awaits the Derby take-off.

Kendall Oil Company fills the crankcase full of oil.

Family and friends at Bobbi's plane to bid her farewell.

ROUTE OF AIR DERBY FROM

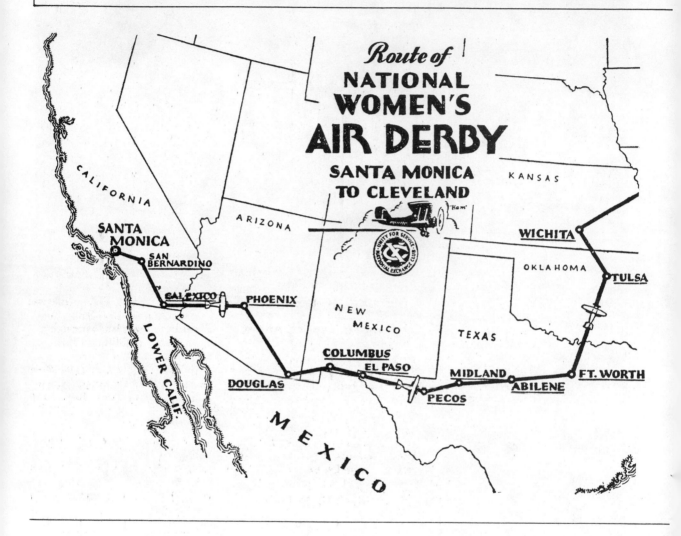

Bobbi watched the first four planes take off and waited in anticipation for hers. She was next. She revved up the engine and rolled down the field. Within moments, Bobbi Trout was airborne.

Although Phoebe Omlie's Monocoupe was a fast plane—and Phoebe a great racer—Bobbi was a contender with the brand new one hundred–horsepower Kinner engine in her new Golden Eagle Chief.

Phoebe, Bobbi's closest competition in her class, had initially been an exhibition pilot who walked wings, transferred from one airplane to another in mid-air, and hung by her knees, toes, and teeth from airplanes during flight. She even stood upright on the upper wing of an airplane while it did loops. Many of her stunts were filmed and used in movie serials. She had rightly earned the title, "Daring Young Woman," and was sure to use all her resources to

SANTA MONICA TO CLEVELAND

This map shows the route that will be followed by the girl fliers between Clover Field in Santa Monica and Cleveland in the nine-day race across the continent. The actual control points and intermediate stops, as taken from the last-minute reports, are as follows: Sunday, August 18—Santa Monica to San Bernardino; Monday, August 19—San Bernardino to Phoenix, overnight; Tuesday, August 20—Phoenix to Douglas, overnight; Wednesday, August 21—Douglas to El Paso, El Paso to Pecos, Pecos to Midland for overnight; Thursday, August 22—Midland to Fort Worth for overnight; Friday, August 23—Fort Worth to Tulsa, Tulsa to Wichita for overnight; Saturday, August 24—Wichita to Kansas City, Kansas City to East St. Louis for overnight; Sunday, August 25—East St. Louis to Terre Haute, Terre Haute to Cincinnati, Cincinnati to Columbus for overnight; Monday, August 26—Columbus to Cleveland.

win the race.

The first leg of the Derby stretched from Santa Monica to San Bernardino. The minute Bobbi was airborne, the oil pressure gauge stayed at zero. She didn't dare fly a straight course. Wondering if she had a broken oil line, Bobbi deviated from the straight course over Los Angeles City Hall. She chose a course that did not carry her over homes or businesses. In case her engine froze up, she had been taught to be where she could easily locate a field or pasture in which to land.

About halfway to San Bernardino, Bobbi's oil pressure gauge suddenly began to work perfectly. Everything seemed to be running fine. It was uncanny; no doubt an air lock in the line. The extra miles cost her a winning time for the first leg of the flight, but that did not upset her too much.

All twenty airplanes landed safely in San Bernardino. The rules stated that the race pilots would stop en route to Cleveland only for fuel, motor testing, rest and food. Each pilot would service her own plane and supervise the fueling of her tanks, leaving her ship during the rest periods where it could be guarded by authorized agents of the National Aeronautic Association (N.A.A.). They could then attend the banquet at the hotel each evening.

Bobbi watched the gasoline being pumped into her plane's tanks until they overflowed. Satisfied that her plane was ready for the next day's flight, she left the plane under the guardianship of the N.A.A. and dashed off to the hotel.

The first day was going well. All twenty pilots completed the first leg and were now discussing the events of the day. At dinner, they were served a super banquet of prime rib. After dinner, the racers sat around at the hotel and visited.

Before long, Bobbi began to get sleepy. She could not wait to get to bed. Meanwhile, the group discussion seemed to center around Pancho Barnes and Vera Dawn Walker, a young woman who came to California to act in the movies. They were debating the course that the race would take. Pancho insisted that she had heard the course was to be changed. Vera disagreed.

Just before the takeoff of the Derby, Vera qualified for the race. She had a few problems with her Curtiss Robin airplane she planned to fly. For one thing, she had not had any time to practice in her plane. She started cold on the first day of the Derby. Despite her disadvantage, Vera did well.

Pancho was the ever fun-loving Pancho Lowe Barnes. She picked up her nickname several years earlier when she rebelled against the duties of a preacher's wife and traveled to Mexico with some pilot friends. It seemed Pancho and some of the pilots wanted to change the route of the Derby. The question of route changes had still not been decided when Bobbi retired to her room. Leaving the final decision up to Pancho and the others, Bobbi went to her room to get some sleep. She quickly showered and called the front desk to leave an early

Only 19 women officially took off.

wake-up call.

The next morning Bobbi awoke to a feeling of impending crisis. Immediately glancing at her wristwatch, she realized the hotel operator had failed to call her at the appointed time. She exclaimed, "Oh bugs! They forgot to call me." Bobbi hurriedly dressed and made her way to the hotel lobby to check out. At the counter she met Thea Rasche, Germany's "Flying Fraulein." She also had been forgotten by the hotel staff.

With no time for breakfast the two last race entrants shared a ride to the airfield, barely arriving in time to take off. The new routing was to fly from San Bernardino, check in at Imperial Airport, and then fly on to Yuma, Arizona. Hurriedly, Bobbi figured her new compass headings and hopped into her plane.

BUILDERS OF THE ORIGINAL STEEL TUBE MONOPLANE "The Lone Eagle"

FEDERAL AIRCRAFT CORPORATION

.. AN EXPANSION OF ..

RYAN MECHANICS MONOPLANE CO.

PHONE FACTORY 321-30

SAN BERNARDINO, CALIFORNIA

August 19, 1929.

*** TO WHOM IT MAY CONCERN ***

\- - - - - - - - -

We, the undersigned pilots of the Women's Air Derby from Santa Monica to Cleveland do hereby wholeheartedly consent to the entrance of May Haizlys in this event, her start to be made this date from Santa Monica.

A. Earhart — Claire Fahy

M. O. Perry — Thea Rasche

Edith Foltz — Gladys O'Donnell

Blanche Noyes — Ruth Elder

Louise Thaden — Neva Paris

Florence Barnes — Vera Dawn Walker

Phoebe Fairgrave Omlie — Ruth R. Nichols

Bobbi Trout — J. M. Miller

Marvel Crosson — Opal Kunz

Mary Van Mack

CREDIT: BOB BEECHLER

Derby contestants agreed to let Mae Haizlip into the race as a late entry.

BELIEVE FLI

YUMA
The most important and strategic site on the Colorado River for a home and profitable investment.

THE YUMA

STARTS THE DAY ON THI
Full Leased Wire Report Of 7

Established 1905----Vol. 26----No. 198

YUMA, ARIZONA, TUES

SEE SABOTAGE

LOST IN DESERT

LANDED ON NOSE

Amelia Earhart, of trans-Atlantic fame was the first of the women fliers to arrive at Fly field. In her orange monoplane, she circled several times and then dipped for the field. She over-shot the cleared section and turned up on the nose of 'the ship... The prop was bent and a new one was rushed by air from Los Angeles... She said something went wrong with the machine's stablizer and blamed the crash on that.

Plunging from an altitude of over 2000 feet, Marvel Crossen, champ woman high flier, is believed to have dropped into a mesquite jungle on the north bank of the Gila river, about five miles from Wellton. Three eye-witnesses saw the plane fo into a nose dive and a spin. Through the thin desert air, the faint sound of a crash reached them. Posses are now scoring the jungle.

ER IS KILLED

MORNING SUN

WEATHER

Generally fair today and tomer-row, little change in temperature.

LOWER COLORADO
he United Press

DAY, AUG. 20, 1929— FOUR PAGES   PRICE FIVE CENTS

IN AIR CRASHES

Search Desert Near Wellton For Crosson Ship, Crash Seen

While the eyes of an anxious nation are turned toward Wellton, Ariz., where the plane of Marvel Crosson, woman flier crashed into a Mesquite jungle in the Gila river valley, yesterday afternoon, United States department of commerce agents last night launched an investigation of ugly charges that several of the airships had been deliberately tampered with to put them out of the woman's air derby.

It was reported from Los Angeles, last night, that the race would be halted at Phoenix until the investigation had been completed.

In the meanwhile, several posses combed the dense thicket on the north bank of the Gila all last night seeking trace of the lost plane. Three witnesses saw it go into a nose dive, yesterday afternoon, and crash to the ground. The searchers, led by Deputy Sheriffs Victor Gael and J. C. Livingston, are combing an area of one hundred square miles.

They were furnished with horses to conduct the search, although in many places the men were forced to crawl over wide areas on the hands and knees. The jungle extends towards Roll, and men of wide desert experience say it is the worst section in Arizona.

Sensational charges that the planes were tampered with were hurled last night by Lieut. Herbert Fahy, husband of Mrs. Clara Fahy, a contestant in the race who was forced down at Calexico because of broken wire braces on her ship.

The wires had been eaten through with crossive acid, Fahy charged.

He dispatched wires to the race officials at Cleveland, Ohio, asking that the derby be called off to protect the lives of the fliers.

continued next page . . .

SAND IN GAS

CREDIT: TERRY ROSS, EDITOR, *YUMA DAILY SUN* AND *ARIZONA SENTINEL*

Forced down at Holtville by a stalled motor, Thea Rasche, German bird-woman, found sand in her gasoline tank. She charges that she received a telegram, Sunday night, warning her to be on guard against sabotage, during the race. Her plane was damaged.

Four aeroplanes will fly over the area this morning.

Miss Crosson's ship, flying at about 2000 feet, wobbled in the air, flopped like a wounded bird and dove towards earth with the tail spinning madly. The sound of the crash could be faintly heard through the thin desert air.

It was the opinion around Wellton, last night, that the flier was either killed instantly, or seriously injured and buried in the wreckage of the ship.

The jungle growth is impassible in many places. Searchers said they could pass within a hundred yards of the ship and fail to notice it because of the denseness and heighth of the mesquite.

Sheriff James Polhamus has all available men in the brush.

Thea Rasche, German air star, who was forced down at Holtville, charges that dirt was placed in her gasoline tank. In an interview, and in making her charges, the Teuton aviatrix exhibited a telegram she received Sunday night at San Bernardino, warning her to be on the lookout for sabotage. She said she did not know the sender of the wire which came from New York. She said her plane was not guarded during the night.

SOMETHING WENT WRONG

Winging along at a good clip, boyish Bobbie Trout, star woman aeronaut of Los Angeles, suffered a stalled motor and was forced to make a landing in a ploughed field near Algodones, Mexico. Her machine turned over on its back. While Bobbie took her tough luck like a gentleman, she declared last night that certain circumstances appeared "queer." Investigation revealed that an altitude adjustment on her engine had been twisted out of place causing the motor to choke.

Bobbie Trout, Los Angeles girl flier, was forced down near Algodones, yesterday, and cracked up in landing. She said that her motor had flooded and with a few coughs ceased functioning.

Investigation by the mechanics revealed that an altitude adjustment on the engine had been twisted so that Miss Trout was unable to operate it from the cockpit. The mechanics said that it appeared as though the connection had been twisted by design.

The boyish woman aeronaut declared that the circumstances appeared queer. She stayed in Yuma last night, after being brought from Mexico by Chief of Police Henry Levy. Her plane was badly damaged.

Although Miss Rasche's ship was damaged considerably in the forced landing, repairs were made and she was scheduled to arrive at Fly field early today.

In making his charges, Lieutenant Fahy declared:

"The wires show evidence of being burned with acid. I am convinced that there is something rotten in this race. I'll do everything in my power to have it called off."

Mrs. Fahy joined her husband in Yuma last night, and they stayed at the Del Ming. They are going to survey the jungle from the air, today, in search for the Crosson plane.

Fahy, who is the holder of the world's solo endurance record, damaged his plane badly when landing at Fly feld. The wheel struck the raised edge of a concrete circle in the center of the field and smashed the landing gear. The machine tipped and damaged a wing.

Amelia Earhart, the American girl who flew the Atlantic was the first to arrive at the field, ran into trouble right after the wheels of her monoplane touched the ground. The plane ran onto a hummock and nosed over, bending the propellor. A new one was rushed from Los Angeles, and she flew to Phoenix a few minutes after the other fliers.

Twelve Women Flyers In Big Race Land in Phoenix

By Associated Press

PHOENIX, Ariz., Aug. 19.—Louise Thaden of Pittsburgh, Pa., was the first to complete the second lap of the Santa Monica-Cleveland Women's Air Derby when she landed at Sky Harbor, the Phoenix airport, at 1:04:36 p. m.

Florence Barnes of San Marino was second, she landed at 1:05:35. Other arrivals were: Gladys O'Donnell, Cleveland, 1:18; Ruth Nichols, Rye, N. Y., 1:18:05; Keith Miller, New Zealand, 1:13:15.

Phoebe Omlie, New York, 1:37:30; Ruth Elder, Beverly Hills, 1:37:53; Vera Walker, Los Angeles, 1:39:04; Amelia Earhart, New York, 1:43:45; Neva Paris, Great Neck, L. I., 1:46:49; Edith Flotz, Portland, Oregon, 1:47:57; Margaret Perry, Beverly Hills, 1:53:40.

Opal Kunz of New York and Marvel Crosson of San Diego, Calif., had not arrived at Phoenix at 3:30 o'clock this afternoon. Miss Kunz left Yuma at 11:53 a. m., while Miss Crosson left at 11:57 a. m.

An escort plane which followed the flyers from Yuma to Phoenix reported that no sign was seen of the missing women pilots between here and Yuma.

By United Press

YUMA, Ariz., Aug. 19.—Lacking three of its most prominent members, the group of women competing in the women's air derby of the national air races, took off for Phoenix today after a brief halt here.

Bobbie Trout, one-time holder of the world's endurance record for women, Thea Rasche, star German aviatrix, and Claire Fahy, wife of the holder of the men's solo endurance flight record, were the pilots who failed to reach this control.

A possibility existed that Miss Rasche and Mrs. Fahy might get back into the race, but Miss Trout faces a longer delay.

Miss Trout made a forced landing six miles west of here. The

(CONTINUED ON PAGE THREE)

WOMEN FLYERS LAND IN PHOENIX

Three Racers Fail To Leave Yuma; 2 Others Are Lost After Leaving

(CONTINUED FROM PAGE ONE)

landing gear on her plane was smashed and the propeller was cracked, but she was unhurt. She will continue the flight when the plane is repaired.

Miss Trout came here, assembled a crew and returned to her plane to make a desperate effort to get it into shape. She said she was forced to land by motor trouble.

Miss Rasche made a forced landing near Holtville, Calif., and was attempting to repair her landing gear in time to reenter the competition.

Supporting struts gave away on Mrs. Fahy's plane when she set her plane down hard at Calexico.

Amelia Earhart nosed over in landing here, but a new propeller was put on her ship and she departed with fourteen other entrants for Phoenix.

She took off and soon flew over the Imperial Airport check-line. Clocking in ten minutes ahead of Phoebe, Bobbi later learned she gained eight minutes over Phoebe's flying time. Proudly, Bobbi turned and headed for Yuma.

Almost in sight of Yuma, Bobbi's engine missed—once, and then again. Her heart skipped a beat. Fear shot adrenalin through her veins. She breathed a sigh of relief the moment the engine caught again. Within a few minutes, however, the engine quit completely. She checked for a safe landing place and spotted a large field to her right. Bobbi thought there must be some dirt in the carburetor and she could clean it out and be on her way. But dirt did not cause the failure: She was out of gas and only six miles from the Yuma Airport.

Bobbi was headed for a field just beyond the town of Algadones, near the Mexican border.

She prepared for a dead stick landing and tried to pancake, to come in slowly and drop down. She discovered, too late, that the field was plowed at right angles to the direction in which she was headed. The wheels caught in the deep furrows, and the Golden Eagle Chief somersaulted, coming to a rest upside down.

As the dust settled, Bobbi slid unscathed out of the cockpit, landed on her head, and began to assess the damage. The greatest damage appeared to be a bent propeller.

Seeing a few Mexican workers some distance away, Bobbi began to walk toward them. "They must have used the biggest plow in the world," she thought, stepping down from one furrow and then up the next. The workers walked toward her, reaching Bobbi in about twenty minutes time. Although she was unable to speak Spanish fluently, she made them understand that she needed a phone to call the

YUMA
The most important and strategic
site on the Colorado River for a
home and profitable investment.

THE YUMA M.

STARTS THE DAY ON THE 1
Full Leased Wire Report Of T

Established 1905—Vol. 26—No. 198 YUMA, ARIZONA, TUESD

FLIER

FOUND KILLED

LANDED ON NOSE

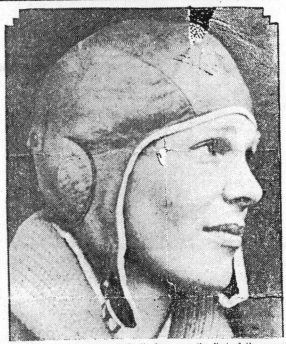

Plunging from an altitude of over 2000 feet, Marvel Crossen, champ woman high flier, is believed to have dropped into a mesquite jungle on the north bank of the Gila river, about five miles from Wellton. Three eye-witnesses saw the plane fo into a nose dive and a spin. Through the thin desert air, the faint sound of a crash reached them. Possts are now scoring the jungle.

Amelia Earhart, of trans-Atlantic fame was the first of the women fliers to arrive at Fly field. In her orange monoplane, she circled several times and then dipped for the field. She over-shot the cleared section and turned up on the nose of the ship... The prop was bent and a new one was rushed by air from Los Angeles... She said something went wrong with the machine's stablizer and blamed the crash on that.

ᴛORNING SUN

OWER COLORADO
e United Press

WEATHER

Generally fair today and tomorrow, little change in temperature.

AY, AUG. 20, 1929— FOUR PAGES

PRICE FIVE CENTS

DEAD

EXTRA!

BULLETIN

The mangled body of Marvel Crosson was found 200 yards from her wrecked plane, six miles north of Wellton. It was found at five a. m. by Deputy Sherif fs Vctor Gael and J. C. Livingston. She was apparently instantly killed as the plane crashed.

Starting out at daylight, after searching almost all night, the searchers came upon the broken plane first. The flier was missing. There was hope that she was still alive and the posse spread out to comb the immediate neighborhood. In a few minutes the body was found, with every bone broken. She had been instantly killed, the flier apparently having been thrown from the plunging machine as it hurtled towards the earth.

Another woman flier, who arrived over Fly Field, late last night did not land and disappeared in the direction of Somerton. She is believed to have crashed. Search is being made for her plane.

Sensational charges that the planes were tampered with were hurled last night by Lieut. Herbert Fahy, husband of Mrs. Clara Fahy, a contestant in the race who was forced down at Calexico because of broken wire braces on her ship.

The wires had been eaten through with crossive acid, Fahy charged.

He dispatched wires to the race officials at Cleveland, Ohio, asking that the derby be called off to protect the lives of the fliers.

factory for parts and help. She remembered her struggle in Spanish and was happy she had learned a few words.

The sun set and rose again. Bone finally sent parts and help. In the one hundred twenty-degree heat, Bobbi, the factory mechanics, and the man from Kinner engines worked feverishly to repair the aircraft. It took twenty-four hours before they had it ready to fly again.

Bobbi was ready to attempt a takeoff. As she was driven through Algadones on the way to her plane, the workers cheered her on and had a great time rooting for her. Bobbi had become the hero of the town. They knew she was a woman flier and discovered she was a contestant in the big Derby.

By the time they got back to the plane, some kind-hearted workers had leveled a takeoff strip for Bobbi. She climbed into the cockpit, ready to start up, when one of the mechanics noticed that the left airfoil, in the left wing section, had been crushed when it hit the top of a furrow.

Bobbi seethed with frustration. Now the mechanics would have to remove the wing and tow the plane to Yuma. In Yuma they opened up the wing and installed new ribs and covering.

While working on Bobbi's ship at Yuma airport: The Trout's met Frances Becerra who became part of their family. Many years later, Frances sold her beauty shop to nurse Mrs. Trout, for 10 years, until their demise, within 2 days of each other.

Bobbi's mother and father came to Yuma to help during the time the plane was repaired. It was at this time Bobbi and her family met a seventeen-year-old Mexican girl, Frances Becerra. Frances was working her way to Los Angeles. Bobbi's family was later to literally adopt Frances. She became like a sister to Bobbi.

It was now Thursday, three frustrating days since she landed in that plowed field. Bobbi's little Golden Eagle Chief was ready to fly again. She got into the cockpit and without a hitch, took off. A Kinner engine man flew "wing man" beside her until the new engine was broken in. He flew with her all the way to Kansas City.

When Bobbi reached Kansas City, she checked in with the race officials. She learned that the majority of the racers had already passed through, but there were several others who had also run into trouble.

All of the trouble had started after the group left San Bernardino. Monday, August 19, Marvel Crosson was found dead in the mesquite jungle within the Gila River Valley, east of Yuma. Marvel, flying a fast Travel Air, had crashed. Marvel was a topnotch pilot. Why the plane crashed was never known.

Thea Rasche, the German aviatrix, was forced down at Holtville, Arizona, because her engine quit. Thea found that there was sand in her fuel tank.

Claire Fahy, in an OX5 Travel Air, was forced down near Calexico with broken wire braces. Her husband, Herb, who held the solo endurance record for men, declared that the wires showed evidence of being burned with acid. He was convinced that there was something suspicious going on in this race, and insisted that the race be called off.

Amelia Earhart, flying her beautiful Lockheed Vega, was the first to arrive at Yuma. She ran into trouble when her wheels touched the ground. The plane ran into a hummock, a concrete knoll extending about six or eight inches above the dirt, to the side of the regular landing area. The plane nosed over and bent the prop. Within hours a new prop was sent from Burbank and Amelia was again on her way to Cleveland.

Update on progress of the Derby.

Bobby Trout Reaches Douglas In Pursuit of Women's Air Derby

PECOS, Texas, Aug. 23 (AP) — Bobbie Trout, delayed early in the women's national air derby by plane trouble, landed there at 6.24 o'clock tonight, having flown here from El Paso in two hours and 10 minutes. She said she would spend the night here.

Miss Bobby Trout, the tom boy aviatrix who landed her Golden Eagle monoplane on its back near Yuma on the second day of the Santa Monica to Cleveland women's derby took off from Yuma Friday morning after a new motor and propellor had been installed in her ship and patches placed on the wings.

She arrived at the Douglas International airport at 10:56:51 a. m., having made the flight from Yuma with a stop at Phoenix in four hours and 25 minutes. She had left Phoenix at 8:34 a. m. The entire official committee of the Douglas control of the derby was on hand to greet the slim young lady when she stepped from her beautiful ship.

Miss Trout was followed by a Lockheed Vega of the Kinner Aircraft corporation with mechanics aboard. The tom boy aviatrix cheered the spaciousness of the airport, ate a sandwich, drank a bottle of soda water, fueled her ship and was flagged out by the timers and starters at 11:8 a. m. for El Paso. She studied her maps carefully and announced that she intended going as far as Fort Worth, Texas, Friday. She expects to overtake the main derby race today.

Miss Trout has been hailed as the most popular woman flier in the west. She so impressed the aviation officials at the International airport. She has the appearance and voice of a 17 year old boy, being very slender with close-cropped brown hair and a gift of spontaneous and unconscious expression. She is unassuming to a marked degree and with half a hundred people standing about eager to do something for her she did nearly everything for herself and then thanked everyone present for their assistance.

She had heard of the handling of the main derby here and spoke of the rigid guard and the efficient servicing of the planes in terms of glowing praise. She said: "It is such a relief to see the guarding of the planes taken seriously after all the accusations that we have heard. Of course no one wants to think that anyone has been tampering with the ships but there has been so much trouble it is hard to understand.

"Sometimes people play little tricks on one another but the sort of tricks that might have been responsible for some things that have happened on this flight would not be very good jokes, would they?" Miss Trout said very little about her own mishaps and only spoke of them after she had been asked if the plane was the same in which she had started. She then said: "I made one landing on my back and we had to put in a new engine so

I am just cruising now until the motor gets worn in." She expressed absolute confidence of making Fort Worth by Friday night and of catching the derby sometime Saturday.

The young lady with the boyish figure and the boyish voice and manners took off and headed for El Paso in the same direct manner in which she met the reption committee and anyone wishing to bet against her would have found a hundred ready to call the bet at the airport.

Bobbie Trout, christened Evelyn, was born in Greenup, Ill., on Jan. 7, 1906. Her father is George E. Trout, and her mother, before her marriage, was Lola Denman. There is a younger brother Denman.

Because of the father's business, the family moved frequently, and the girl attended many schools. The first was Deleplane, Ark.; with Greenp, Ill.; Oak Creek, Colo.; Seattle, Wash.; Hamilton, Ont.; St. Louis, Mo.; San Diego, Huntington Beach and Chula Vista, Calif. following. She graduated from the Roosevelt high school in Los Angeles in 1926. This was followed by attendance at the University of Southern California where the girl was interested in the architectural course.

In St. Louis, the girl was the only member of her sex in the manual training school. This fact may be understood when it is told that as a child, she was far more interested in mechanics than in dolls, etc. She preferred building tables, chairs, etc., fo rthe dolls to playing with them, and now, since growing up, there is definite dislike for any sort of housework—almost sheer inability in fact—but as a mechanic she is an amazing success for one of her sex.

When in high school, she was one of the first to have her hair bobbed. It was such a terrible hair cut that in fun she was christened Bobbie. The name has stuck ever since and her own name is practically forgotten.

In 1922, Bobbie had an opportunity to take a flight with "Tommy" Thomas, then at the old Rogers airport in Los Angeles. From the first minute off the ground, she has been an aeronautical enthusiast.

After selling a service station which she operated herself, Bobbie took a course of flying with Burdette Fuller. She soloed on April 30, 1928 and soon after her family bought her an airplane for commercial work. In June, 1928, she received her commercial license. It was not long until she was a regular employe of the R. O. Bone company of Inglewood, Calif., builders of the Golden Eagle airplane, soon serving as their demonstrator. As such, Bobbie established the first notable endurance flight for women. It was but a matter of time until she received her transport license, being one of the very few women possessing this form of license.

How Fliers Stand

The total elapsed time at Phoenix.

Florence Lowe Barnes, San Marino, Calif., 3:21:10.

Louis McPhetridge Thaden, PPittsburgh, 3:37:20.

Gladys O'Donnell, Long Beach, Calif., 3:38:48.

Amelia Earhart, New York, 3:34:15.

Ruth Nichols, Rye New York, 3:56:40.

Phoebe Omlie, Memphis, Tenn. (light) 4:17:15.

Ruth Elder, Hollywood, 4:37:-27.

Neva Paris, Great Neck, L. I., 5:01:51.

Vera Dawn Walker, Los Angeles, 5:02:38.

Margaret Perry, Beverly Hills, Calif., 5:08:44.

Edith Foelts, Portland, Ore., (light) 5:10:52.

Mrs. Keith Miller, New Zealand (light) 5:28:14.

Opal Kunz, New York, 7:26:-41.

Update on Derby participants.

A number of people claimed to have seen a man or group of men tampering with the planes the night before the racers left San Bernardino. There was growing concern among the pilots that the aircraft were sabotaged. Bobbi, too, realized that she had somehow been victimized. Despite the controversy and threat of disaster, however, she decided to continue.

Everything was working better now. Bobbi left Kansas City alone and proceeded at full speed toward Cleveland. Before she could reach Cincinnati, at Greensburg, the engine quit again. It was an electrical problem this time. She surmised it wasn't sabotage or misfortune, just dumb luck.

Forced to make another dead-stick landing, she found a little field that was outlined with tall poplar trees. The field was enclosed with a fence which she knew would be impossible to avoid, but it was the only available place to land. To lose altitude fast she slide-slipped down to a small space to land and told herself, "Well, when I roll close to the fence, I'll ground-loop." She set the airplane down, and ground-looped as planned.

During the ground-loop maneuver, the aileron on the right wing caught on a fence post, which tore a large hole in it. Bobbi could fix that. She used a piece of tin can and some baling wire and made a temporary patch. This was an easy repair in those days. She did this repair while an electrician from town came out to see about her electrical problem. He put in a new electrical switch.

Another day had been wasted, but on the morning of August 22, Bobbi was able to take off and continue the race. She knew that she was out of the running, but continued despite her standing in the official race. Too much time had elapsed for her to have a chance at any of the prizes. In Columbus, Ohio, however, she was pleasantly surprised to see that the last of the other contestants were just departing for Cleveland.

Bobbi's competitive spirit came once more to the fore. She pushed the Kinner engine to the maximum and arrived at Cleveland before Ruth Elder and one other entrant. Ruth told Bobbi that she made an unscheduled landing in a cow pasture to ask directions because she lost her maps. While both of her hands were occupied trying to steady the controls during some rough weather, her maps blew out of the plane.

Louise Thaden won in the "DW" Class, the heavier planes with larger engines, with a time of twenty-one hours, twenty-one minutes and forty-three seconds, averaging a speed of one hundred twenty-seven point fifty-two miles per hour. She won the one thousand nine hundred-fifty dollar prize. Gladys O'Donnell, from Long Beach, California, was second in the "DW" Class, and Amelia placed third.

In the "CW" light plane class, the winner was Phoebe, with a time of twenty-five hours, ten minutes, thirty-six seconds at one hundred-eight point nineteen miles per hour, Edith Foltz was second and Chubby Keith-Miller, who had completed the longest flight to date by a woman when she made the trip from London to Australia in March of 1928, came in third. Since Bobbi was out of the competition, she was happy for Phoebe.

Though out of the race, Bobbi completed the course. Most pilots stayed on for the week of the Cleveland National Air Races. When not at the airfield, most pilots had fun and relaxed at

WOMEN READY FOR FINAL AIR DERBY DASH; MEN IN ST. PAUL

COLUMBUS, O., Aug. 25.—(U.P.)—Leaving two of their number behind on the 408-mile jump from St. Louis today, the 14 remaining contestants in the women's air derby from California to Cleveland landed late today, to the plaudits of 20,000 spectators

Mrs. Louis M. Thaden, of Pittsburgh, practically assured herself of the $8000 first prize for finishing first when she again led the parade, dropping down at 6:15:10 p.m. Her elapsed time for the flight so far is 19:35:04.

Gladys O'Donnell, of Long Beach, Calif., who is running second to Mrs. Thaden in the heavy class, came in five minutes later. She was followed by Blanche Noyes, of Cleveland; Ruth Nichols, of Rye, N. Y., who is third in elapsed time, and Amelia Earhart, of Boston, who is fourth.

2 STOPS EN ROUTE

Others finished in order were Ruth Elder, of Hollywood; May Haizlip, of Kansas City; Edith Foltz, of Portland; Opal Kunz, New York; Mary Von Mack, Detroit; Neva Paris, of New York; Vera Walker, Thea Rasche, Germany, and Mrs. Phoebe Omlie, of Memphis.

The flyers stopped at Terre Haute and Cincinnati en route and reported weather conditions near perfect. Miss Foltz failed to locate the Cincinnati airport and came on without stopping. As a result she may be disqualified, if officials decide.

ALL APPEAR TIRED

Miss Bobbie Trout, whose plane was damaged at Yuma, Ariz., caught up with the flyers, but had more trouble at Cincinnati and remained there.

Mrs. Miller, of New Zealand, was forced down at Xenia, O., by motor trouble

The aviatrices appeared tired when they arrived and hurried to hotels for dinner and bed. They leave at 12:30 p. m. tomorrow for the finish dash to Cleveland.

Army, Navy Planes Feature Ohio Meet

MUNICIPAL AIRPORT, CLEVELAND, Aug. 25.—(U.P.)—America's first line of defense—the air corps—demonstrated its skill and daring today to open the racing program of the 10-day national air meet here. The army, navy and marine corps sent their crack pilots to dive and loop, singly and in intricate formation, to thrill an opening day crowd of 25,000.

Besides the military maneuvers, the start of a derby, two races, a parachute jumping contest, balloon bursting and acrobatics filled out an afternoon for the air-minded.

The military flyers took the limelight of the afternoon. Six marine corps planes from Quantico, commanded by Capt. Arthur Page, appeared out of the east at 1:45 p. m., the exact time they were scheduled to arrive.

Before the marines had landed, a navy squadron from San Diego numbering 17 planes, roared past the grandstand, led by Rear Admiral William A. Moffat, in charge of naval aeronautics, and Assistant Secretary of the Navy David Ingalls, with their aides, in three civilian planes.

The naval flyers took a few minutes' more time than they had been allowed and before they had maneuvered to land, 36 army aces bore down on the field from opposite directions, 18 from Selfridge field, Mich., and 18 from Fort Crockett, Texas.

Lee Shoenhair Off On Non-Stop Flight

Through darkened skies sped Lee Shoenhair last night from Metropolitan airport, Glendale, as the men's non-stop race to Cleveland, O., and the national air races got under way.

Shoenhair hopped off at 12:35 a. m. in a new streamline Lockheed Vega monoplane.

The event, one of the outstanding speed contests of the national air races, is expected to be one of the most hotly contested transcountry battles in aviation history. Entrants in addition to Shoenhair include Capt. O. C. Le Broutillier, Henry Brown, John Woods, Roscoe Turner and Art Goebel.

Anticipated time for the trip was placed yesterday by the pilots as about 14 hours.

6 Flyers Race From Oakland to Cleveland

OAKLAND AIRPORT, OAKLAND, Calif., Aug. 25.—(U.P.)—Six airplanes started a race from here to Cleveland for the national air races today.

The entrants were to stop overnight at Salt Lake City.

D. C. Warren, local pilot, was first to take off, leaving at 9:46:25. Then at brief intervals Joe Barrows, Oakland; Loren Mendell, Los Angeles; J. C. Donaldson, Newark, N. J.; Bob King, Los Angeles, and Bob Nagle, Oakland, followed.

BOBBY TROUT LANDS AND TAKES OFF AGAIN

EAST ST. LOUIS (Ill.) Aug. 25. (P)—Bobbie Trout of Los Angeles, contestant in the Women's National Air Derby, who was delayed after being lost several times, landed at Parks Airport near here at about 11:30 a.m. today and took off for Terre Haute, Ind., at noon. She left Wichita, Kan., at daybreak and Kansas City at 8:07 a.m.

Update on participants on August 26, 1929.

the home of the Rex family, who were prominent people in Cleveland. They proved to be gracious hosts, doing everything possible to ensure the fliers' comfort.

During the mishaps, Bobbi inconveniently lost her luggage. She arrived in Cleveland with only the clothes she had worn throughout the trip. Elinor, who had come from New York for the Cleveland Air Races, learned of Bobbi's dilemma and loaned her a white shirt.

On August 26, Bobbi attended the end of-race banquet in her old breeches, boots, and Elinor's white cotton shirt. The other pilots arrived in evening dresses. Self-conscious, but still trying to maintain a relaxed composure, she realized that she was probably the most comfortable person there. She had just begun to relax and enjoy herself when from behind her a stern male voice announced, "I see you're making a habit of this." It was Jack Helm, the Golden Eagle distributor, who was with her in Oakland when she had gone into a posh night club in similar attire. Her cheeks burned while he told the group of Bobbi's previous pants-wearing antics.

The next morning, at the start of the Cleveland National Air Races, Bobbi returned Elinor's shirt. Bobbi remembered her promise to Sherrill about finding a refueling partner. Bobbi decided to ask Elinor if she would come to California and help set the record. Bobbi wanted Elinor to join her instead of competing against her as they had been doing the past year on the solo endurance records. It would be a good opportunity for Bobbi and Elinor to join forces. Elinor agreed that it was a good idea. They arranged a time and date when plans for the flight were finalized.

The National Air Races and Aeronautical Exposition in Cleveland, Ohio, were to run from August 24 through September 2, 1929. During the first few days at the National Air Races, several of the women pilots got together for some hangar flying. While standing under the bleachers and discussing the events, they all wondered if it would be a good idea to form a woman's flying organization. Bobbi, Amelia, Phoebe, Louise, Blanche Noyes, and several other eastern women decided to make up a set of by-laws and try to get the group started.

AVIATION ACHIEVEMENT DINNER
SPONSORED BY THE
EXCHANGE CLUBS OF GREATER CLEV
HOTEL STATLER — AUGUST 26, 19
CLEVELAND, O.

The big banquet at the Hotel Statler in Cleveland, Ohio, Aug. 26, 1929, at the end of the first Women's Transcontinental Air Derby.

Charter Members of the Ninety-Nines
(Organized Winter 1929)

Pilot	License No.		Pilot	License No.	
Alexander, Mary C. (Held)	*1955	8561	Lay, Eleanor B. (Ross)	*1981	8343
Bacon, Mary Ellen	*1936	9969	Lange, Eva Mae	*1963	8189
Bancroft, Barbara W.		6200	LaRene, Jean (Foote)	*1960	5700
Blake, Bernice C. (Perry)		9138	Leh, Dorothea Backenstoe	*1955	3961
Bridewell, Ruth T.		6793	Lesser, Marjorie M. (VanAntwerp)	*1969	7200
Brown, Margery H. (Sanford)	*1961	6945	Lovelace, Ethel		5766
Brown, Myrtle	*1934	7701	Lutz, Lola L.	*1968	7806
Brown, Vera	*1976	10591	McConnell, Edwyna (Thro)		7500
Burleigh, Thelma R.(Johnston)	*1982	6761	McCulloh, Retha (Crittenden)		5260
Caldwell, Myrtle R.		7718	Manning, Helen (Mathews)	*1963	9241
Camp, Ruth Elder (King)	*1977	675	Mathews, Olivia (Maugham)		9159
Chase, Mildred H. (MacDonald)	*1982	7455	Miller, Jessie M. Keith-(Pugh)	*1973	6014
Chassey, Irene J. (Green)		8587	Mills, Agnes A.		5711
Chittendon, Bonnie (Whitman)		8589	Nelson, Sylvia Anthony	*1984	6456
Clark, Marion		6763	Nichols, Ruth Rowland	*1960	326
Cox, Helen V. (Cohecy)		7767	Noyes, Blanche Wilcox	*1981	6540
Davidson, Jean		9400	Nicholson, Mary	*1943	9562
Dodge, Jane	*	7930	O'Donnell, Gladys	*1973	6608
Doig, Margery L.(Greenburg)		10073	O'Mara, Margaret Frandee		2175
Earhart, Amelia (Putnam)	*1937	5716	Omlie, Phoebe Fairgrave	*1975	199
Elliott, Thelma (Giesin)		7732	Paris, Neva Findley	*1930	5073
Ferguson, Frances (Leitch)		8695	Paxson, Peggie J.		8551
Fenno, Sarah S.	*	9920	Peacock, Achsa B. (Holfelder)		3289
Fiset, Adeline F. (Anderson)		8613	Perry, Margaret C. (Manser)	*1951	4049
Fleet, Phyllis (Crary)		8097	Place, Elizabeth F.		8716
Foltz, Edith (Sterns)	*1956	5600	Porter, Lillian		4229
Fox, Ila (Loetscher)		7738	Rasche, Thea	*1971	6700
Gentry, Viola		1822	Ray, Mathilda J.		7591
Gillis, Fay (Wells)		9497	Rothholz, Meta	*1974	10169
Goddard, Phyllis M. (Penfield)	*1984	5487	Ruland, Gertrude (Oberlander)	*1972	8322
Goodrich, Mary H.		9410	Shankle, Joan Fay (Davis)	*1951	7838
Gorby, Melba (Beard)		9116	Spangle, Hazel Mark		9260
Gray, Geraldine (Loffredo)	*	1788	Stewart, Ruth Woerner	*1932	5375
Hall, Candice I. (Gullino)		6500	Stinson, Marjorie C.	*1975	1600
Hall, Sacha Peggy (Martin)		2500	Stinaff, Mildred	*1931	10491
Halliburton, Ruth E.(Seitz)		8031	Stocker, Dorothy L.		7973
Harrell, Frances (Marsalis)	*1934	7346	Thaden, Louise McPhetridge	*1979	1943
Heath, Lady Mary (Williams)	*1935	5333	Thomas, Margaret (Warren)		6180
Hopkins, Nancy (Tier)		5889	Trout, Evelyn "Bobbi"		2613
Hoyt, Jean D.		4851	Vance, Ester Combes	*1983	3180
Huyler, Betty (Gillies)		6525	Von Mach, Mary E.	*1980	4117
Johnson, Katherine F.	*1967	7793	Walsh, Wilma L.		4272
Joseph, Angela L.	*1930	8947	Walker, Vera Dawn	*1978	5265
Kauffman, Mildred E.(Workman)	*1932	6447	Webb, E. Ruth		8240
Kelly, Betsy (Weeks)	*1985	9948	White, Nora Alma	*1931	9270
Kelly, Madeline B. (Royle)		5919	Willhite, Nellie Zabel		8242
Kenyon, Cecil W. "Teddy"	*1986	9949	Willis, Margaret (Smith)	*1971	5018
Kenny, Cecelia Roy	*1980	7143	Wood, Josephine C. (Wallingford)		9129
Klingensmith, Florence E.	*1933	7096	Worley, Alberta B.		9286
Kunz, Opal Logan	*1967	6830	*year of death		

Aviator Bobbi Trout, Circa 1929.

Before the first meeting, a set of by-laws were sent out to all licensed women pilots. Ninety-nine women approved the by-laws and sent in their checks by a deadline date, to become Charter Members. Since ninety-nine members joined, the eastern women made the decision to call the group the Ninety Nines.

Amelia was elected the first president and served from 1929 to 1933. Their constitution stated their purpose: "We propose to assist women in aeronautical research, air racing events, acquisition of aerial experience, administration of aid through aerial means in times of emergency arising from fire, famine, flood, or war." The only requirement for membership was, and still is, an active pilot's license.

The week in Cleveland with the National Air Races, the excitement at the field, and the fun at Rexes' was delightful. At week's end, Bobbi and Helm departed in the Golden Eagle Chief. Bobbi flew to East St. Louis, where she and Helm had to set down for the night before resuming their flight home the next day.

The next morning, September 7, Bobbi took the front seat because Helm wanted to pilot the plane. Shortly after passing over the west side of St. Louis, they ran into a blinding rain storm and heavy, black rain clouds. Helm attempted to land in a small, muddy field, but as the Golden Eagle Chief touched down in the mud, it ground-looped. The airplane stuck, nose-up in the mud, the wing was damaged and the entire plane was in no condition for a quick repair, so they left it behind. Luckily neither was hurt in the mishap, but it seemed to Bobbi that the beautiful airplane had been doomed from the start.

Bobbi had been a wonderful representative for the Golden Eagle Chief. Its beautiful, streamlined red and gold fuselage now lay crumpled in the Missouri mud. To her, seeing the end of such a thing of beauty was like losing a member of the family. Bobbi and Helm finished the trip home by train, again traveling in their flying togs.

Bobbi's guest passes to the 1929 Cleveland Air Races.

Chapter Nine

First Refueling Endurance Flight

REMEMBERING the beautiful Golden Eagle Chief lying crumpled in the mud, Bobbi wondered how she and Helm would explain the final disaster to Bone and what would result with the sales of the Golden Eagle. She never learned why the plane ran out of gasoline; it is still a mystery. Could it have been sabotage?

Bone knew she had done her best and was more understanding than Bobbi had anticipated. He was glad they had escaped uninjured. Bobbi wished she could have won the Derby for him, especially since they had the fastest ship in the light class. He told her that it should not adversely affect the company.

Within a few weeks however, the stock market crash of 1929 wiped many people out of business. Selling airplanes became an impossibility and it forced Bone to move back to Columbus, where he sold his company.

The race, however, was not a complete loss. Bobbi did finish and found a partner with whom to make the refueling endurance flight. At their last meeting Bobbi told Bone how she wouldn't rest until she set the first women's refueling endurance record. Bone couldn't let Bobbi go without his best wishes for success. Bobbi got a sudden nostalgia for all the wonderful and exciting times associated with Bone. She swallowed to clear the sudden lump in her throat and said, "I'll never forget you or your wonderful Golden Eagle Chief." They shook hands and she gave him a parting hug. It was the last time they would see each other.

Jack Sherrill, promoter for Ullman & Associates, discuss some last minute arrangements of the refueling endurance flight in the Sunbeam.

Photograph of one of the last Golden Eagles, taken about 1939.

Mark Britt

Stone Mountain, Ga.
30083
Ox 5 # 2647

Dear Miss Trout:

I was reading my ox5 news for Feb 79 and noticed your interest in a Golden Eagle. I was once the Proud Owner of NC56W Golden Eagle Chief and I think I was next to the last owner of this plane, I'm also of the opinion that this was the last of the Golden Eagle Chief built, I was informed when I Purchased this Plane in either 1938 or 39 that B.T. Bone Aircraft Co. somewhere in Calif had built only 3 of these Ships and that the other 2 had been distroyd, This was only verbal information I received and have no actual proof of any of this except the following history of NC56W. In 1932 – Ben Seigle Hickory NC° owner. He sold it to a Mr. W. R. Reese in Greensboro N.C. With the understanding it would be relicensed. A Mr. Jim Noll who was the CAA Inspector in the Greensboro area at this time would not issue a license as he said the Plane had a very bad spin Carastic, In 1934 "Squeak" Burnett bought it and used in in air Shows with the Flying Aces. He then sold it to a Mr ? (I don't remember his Name) Who wrecked it, It was repaired and I bought it in 38 or 39 and completly rebuilt it, Flew it for a while and sold it to a Mr. Charles Boden

A sad letter relating the fate of one of the last known Golden Eagle Chief airplanes owned by Mark Britt of Stone Mountain, Georgia.

in Ashland, Va. Mr. Boschen and his Instructor Mr. Floyd G. Clark spun it in into the top of a tree either in 40 or 41 as Mr. Clark was checking Mr. Boschen out on the ship. Neither man was injured badly but I'm told Mr. Boslen removed the rudder from the plane and burned the balance while it was hanging up in tree.

I thought you might want the picture of NC56W I cut out of my Scrap Book. This picture was made just prior to my rebuilding and I have only 1 photo in my book after I rebuilt and I would like to keep this one. I also have 1 6 x 8 glossy photo of the original plane as it was in 1932.

I sincerely hope this history will be of some interest to you.

Sincerely yours,
Mark Britt

P.S. I am a retired Eastern Air Line Pilot retired Sept 21-1972 after 30 1/2 years of flying with E. A. L. I have 29,000 hrs logged but due to physical reasons I haven't flown since 1974. I retired on the Boeing 727 Started flying in OX Eaglerock & OX Challenger, in Richmond, Va. 1932

Mark

History of NC56W
Golden Eagle Chief—110 LeBlond engine. Purchased from R.O. Bone, Columbus, Ohio in 1930. The purchaser was Ben Seagle Flying Service, Hickory, North Carolina.
1932—sold to W. R. Reese, Greensboro, N.C.
1934—"Squak" Burnett bought it for shows and later sold it to unknown person. While owned by third party, it was wrecked and repd.
1939—Mark Britt bought it and rebuilt it. Mr. Charles Boschen bought it about 1941 and while taking lessons, spun into a tree top (no one seriously hurt), but he removed the rudder and set fire to the rest!
What a life this poor little Chief had!!

At Home in Air

Miss Bobbie Trout

GIRL PLANS RECORD FLIGHT

Bobbie Trout Will Attempt to Beat World's Endurance Record

Miss Bobbie Trout, 24-year-old Los Angeles aviatrix, who, with Miss Elinor Smith of New York, holds the world's endurance mark for women, announced here yesterday that she is planning with another girl pilot an attempt to best the men's record, now held by Dale (Red) Jackson and Forest O'Brine, some time in April.

Miss Trout, who formerly held two solo records for her sex, left San Francisco for Los Angeles in a Maddux plane yesterday, after making tentative arrangements for the proposed flight Thursday at Stockton, where she plans the takeoff.

She declined to state whether she has yet approached another girl to act as co-pilot, but she said Miss Smith will not be associated with her in the venture. She hopes to enlist Stockton business men and civic associations as backers for the flight, she said, although no definite arrangements have yet been agreed upon.

Her flight with Miss Smith at Los Angeles last November ended after 42 hours and 5 minutes in the air, when the motor of the refueling plane was damaged beyond immediate repair. Her latest solo mark was eclipsed by Mrs. Louise Thaden McPhetridge at Oakland last March. She is one of the few women in the country holding a transport pilot's license.

GIRLS PLAN REFUEL FLIGHT

Two Southland Misses Will Go Up Next Week to Set Sky Target for Women

The world's first women's refueling endurance airplane flight will take place over Los Angeles next week when Peggy Paxson, 17 years of age, and her 19-year-old flying partner, Lucille Wallingford, leave the ground from the Lincoln Airline field in a light plane.

Meanwhile Bobbie Trout, one of the few women transport pilots in the country and a participant in the Santa Monica-Cleveland air derby, is rushing arrangements for another endurance attempt at Los Angeles Metropolitan Airport.

BOBBIE TROUT.

Vern Durrell probably will have charge of refueling the Paxson-Wallingford ship while it wings its way around Southern California with the two young flyers aboard. The girls believe they can remain in the air at least 150 hours in the light plane, but regardless of their mark they plan to take off again after a few days' rest in a Curtiss Robin, powered with a Curtiss Challenger motor, in an attempt to set a heavy-plane record.

FLYING SIX MONTHS

Both girls have been flying six months and expect to hold limited commercial transport licenses before they go aloft. They are busy flying to fulfill the Department of Commerce requirement of fifty solo hours for a license.

Miss Paxson is the daughter of L. W. Paxson, local representative of Pratt-Whitney airplane motors, and resides at 1723 Longwood avenue, while Miss Wallingford resides at 720 Guadalupe Place, Redondo.

"Reports that we will make the flight to reap a reward for indorsing cigarettes and other articles are untrue," Miss Paxson declared. "Neither of us smoke. We are going up to show the world that women are equal to men in the air."

SEVERAL AFTER PLACE

Although Mrs. Louise M. Thaden of Pittsburgh, winner of the Cleveland air derby, was scheduled to be Miss Trout's flight companion, her husband refused to allow her to come here, telling her she had been away from home long enough, according to Miss Trout.

Several local girls, however, want to take Mrs. Thaden's place, and Miss Trout will select one within a few days. This pair will fly a Sunbeam biplane, powered with a Wright Whirlwind 325-horsepower J-6 motor. The ship is being especially built for the endurance trial. It has an open control cockpit near the tail, but a roomy closed cabin forward in the fuselage. The Commercial Aircraft Corporation at Metropolitan is building the plane and expects to have it in the air within three weeks.

Bobbi meditates by the Sunbeam biplane before her flight.

Air-Cooled Motors Win Interest

BOBBIE TROUT and Eleanor Smith, girl flyers, with Franklin air-cooled car which they highly praise.

THEY are shown near demounted whirlwind motor and plane in which they seek endurance record.

2 GIRL FLIERS PLAN L. A. ENDURANCE HOP

SEVERAL AFTER PLACE

Although Mrs. Louise M. Thaden of Pittsburgh, winner of the Cleveland air derby, was scheduled to be Miss Trout's flight companion, her husband refused to allow her to come here, telling her she had been away from home long enough, according to Miss Trout.

Several local girls, however, want to take Mrs. Thaden's place and Miss Trout will select one within a few days. This pair will fly a Sunbeam biplane, powered with a Wright Whirlwind 325-horsepower J-6 motor. The ship is being especially built for the endurance trial. It has an open control cockpit near the tail, but a roomy closed cabin forward in the fuselage. The Commercial Aircraft Corporation at Metropolitan is building the plane and expects to have it in the air within three weeks.

Bobbie Trout Tests Plane for Record Hop

By International News Service.
LOS ANGELES, Oct. 13.

BOBBIE TROUT, aviatrix, today tried out a special airplane in which she and Eleanor Smith, New York society girl flier and former rival of Miss Trout, will attempt to break refueling endurance records held by both men and women.

Bobbie Trout.

The attempt is scheduled for late this month. Miss Trout expressed herself as well pleased with the new airplane.

Bobby Trout Soon to Seek New Records

Los Angeles Girl Spends Day in Santa Barbara; Likes City

An indomitable optimist. That in brief describes Miss Bobby Trout, twice holder of the women's solo endurance flight record, who was a visitor in Santa Barbara Saturday and yesterday.

When asked yesterday what her plans are for the future, Miss Trout said that she is planning within three weeks to make another attempt at lowering the world's record now held by Miss Elinor Smith, New York girl, at 26 hours.

Miss Trout was the first to establish a mark for women's solo airplane flights when she flew over the San Joaquin valley for an eight-hour period several months ago.

Another Record

Within a few weeks following, and probably as a result of the nation-wide mention given to Miss Thout's initial achievement, a new candidate for women's laurels, Miss Elinor Smith, rose into the air on the Atlantic coast to stay aloft for 12 hours and 11 minutes.

In response to this challenge, the unconquerable Bobby took to her wings at Los Angeles and flew alone for a period of 17 hours and 24 minutes.

Then a new rival took off from the Oakland airport, and Miss Louise Thaden smashed the record

flight when her wheels touched the ground after a period of 22 and one-half hours in the air. Two weeks ago Elinor Smith closed the door of her cabin plane and took off to a new goal of 26 hours.

To Try Again

Air-minded femininity of the Pacific coast is now looking to Bobby Trout to regain her twice-lost honors and reestablish California renown in aviation.

"I don't believe that it will be long before you are reading of my new record," Miss Trout said yesterday.

She explained that she is having a new plane built in Los Angeles and that the flight will center at Mines field. The new ship will be a Golden Eagle monoplane powered with 90-horsepower motors. It has more wing space than her first plane and will be supplied with an N.A.C.A. type of cowling, used by the famous Hawks in his transcontinental flight to produce greater speed.

Likes City

"Santa Barbara is the most delightful city I have visited," said the petite aviatrix. "Everyone and everything here seem so hospitable that it leaves an unforgetable impression of happiness."

She stayed with Mrs. N. V. Horning, 601 1-2 West Carrillo, and Mr. and Mrs. George Bokes of Montecito. Her home is in Los Angeles, and she motored northward on Saturday.

"Santa Barbara should not have to go to Carpinteria for its airport," she declared. "There are sites nearer the city which if improved would provide all the necessary air terminal facilities."

As Bobbi made plans for the flight and prepared for Elinor's arrival from New York, Jack Sherrill arranged for them to fly the Commercial Aircraft Corporation's Sunbeam biplane, powered with a Wright Whirlwind three hundred horsepower engine, for the endurance flight.

Elinor arrived at Grand Central Airport in October 1929, via train and plane, the year the new Transcontinental Air Transport, Inc. (T.A.T.) was formed. T.A.T. was the first coast-to-coast passenger service and the trip took forty-eight hours. Upon her arrival in California, Elinor was welcomed into the Trout home for the duration of her stay in the southland. Bobbi filled Elinor in on the details of their upcoming try for the endurance record. Elinor was anxious to go over to Metropolitan Airport and take a look at the Sunbeam.

At Metropolitan, Bobbi and Elinor walked into the airport manager Waldo Waterman's office. Jack Sherrill was there to meet Elinor. They talked to Waterman and a man named Green, owner of the Commercial Aircraft Corporation. Green showed them into the hangar where their airplane was being worked on. The two ladies met aviator Roman Warren, Green's mechanic, and he assured them that the plane would be ready and in perfect shape for the next day's practice flight.

Bobbi and Elinor, partners in record breaking.

DETERMINED to shatter the world's endurance flight record of 400 hours and 21 minutes now held by the St. Louis Robin, Elinor Smith, 18, of New York city, and Bobby Trout, 23, of Los Angeles, intrepid aviatress, are scheduled to take off from the Metropolitan airport, Van Nuys, at 8 o'clock Friday morning.

The young women, eager and confident of victory, expect to keep their giant Sunbeam six-passenger bi-plane aloft over San Fernando valley for 500 hours. This is the first time in the history of aviation that women have attempted an endurance flight of such length.

The Sunbeam, built by the Commercial Aircraft corporation, is equipped with a Wright J-6 300 horsepower motor and has a cruising radius of 115 miles an hour and a maximum speed of 145 miles an hour.

A gasoline load of 300 gallons will be carried by the plane and the giant aircraft which Miss Trout and Miss Smith hope will carry them to victory in their endurance flight, will be refuelled twice every 24 hours. During the refuelling periods Miss Smith will handle the controls and Miss Trout will handle the loading of gasoline, oil and water.

Miss Smith and Miss Trout will decide which one will have the honor of handling the controls at the takeoff by tossing a coin. The same method will be employed in deciding which one of the young women will handle the landing of the plane.

Paul Whittier, millionaire aviation enthusiast and pilot, and "Pete" Reinhart, the latter a famous endurance flier, will have personal charge of the giant refuelling plane that will supply the precious liquid to the big green Sunbeam as it circles over San Fernando valley.

The pilots wave goodbye.

CREDIT: D.B. HATFIELD

CREDIT: D.B. HATFIELD

Bobbi and Elinor, happy that the radio Freeman Lang made for the flight, has arrived. They are anxious to install it in plane.

Bobbi and Elinor receiving a movie camera to use to capture pictures of their flight.

Bobbi's notification of passing radiotelephone class.

DEPARTMENT OF COMMERCE
RADIO DIVISION

U. S. Asst. Radio Inspector's Office,
(Office of examiner)

Miss Bobbie Trout,
(Applicant)

Los Angeles, California.
(Place of examination)

418 So. Soto St.,
(Address)

Oct. 2nd, 1929.
(Date)

Los Angeles, Calif.

Sir:
    You are hereby notified that you _____ PASSED _____ in your examination for license as radio
(Passed or failed)

operator, Radiotelephone _____ class. Code speeds, _____ words per min. Percentage _____ 76
(Insert class)

    If you have passed you will find your license inclosed herewith, *unsigned*. The oath of secrecy must be executed and the license returned to this office for my signature before it is valid.
                        Respectfully,

_____ James M. Chapple _____
(Signature of issuing officer)

1F—9287   Asst. Radio Inspector.
(Title)

The United States of America
DEPARTMENT OF COMMERCE
RADIO DIVISION
NUMBER 1511
LICENSE
TO
RADIO OPERATOR, RADIOTELEPHONE CLASS

This certifies that ___ BOBBIE TROUT ___
has been examined and passed, pursuant to the Radiotelegraphic Convention, in

(a) knowledge of the adjustment and operation of radiotelephone apparatus,
(b) ability to transmit and receive clearly conversation by telephone apparatus,
(c) knowledge of international regulations and Acts of Congress to regulate radio communication;

and is hereby licensed, as required by law, a Radiotelephone Operator.

The holder of this license is authorized to act as operator at any licensed radiotelephone station of three hundred watts or less input power.

James W. Chapple
(Examining Officer)
Asst. Radio Inspector.
(Title)

R. P. LAMONT
WILLIAM P. WHITING,
Secretary of Commerce.

W. D. TERRELL,
Chief, Radio Division.

Place Los Angeles, Calif. Date October 2nd 19 29.

Bobbi's Radio Operator Radiotelephone Class License.

"I see my way as birds their trackless way.
I shall arrive,—what time, what circuit first,
I ask not; . . .
He guides me and the bird. In His good time."

Notes from friends.

Such a Faux Pas!

Mrs. Ebright: (in corset department, seeing smart young man in riding attire wandering around fitting room aisle) "Pardon me, you are looking for someone?"

Smart Young Man: "I'm looking for Mrs. Trout."

Mrs. Ebright: "I'll try to find her. Please step out in front of the counter." Mrs. E. begins opening each door to locate the lady and is amazed to find the young man right at her side. "I will have to ask you to stay out in front," says Mrs. E. "These are fitting rooms."

Smart Young Man: "Oh, that's all right. I'm Bobbie Trout and I'm looking for my mother—she's back here somewhere getting fitted."

(In case you don't know it, Bobbie Trout is the famous young Glendale aviatrix who holds the world's endurance record for women.)

CREDIT: DAVID D. HATFIELD AVIATION COLLECTION

TO TELL ABOUT THEMSELVES—Bobby Trout (right) explaining to Anita Page, Metro-Goldwyn-Mayer actress, how she will broadcast from air during endurance flight she and Eleanor Smith (in cockpit) will undertake this month. KMTR will broadcast flight.

(top right)
Pete Reinhardt (c) demonstrates how he will drop the refueling items and equipment.

(lower)
Bobbi and Elinor relax during refueling practice sessions.

Bobbi and Elinor wanted to make sure everything was working and that they were capable of receiving the fuel and supplies without problems before they attempted to remain aloft for an entire month. When they returned home, Bobbi's mother had their dinner ready for them.

The next morning Bobbi and Elinor arose early for the one hour drive to Metropolitan Airport. They watched Pete Reinhardt and Paul Whittier take off down the runway in the Curtiss Carrier Pigeon that was going to make the fuel deliveries. The Pigeon was capable of delivering one hundred eighty-five gallons of fuel to the receiver aircraft in only four minutes during each refueling contact. The refueling was planned twice a day—early morning and before sunset.

When Bobbi and Elinor arrived at the airport, they completed their pre-flight inspection of the Sunbeam. They flipped a coin to determine who would pilot the plane: Elinor won. When the Pigeon was in the air, Elinor steered the Sunbeam down the asphalt runway. Time after time, when Bobbi and Elinor got into refueling position under the Pigeon, they were blown from side to side by the strong prop wash from the Pigeon's Liberty engine. They swayed from side to side until Elinor was forced to take the plane down for re-rigging.

This re-rigging scenario was repeated with each takeoff and subsequent landing in order to adjust the flying attitude of the wings. Warren made adjustments of the wing wires after each flight attempt. Each re-rigging helped, but was not perfected until many changes were made. The rigging had to be perfect so the Sunbeam could stay in position under the refueling ship.

At the field they were greeted by Waterman, the airport manager, who insisted on sending them off with a kiss—and welcoming them back the same way. That would have been all right, except that he was the proud possessor of a big, bushy mustache.

Several days later a radiotelephone was installed in the baggage compartment, the only space available. Freeman Lang, master of ceremonies for all the big movie premiers, had built this radio especially for their flight. Bobbi and Elinor took the plane up to test the radio. When they were airborne, they discovered the plane

CREDIT: D.D. HATFIELD

to be tail-heavy, even with the stabilizer at its maximum position. This was not successful and they decided to circle the field and land. Elinor safely landed the airplane and taxied back to the hangar.

After discussing the stabilizer problem with Warren, they all agreed that the radio made the tail too heavy and had to come out. Warren opened the baggage compartment and unloaded the Freeman Lang radio. Bobbi could not help thinking of Freeman's work building the radio and all her time and effort involved in getting her Department of Commerce license and obtaining the Radiotelephone Class certificate. She watched in stoic silence while their verbal link to the ground was severed; they had planned to broadcast eight times a day with a local radio station, KMTR.

Bobbi and Elinor were still determined, however, to continue preparations for the flight. They were sent off again with another kiss by Waterman. Removing the radio made flying the Sunbeam a real joy. The changes finally allowed Elinor to maintain a controlled, steady position beneath the Pigeon long enough for Bobbi to grab the bag of food, oil, and mail attached at the rope's end.

The next time Bobbi was able to grab the bag and and pull in about twenty-five feet of hemp rope. Suddenly, the Sunbeam broke contact. Bobbi realized, in terror, she must guide the coil of rope out of the plane. Fearing she would be caught up in the rope and pulled out of the plane, Bobbi held the rope and guided it with her bare hands as it spun out. With no hand protection, Bobbi grimaced in shocked anguish as blisters formed immediately on her palms. Her groan of pain was covered by the engine noise as Elinor again brought the Sunbeam in to land. Fearing that Elinor might insist on giving up the try for a record, Bobbi controlled her agony and prepared to try again the next day.

Jack Sherrill, manager, discuss some flight plans with Bobbi. Bobbi was eager to establish a new record for women and men.

Simulation of Bobbi receiving the bag of oil, food and mail, which was tied to a 25 ft. rope and led the gasoline nozzle and hose to Bobbi. Bobbi inserted this nozzle into a pipe through which the gasoline flowed into the cabin gasoline tanks. Gasoline was pumped through wind driven pumps, attached to the struts, up to the wing tanks for gravity feed to the engine.

Bobbi examines pipe opening to receive the refueling gasoline nozzle.

Bobbi and Elinor posing for publicity.

Bobbi Trout in her fuchsia suede flying suit especially made for her by HOOK TAILORS, 1929.

They attempted to refuel again the next morning. The bag was the guideline for their fuel supply from the Pigeon. The thick hemp rope coiled carefully as she reeled it in, and at last Bobbi got hold of the gasoline nozzle. With a sense of triumph she placed it in the pipe which led into their gas tanks in the front cabin of the plane. She signaled Reinhardt to open the valve and let the gasoline flow. As it began to pour into the Sunbeam tanks, Bobbi glanced upward and laughed. Success was at hand.

Suddenly the ships broke contact again. The hose, still gushing gasoline, flipped out of the pipe and trailed across Bobbi's open mouth before she could react. She gasped, gulped, and swallowed what seemed like a pint of gasoline.

Elinor hurriedly landed the ship, whereupon Bobbi, who was now having trouble breathing, was rushed to her doctor. Her head and ears felt as if they were miles out and she labored to breathe medicated steam under the oxygen tent. After most of the night had passed, the burning and nausea receded and she was able to rest comfortably.

The next morning when Sherrill arrived at the house to check up on her, he found Bobbi packed and ready to head for the airport. Sherrill tried to convince her that they should either wait, or even call the whole thing off: Bobbi would not hear of it. He finally gave up trying and drove with her to the airport.

On November 27, 1929, Bobbi and Elinor took off again and began their attempt to set a new refueling endurance record. Waterman, with his big, bushy mustache, was there to send them off, as well as Sherrill, their thoughtful manager. This time the refueling went perfectly and they took shifts of four hours each, alternately sleeping atop the gasoline tanks and flying the Sunbeam. Bobbi's other jobs were to change the engine oil twice a day. She also had to use the Alemite grease gun on thirty-six Alemite connectors leading to the small copper tubing outside the cabin that greased the rocker arms on the Wright J-6, nine-cylinder, three hundred–horsepower, radial engine. If she got two hours sleep out of four she was lucky.

They continued this routine for two days with everything going along smoothly. Bobbi began to think their problems were behind them.

On Thanksgiving Day they had been up thirty-nine hours and were in the process of taking on gasoline from the Pigeon when black smoke began to pour out of the refueling ship's exhaust. It looked like a typical smoke scene from a war movie. Bobbi quickly pulled the gasoline hose, still gushing gas, from the Sunbeam's filler pipe and tossed it over the side.

The rope quickly followed, for after the first accident when she suffered rope burns, while trying to get it out of the airplane, Bobbi devised a way of coiling the rope that enabled her to get rid of the whole coil in one quick toss.

Elinor's reaction was just as swift. She immediately nosed down toward Mother Earth, banked to the left, and got out from under the Pigeon.

The gasoline hose was still trailing like a gigantic fish line as the Pigeon spewed dark clouds of smoke and went into a steep glide. It appeared that they were not going to clear the barbed-wire fence surrounding the field. The Pigeon glided safely past the fence, but the dangling gasoline line caught securely on the fence. The Pigeon dragged post, wire, and underbrush in its wake. The plane eventually came to rest in the field without catching fire, and Reinhardt and Whittier got out of it without receiving a scratch. The aircraft also sustained very minor damage, but the engine had to be completely overhauled. Elinor made a pass over the "dead" Pigeon. Seeing that all was well with the two men, Bobbi and Elinor continued to circle the field.

Before the mishap, the Sunbeam had managed to get enough gasoline to keep them airborne until 3:47 a.m. when their fuel supply gauge showed almost zero. Elinor made a nice landing onto the field. The crowds were cheering them in as they landed.

The official time was forty-two hours, three and one-half minutes and they refueled three and one-half times. This was the first refueling endurance flight record ever made by women, and thus set a world's record.

About to refuel over San Fernando Valley while various ships look on.

Bobbi shows sleeping arrangement on top of the gasoline tanks.

CREDIT: D.D. HATFIELD

Refueling in progress.

Dr. Peterson giving Bobbi a chiropractic treatment before flight.

Simulation of Elinor piloting while Bobbi sleeps on top of gasoline tanks.

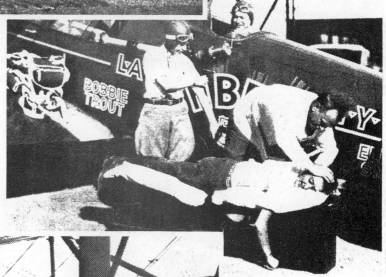

CREDIT: D.D. HATFIELD

CREDIT: D.D. HATFIELD

TRANSCONTINENTAL AIR TRANSPORT, INC.

AMELIA EARHART
ASS'T TO THE GENERAL TRAFFIC MANAGER

959 EIGHTH AVENUE
NEW YORK CITY

December nine
1 9 2 9

Dear Bobby:

I called on Porter Adams in Tuscon the
other day and found him laughing over
the enclosed. The issue from which he
had cut it had the picture of two one armed
aviators with Portugal's President's
inscription under it, and the President
of Portugal, you see, was being refuelled
by two aviatrixes. There was no picture
of you or description of the one armed flyers.

How goes the refuelling, anyway? It was
a tough break that the other ship failed
you. You have a record, anyway.

Sincerely yours,

Amelia Earhart

*Interesting mail and enclosure
from Amelia Earhart.*

Portugal's President Visits Spain

Refueling is one of the most important factors in a successful endurance flight, and Elinor Smith is standing alongside while Bobby
Troutt shows the refueling funnel alongside the cockpit of their
Sunbeam plane which the girls will use in their endurance attempt
over Los Angeles

CREDIT: AMELIA EARHART

WOOD DAILY CITIZEN

HOLLYWOOD, CALIFORNIA, THURSDAY, NOVEMBER 28, 1929   Price 2 Cents Per Copy

SET MARK, STILL IN AIR

China Differences Doubted

2 GIRL FLIERS DOWN AFTER 42 HOURS

The fifth attempt of Bobby Trout and Elinor Smith to establish a new world's record for endurance flying ended dramatically early today through no fault of their own.

The girl flyers were forced to land at 3:45 a. m. after 42 hours and 5 minutes in the air because their refueling plane's motor was wrecked and they were forced to come down in a dead stick landing when they ran out of gasoline.

Failure of the "mother" ship's motor was taken philosophically by the girl fliers and they announced they will make a new assault upon the world's endurance record next week.

TO TAKE NO CHANCES

"We will have two refueling ships ready for the next try," said Miss Trout. "If one fails, the other will be able to supply us."

The motor of their own ship is to be overhauled while mechanics are installing a new motor in the refueling plane. An emergency refueling plane will be outfitted with necessary apparatus.

Thousands watched the heartbreaking attempt of the young girls to keep their plane aloft last night until an emergency refueling ship could be commissioned. A substitute plane was taken up and made one hazardous contact, but the flight managers ruled against further use of the makeshift.

Danger lurked in the upper air lanes through the long night as fog and chill winds enveloped the ship and a huge crowd spurred the ground crew to rig up a substitute "mother" plane.

CALL OFF CONTACT

Finally Roman "Cowboy" Warren and "Pete" Reinhart, the refuelling crew, fitted up another ship with a 15-foot contact hose and went aloft. They succeeded in transferring 50 gallons of fuel under the most hazardous of conditions. But when they reported to Flight Managers Jack Sherill and A. B. Green they were forbidden to go aloft again with the short hose.

The girls flew on through the night with their meager load of fuel and finally at 3:45 a. m. they came to earth, out of gas, amid a burst of cheering.

Former Rivals United In Aerial Venture

ELEANOR SMITH (left insert) and BOBBIE TROUT, Los Angeles birdwomen, who once were rivals in the air, were circling Metropolitan Airport today in an endurance flight which early this morning had broken all records for their sex. Their plane, "Sunbeam," is shown above, with Miss Trout standing beside it.

WOMEN UP 42 HRS.; FUEL GONE

Eclipsing their previous mark of 18 hours and 26 minutes in the air, but falling far short of establishing a new world's record for refueling endurance flight and with gas tanks empty, Bobbie Trout, Los Angeles, and Elinor Smith, New York, landed at 3:45 a. m. after forty-two hours and five minutes aloft.

The new mark sets a record, as the two girl flyers are the first of their sex to attempt a refueling endurance record. The official men's record is 420 hours 21 minutes and 58 seconds, held by Dale Jackson and Forest O'Brine of St. Louis.

Both flyers expressed keen disappointment because of their inability to replenish their gasoline supply before dark last night. An attempt shortly before dark was balked when the Carrier Pigeon, refueling plane, developed trouble and landed in a plowed field.

TWO AVIATRICES TO TRY FOR ENDURANCE RECORD AT LOS ANGELES.

RECORD MADE WITHOUT SIGN OF FAILURE

Elinor Smith, Bobbie Trout Continue Circling Field On Endurance Flight

After flying steadily in wide circles throughout the night over Metropolitan Airport the two young women endurance flyers, Elinor Smith and Bobby Trout dropped a message on the field this morning stating everything was running fine and that they felt great.

A breakfast was lowered the girls from another plane about 6 a. m. and an hour later the refueling plane, Carrier Pigeon, took off and transferred 100 gallons of gasoline to the giant Sunbeam.

It was the third refueling since the girls took off yesterday morning at 9:40 a. m. The first contact was made yesterday noon when 50 gallons of fuel were taken on and the second contact at 9:30 p. m. last night when they took on 100 gallons more of fuel.

Breakfast this morning consisted of a pint of orange juice each, four pieces of dark toast and a slice of ham. With the breakfast was lowered 83 letters and 16 telegrams congratulating them and wishing them success in their flight.

At 7:30 a. m. this morning the girls had been aloft 21 hours 50 minutes, setting a world's record for women for sustained flight.

No word came from the plane during the forenoon, but there was no indication of trouble and field attendants predicted the flight would continue through the day without interruption. It was not known when the girls would need more gasoline.

Gathering of many noted pilots, November 1929, to celebrate Amelia Earhart's aviation feats at Grand Central Airport. (from left) unknown, Waldo Waterman, Charley Babb (man with hat), Earle Ovington, Vic Clark, unknown, unknown, Amelia Earhart, unknown, unknown, Elinor Smith, unknown, unknown, unknown, Bobbi Trout and Roscoe Turner.

Although the flight had been a success, both in performance and publicity for the two aviatrixes, Elinor informed Bobbi that she did not want to wait until either the Pigeon could be repaired or another refueling ship could be found to try to make a longer endurance record.

Sherrill located a Buhl Aircraft Company airplane to replace the Pigeon, but it had a much lower gallons-per-minute delivery capacity. It was therefore a less desirable refueling airplane. Bobbi tried to talk Elinor into making another try at a longer record. Because Elinor's finances were running low, and her grandmother was seriously ill back east, she left shortly after and hurried back to Long Island.

Bobbi was once again riding the crest of the newest wave of publicity. She was thrilled to be recognized on the street and asked for her autograph. The Los Angeles City Council proclaimed her "Sweetheart of Los Angeles." Other awards proved to be more practical. Dr. Burton Charles of Radium Products Laboratory, in conjunction with the Stewart Leather Manufacturing Company, presented her with a beautiful, electrically heated leather flying suit. Dr. Charles had read where she complained of being cold during flights and this was his answer. Another gift was fur-lined boots from the G.A. Bass Company.

*Richfield Oil sent Bobbi an
official record of the
refueling flight.*

Richfield Oil Company

of California

GENERAL OFFICE RICHFIELD BUILDING
555 SOUTH FLOWER STREET

Los Angeles

February 13th, 1930.

ALL COMMUNICATIONS SHOULD BE
ADDRESSED TO THE COMPANY

ALL QUOTATIONS SUBJECT
TO CHANGE WITHOUT NOTICE

Miss Bobby Trout,
418 Soto Street,
Los Angeles, California.

Dear Bobby:

We are enclosing copy of Department of
Commerce, Bureau of Standards report on recent attempted
refueling endurance flight, made by yourself and Elinor
Smith, which has just been received.

This report gives the duration of the
flight as 42 hours, 4 minutes and 41 seconds.

Our sincere best wishes go with you in all
future flights.

Very truly yours,

SALES DIVISION

DUDLEY M. STEELE, Mgr.,
DEPARTMENT OF AVIATION.

DEPARTMENT OF COMMERCE

BUREAU OF STANDARDS
Report
on
Refueling Endurance Flight
made by
Miss Elinor Smith & Miss Evelyn D. Trout
at
Los Angeles, California
on
November 27 - 29, 1929
requested by
Contest Committee, National Aeronautic Association,
Washington, D. C.
on
January 13, 1930.

Data and Instrument

A. Julien P. Friez barograph and data relative to a refueling
endurance flight made by Miss Elinor Smith and Miss Evelyn D. Trout in
a Sunbeam biplane, powered with a Wright Whirlwind J6-9 cylinder, 300
horsepower motor, were submitted in order to determine the endurance
time and whether or not an intermediate landing had been made during
the flight. The range of the instrument carried, B. S. Serial No. 3330,
Ident. No. 2, is 10,900 feet P.A.X. standard altitude. The duration of
the flight as given by the official timer was 42 hours 4 minutes 41 seconds.
The instrument was received at the Bureau of Standards with the seal
unbroken.

Test.

The smoked chart was "fixed" by immersion in a solution of collodion
and Duco solvent and then replaced on the barograph drum. The time scale
was checked against a standard time piece and it was found that the recording
drum made one revolution in 24 hours. The duration of the flight as recorded
by the barograph was 42 hours. The excellent barograph trace clearly
indicates that no landing was made between the start and finish of the flight.

George K. Burgess, Director.

Washington, D. C.
February 3, 1930.

*Artist Gertrude Orde chose
Bobbi as her subject
(opposite page) in a theme
contest on "Peace Around
the World Through
Aviation." This was in
response to Elizabeth
McQueen's painting
contest, circa 1930.*

A letter and rhyme from a fan, Downie Tepsic Zatko. Downie came to California about 1944 and worked for Bobbi, in her De-Burring business, during WWII. They are still very good friends today.

```
                          Conway, Pa.
                          1-28-31.-

Dearest "Bobbie"
              I don't know how to thank you,
dear-for, the wonderful letters, you write
to me. Speaking of 'clever people'- why
Bobbie dear- I'm nothing compared to you.
              Would I like to meet you, ????
you bet, and how????. I'll do everything
I can for such a chance. Then I'd be the
happiest girl in the world.
              I want to congradulate you, on
the fine record you established. That's a
record, that will make the whole world sit
up, and notice. Saw your picture, and that
of Edna and Mr. Martin, in the Sunday pap-
ers, and if you aren't the sweetest person
in the world, "I'll eat my hat". You look
so cute, and was I proud, to show everybody
your picture???. They all say, "My, but is-
n't she the sweetest little thing". Now you
can imagine, how proud I feel, as your true
old pal.
              Bobbie dear, if there is any-
thing I can do for you, just let me know.
I'd be glad to help you in any way, I can.
I have a little verse for you, dear- so here
                                        goes--

              "My Pal Bobbie"
       I have a pal, whom I love well
I love her more then tongue can tell
She's always willing and trying to be
The dearest 'friend' in the world,to me.

She possesses, beauty, charm, and grace
The "sweetest" smile, lurks on her face
The Endurance Record Holder, of world
                              wide fame----
You bet, "BOBBIE TROUT" , is her NAME.

P.S. Will have more for you the next time,
     Bobbie dear- and I'll sign off, and
     tune in, on station "SWEET YOU"......

              Loads of love,
```

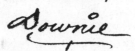

```
      "Mrs.Beryl Hart--&--William S.MacLaren"
          "The-Lost*Ocean-Flyers"

At break of dawn--like a beautiful swan
The "Tradewind" hopped off across the waters,
Carrying into-------------'the unknown'-
Two of America's 'interpid fliers'.....

The world awaited, news of the flight-
As 'ocean liners', reported them no where
                              in sight--
Day passed on,-------and night set in-
While-hope-for the fliers- was growing dim.

The 'little red headed widow', who strived
                         to gain-
Was at the 'controls, of the trim little
                              plane-
And her co-pilot, and navigator-'a former
                         navy flier'--
To fly the first payload, to Europe,---
Was his----------------'utmost desire......

Lost---but not forgotten,-forever they'll be
For-they've added a 'new page', in aviation
                              history-
Their's was the fate, of so many pioneers-
Who "bravely", ended-their 'Flying Careers."


                         D.Tepsic.
```

Downie by her ship.

A fan's reaction to flyers lost at sea. The "Tradewinds" and crew were forever lost at sea, like so many other ocean adventurers, in the early days. Written in 1931 by Downie and sent to Bobbi.

IMPORTANT . . . Finder Please Telephone This Message to L. A. Metropolitan Airport . . . Van Nuys 1145

ON BOARD
THE
L.A.   N.Y.

BOBBIE   ELINOR
TROUT   SMITH

WOMEN'S REFUELING ENDURANCE FLIGHT

418 So. Soto St.
Los Angeles, Calif.

Pitcairn Aircraft, Inc.
Willo Grove, Pa.

Gentlemen;

    I am working on an aerial advertising proposition
which requires three ships that are strong and sturdy enough
to withstand a reasonable amount of stunting. I believe that
your PA-7 J6 would meet our requirements perfectly.

    Since the Sea Hawks proved to be the sensation of
the '928 National Air Meet I have had an ever growing desire
to get two more girls and three ships of this type and do the same
same stunt excepting the extreme hazardous parts. After one
public performance at a big air meet or any large open-air
assembly of the public this trio would be"Made",it would be
in demand all over the country and being the first of its kind
and girls doing the flying would make it the"drawing-card"of
any affair. The money would either be made on the "Gate" or
flat sum and various advertisers would use the space on the
the ships and"Pitcairn" did it, which, as you can see would
be an enormous advertisement for your ships.

    I can obtain finances up to two-thirds on this
project or approximately thereof. Surely you can see the
advantages of this proposition as well as entering the ships
in the Women's Air Derby and meets of every type.

    Now, that you can see the wonderful advantages
offered your product will you help me in making up the defi-
siency in financing our project?

    Trusting you will meet this favorably, I am

        Sincerely,

Using Richfield Products Exclusively

Bobbi writes Pitcairn Aircraft for sponsorship of aerial advertising.

Bobbi models her new electric heated leather flying suit and the warm Bass boots.

Letter from the Bass Company who donated warm aviation boots to keep Bobbi's feet warm.

THE BASS SHOE
FOR HARD SERVICE
MOCK-MOCCASINS

G. H. BASS & CO.
WILTON, MAINE
SHOEMAKERS
SINCE 1876

RANGELEY
MOCCASINS
WOC-O-MOCS

February 14, 1929.

Miss Bobby Trout, Aviatrix,
Los Angeles,
California.

Dear Miss Trout:

We were very much interested to note that you had not only broken the women's endurance flight record but also the men's night flying and distance records. This certainly was a great accomplishment for one night.

However, we felt very sorry that you had trouble with your feet being cold and that you could not keep them warm without their getting very tired.

We wonder if the moccasins referred to in the newspaper were Bass Aviation Moccasins with wool lining. We are now making Aviation Moccasins especially for women, to be put on over the ordinary shoes or boots. We are also making a flexible moccasin that can be worn beneath the wool lined moccasins.

B. H. Dyas Company of Los Angeles and Hollywood have an order in with us for Aviation Moccasins, and we would be very glad to present a pair to you through them. We hope very much that you will avail yourself of this offer as we certainly do not want you to run any chances of not breaking records in the future on account of cold and tired feet.

Very truly yours,

JRB.G   G. H. BASS & CO.

SECOND NEWS
SECTION
FINANCIAL REPORT

MARINE INFORMATION—VITAL STATISTICS.   (R)

The San

AND DAILY BEE — THE

SAN DIEGO, CALIFORNIA,

STORMS FAIL TO DAUNT NOTED

HAS BUMPY HOP BUT NEGOTIATES PERFECT LANDING

Miss Bobby Trout Sets Plane Down on Lindbergh Field With Two Passengers.

Storm Queen

Rain storms and squalls did not mean anything to Bobby Trout, intrepid girl flier, yesterday when she piloted a plane and two passengers from Los Angeles to San Diego in the face of adverse weather conditions. Miss Trout is shown here in high flying costume. (International Newsreel).

While at least one aerial transportation company cancelled its service to San Diego yesterday because of inclement weather, Bobby Trout, pretty 23-year-old aviatrix and internationally known flier, battled a series of rain storms and squalls to make a flight from Los Angeles to San Diego.

Miss Trout, one-time holder of the solo endurance record for women and who with Miss Elinor Smith still holds the refueling record of 42 hours and five minutes for women, set the plane she was piloting down to a perfect three-point landing on Lindbergh field at 11:20 o'clock yesterday morning. With her were William George, aviation promoter, and Ted Scoff, jr., owner of the biplane in which the trio made the flight to San Diego.

AIR RATHER ROUGH

"Mr. George had a business appointment in San Diego with Col. D. L. Roscoe, so I just helped him fill it by piloting him and Mr. Scoff here," Miss Trout said when found at a down town hotel. "It was a rather "bumpy" trip down and the air was plenty rough, but that didn't mean anything. We got through without mishap."

George and Colonel Roscoe, who were with Miss Trout, refused to discuss the nature of their business. They did reveal, however, that clearance papers to permit the plane piloted by Miss Trout to cross the international boundary into Mexico have been obtained and that the entire party this morning will leave for some place in Lower California.

PLANS AIR SPECTACLE

"What we are working on," said George, speaking for himself and Colonel Roscoe, "in a short time will mean a great deal for San Diego, we hope, but at this time we cannot reveal our plans."

George also hinted that Miss Trout is planning soon to attempt a new aerial spectacle and that she will make San Diego her base of operations.

To Aid Altitude Attempt

Dr. Charles is shown here with the wire and a piece of the pliable stitched lining which is put into the arms, legs, boots, helmet and gloves of the flying suit. Attached to the battery of Miss Trout's plane, the suit will be warmed no matter how cold the atmosphere gets. The mesh lining weighs only eight ounces.

Charles and Anne Lindbergh copied this electrically heated flying suit for their round-the-world flight.

Diego Union

PIONEER NEWSPAPER OF SOUTHERN CALIFORNIA

MONDAY MORNING, MAY 5, 1930

AVIATRIX IN TRIP FROM L. A.

Girl's New Flying Suit ✠ ✠ Heated by Electricity

When Bobby Trout, girl flier, attempts to make a new altitude record for women by reaching 21,000 feet, she will be able to stay warm, no matter how cold the air becomes, in her electric heated flying suit invented by Dr. Burton Charles of Los Angeles. She points to the wired lining which carries the heat.

Diamond drawn copper wires, made into a cable, insulated and wound around soft seine cord, form the heating mesh. An electric cord is attached at one end.

This machine, invented by Dr. Charles, winds the copper cable spirally around the pre-shrunk cord. The arrow points to the finished cord with the cable around it. The mesh is pliable and unbreakable, it is claimed, the spiral curves of the wire around the cord taking up the strain in bending any part of the lining.

Lindbergh read about her electrically heated flying suit and called. He and his wife, Anne, were making preparations for several upcoming flights and since he had experienced similar problems with cold during his flights, he expressed a wish that she meet them at a mutual friend's home. Anne wrote in 1982:

> Thank you for your letter of April 21 reminding me of our meeting in the Maddux [Helen Maddux] home when we were waiting for our Lockheed Sirius to be built. . . . I am grateful to you for your showing us your new electric flying suit so long ago which we copied and used so many times on our flights in the thirties. . . .

The Lindberghs' suits were made of waterproof canvas instead of leather, no doubt to lessen the weight.

This was not the end of refueling flights for Bobbi.

authorize:s us
to say that a
TELEGRAPHIC reply
is desir:

via
WESTERN UNION
3936

UNION

NEWCOMB CARLTON, PRESIDENT   J. C. WILLEVER, FIRST VICE-PRESIDENT

NLT = Cable Night Letter
WLT = Week-End Letter

the date line on full-rate telegrams and day letters, and the time of receipt at destination as shown on all messages is STANDARD TIME

So. Spring St., Los Angeles, Cal. **ALWAYS OPEN**   1930 JUN 17 AM 7-23

NB31 70 NL XU=NEWYORK NY 16

EVELYN TROUT=
    418 SOTO ST LOSANGELES CALIF=

TO ALL WOMEN TRANSPORT LICENSEES CARL EGGE REPORTS RACE

COMMITTEE WILL AUTHORIZE ADDITIONAL CLASSIFICATION EIGHT

HUNDRED UP IF FIVE ENTRANTS ASSURED IF COMPETING PLEASE

ANSWER COLLECT EARHART 959 8 AVENUE TWO QUESTIONS WHAT

DISPLACEMENT YOU WOULD PROBABLY FLY IF THREE CLASSES ALLOWED

FIRST IF RACE FROM WEST SECOND IF RACE FROM EAST REMEMBERING

ATC REQUIRED ON ALL SHIPS STOP MATTER OF PRIZES FOR

TENTATIVE CLASS BEING WORKED ON=

    NOYES THADEN EARHART.

Obituary of Joe Harrison, a dear friend and great mechanic.

AIR PILOT CRASHES IN TEST SPIN

Soloing for his limited commercial aviator's license, Joe Harrison, 38, of 3661 South Grand avenue, sent his biplane into a spin to crash to earth yesterday from an altitude of 3000 feet in a field west of Inglewood.

At Centinella hospital last night physicians said the flyer would die from a skull fracture.

The accident occurred a few minutes after Harrison had taken off from Mines field in Inglewood in view of department of commerce inspectors, who were present to pass on his requirements for the license.

Joe Harrison

Harrison, who already held an ordinary pilot's license, had his parachute strapped on, but apparently made no move to use it.

FLYING FOR YEAR

Friends of Harrison were unable to account for the accident. They said that he had been flying since a year ago, when he and his wife came to Los Angeles from Kentucky.

When Bobbie Trout, aviatrix, broke the women's solo endurance flight, she gave much of the credit to Harrison, who acted as her mechanic.

Congratulations Bobbie !
I hope you've hung a record
up there on the Suns whiskers
that will be a mighty
long time in falling back
to the landing field.
Yours for places
nearer heaven
EVE

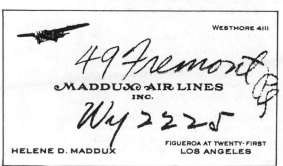

Obituary of friend, Jack Maddux, circa 1935. His wife's, Helene, business card to the left.

Jack Maddux, Aviation Pioneer Here, Dies

Jack Luther Maddux, 49, noted pioneer Pacific Coast air line promoter, who was one of the organizers of the Transcontinental and Western Air, and who induced Col. Charles A. Lindbergh to become technical adviser of the line, died in New York today of a heart attack.

While Mr. Maddux was Los Angeles agent for Lincoln automobiles in the late 20s he became interested in aviation and founded the Maddux Air Lines between here and San Francisco.

Maddux, a pioneer in air transport, organized the Maddux Air Line between Oakland, Los Angeles and San Diego, using Ford planes.

In 1929, Maddux reorganized his line as the Transcontinental Air Transport, and started an eastward extension of service to Winslow, Ariz., where connection was made with transcontinental train service. T. A. T. had the personal financial backing of Henry Ford, whose planes it used.

Later, T. A. T., through the influence of Maddux, signed Lindbergh as technical adviser, and a combination air-rail service was organized between Los Angeles and New York. Planes flew by daylight between New York and Columbus, Ohio, and between Amarillo, Tex., and Los Angeles, with intervening sleeper service by rail.

Meanwhile Western Air Express had branched out to Kansas City, but when the government in 1931 refused to permit mail subsidies on parallel lines, T. A. T. and the Kansas City line of Western Air were merged to form Transcontinental & Western Air. Shortly after this Maddux sold out his controlling

JACK L. MADDUX
Air Lines Founder Dies in East

interest to the Pennsylvania railroad, although retaining a large block of stock.

Maddux was one of Lindberg's few close personal friends, having become acquainted with the flier before he flew to Paris. Whenever Lindbergh was in Los Angeles he stopped at the Maddux Fremont place home.

More recently, Mr. Maddux has been interested in the Maddux Electric Brake Corp. With Mr. Maddux when the end came were his second wife, Mrs. Rowena Maddux, and their child, Jimmie, 2. His first wife, Mrs. Helen K. Maddux, died here in 1932. Their child, Jack Jr., now 13, survives. The family home is at 49 Fremont place, Los Angeles.

LIST OF OBJECTS RECEIVED BY MUSEUM

ACCESSION NUMBER   A.5665

THE objects indicated below, or on the attached list, are at all times subject to the conditions of acceptance on the reverse of this sheet.

Woman flyer's suit. Coverall style with sheepskin collar and light brown sateen lining. Wired throughout, with the electric plug in the left knee pocket. The first electrically heated suit made.

The Board of Governors of the
LOS ANGELES COUNTY MUSEUM OF HISTORY, SCIENCE AND ART
GRATEFULLY ACKNOWLEDGES
the generosity of

MISS BOBBIE TROUT

Bobbi's electrically heated flying suit which she donated to the Los Angeles County Museum of History, Science and Art, where it remains today.

Chapter Ten

Bobbi's Second Refueling Endurance Flight

THE Depression of the 1930's started with the terrible stock market crash in late 1929. Bobbi's family was fortunate, however. The Trouts' service station was doing business, almost as usual. Even though some of their customers were unable to pay their bills, the Trouts' business income was still adequate for their needs. In addition, Bobbi made several trips in the airplane, dropping thousands of leaflets advertising gasoline at a dime-a-gallon. Each time she returned to the station, she could hardly get in because of the lines of cars waiting for the ten-cent gasoline.

Bobbi had so many invitations to luncheons and banquets she didn't have to worry about food, even if the family business should decline. Free food, however, did not appeal to her because she would have to give a speech about her flying experiences—in other words, she had to "toot her own horn." She was much more comfortable working at the family business during her free time.

The Depression also affected sponsorships. Bobbi spent 1930 trying to find sponsors to back new business ventures using airplanes. One of her brainstorms was to fly oysters from Chesapeake Bay on the east coast to Los Angeles and to fly flowers from California on the return trip. She finally interested a large distributor of sea foods in Los Angeles in backing the venture, only to have the president of the company die of a heart attack before they completed the deal.

Publicity picture of Bobbi in 1930.

IMPORTANT . . . Finder Please Telephone This Message to L. A. Metropolitan Airport . . . Van Nuys 1145

ON BOARD
THE
L.A. ▓ **N.Y.**
SUNBEAM

BOBBIE   ELINOR
TROUT   SMITH

WOMEN'S REFUELING ENDURANCE FLIGHT

Gentlemen:

Every one is interested in a lucrative and spectacular enterprise. The entire world has become air-minded, so each major event is looked forward to with great anticipation by everybody.

It is with these thoughts in mind that I have taken the liberty of writing this letter to you, as I am sure will realize the tremendous possibilities to the right person that can successfully manage aeronautical events, as outlined in the attached prospectus.

As you probably know that I have been very successful in endurance flights, re-fueling, altitude, cross-country flights and many rades. In addition to this I am one of the few women to hold a transport pilot's license and Federation Aeronautic International license.

At the present I am not under contract, so I am open to any good proposition that you may care to offer, regardless where it may be. As I am not confined only to local activities. All that I request is proper financial support and a fair proposition.

Thanking you for your kind consideration and an early reply, I remain

                                  Sincerely

Address
418 South Soto St.
Los Angeles, Calif.
Phone Angelus 4550.

Using Richfield RICHLUBE *Products Exclusively*

Re-Fueling Flight

There are unlimited possibilities for making thousands of dollars in putting on an endurance flight with two girls handling the endurance ship.

I am sure that with my experience in Re-Fueling and endurance flights together with my knowledge in motors and general flying experience that I can easily make a success of any refueling flight. All that is needed is a very good ship and motor. As far as my Co-pilot I can very easily obtain another girl to assist me in this flight.

Gasoline and Oil Companies as well as Radio Broadcasting Stations are always ready and willing to assist in an event of this kind. Incidentally I might mention that I hold a license to operate Radio Telephone Broadcasting from an airplane making it possible to tie up many advertising programs with the refueling flight.

There are really too many details to elaborate on at this time. I will confer with anyone giving them further particulars regarding such a flight.

"Around the World Flight"

After establishing a new record for refueling it would be quite a simple matter to promote a refueling flight around the world. This would be the first flight of its kind and would be an epoch in aviation history.

"Other Events"

Non-Stop from Vancouver to Agua Caliente
Non-Stop From Los Angeles to New York
Woman's National Dreby
Ocean hop from Honolulu to here (Los Angeles)
Countless other events that come up from day to day in aviation.

Bobbi was always looking for flying activities in the 1930's.

Bobbi's prospectus and Transport License (below) reflect her courage and ability.

Another idea was with her brilliant and special friend, Dick Costello, who learned to fly at Burdett's when Bobbi was learning. Costello, comptroller of Wurlitzer Music Company in Los Angeles, would come over to Bobbi's home often and talk business and flying. Costello also took Bobbi out on many nice dinner dates. During the Depression, Wurlitzer went out of business and Bobbi and Costello talked of opening up a business together.

They wanted to open up what they called, a "Foultarian," a high-class chicken business. In those days, to buy a chicken, one would go into a chicken establishment and pick out a live chicken housed in a wire cage. The owner would kill and dress the chicken while the patron stood around waiting and smelling the miserable chicken odors.

The "Foultarian" idea fell through when Costello was offered a very good position managing a large department store in the south part of Los Angeles.

Bobbi's next idea was to convince a man named Beesemyer, an official of Gilmore Oil Company, to purchase Jack Northrop's new, all-aluminum Beta monoplane, in which she hoped to make speed flights from city to city advertising the company's product, similar to the work Roscoe Turner was doing. After Beesemyer looked at the ship with her, he agreed to put Bobbi under contract for Gilmore Oil, and they were scheduled to meet the following day to finalize plans. Unfortunately, a gas-price war erupted overnight, and Bobbi did not become the "speed-queen."

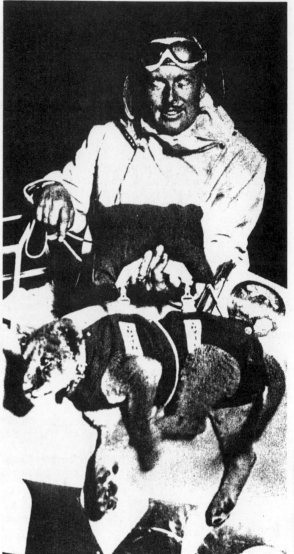

PHOTO CREDIT: DICK COSTELLO

Roscoe and his lion.

Roscoe Turner, Flier, Dies at 74

INDIANAPOLIS, Ind.

Col. Roscoe Turner, 74, flamboyant air racer and aviation executive who helped put glamor into post-World War 1 aviation, died in an Indianapolis hospital Tuesday after a long illness.

Turner was America's foremost speed flier in the 1930s. He won the annual 300-mile Thompson trophy race three times and also captured the Bendix cross-country race.

He took the Harmon trophy given to the country's top speed pilot, in 1934, 1938 and 1939.

Turner's waxed mustache and the natty blue uniform he designed for himself were familiar for decades to American aviation enthusiasts. A set of $5,000 diamond-encrusted wings set off the unofficial uniform.

He added spice to his speed flying by carrying a tame lion named Gilmore in his cockpit. At hotels he registered simply, "Turner and Gilmore."

Turner set transcontinental records in both directions in the 30s by going more than 250 miles an hour. His best time, west-east was 11 hours 30 minutes in 1930.

He was a stunt flier, both in barnstorming tours and in the movies. He performed in the film, "Hell's Angels," once flying so low he knocked down a camera.

Turner was board chairman of Roscoe Turner Aeronautical Corp., a flight school and aircraft sales and service facility at Indianapolis Weir Cook Airport.

He and Jimme Doolittle were the only pilots ever to win both the Thompson and Bendix trophies.

Turner estimated he flew 3 million miles during his career and logged 18,000 hours.

A friend recalled Turner once saying: "When I get so old I can't come here and look over the field and hear the engines, I want to die."

The Trout's remodeled service station in 1927.

Bobbi and brother, Denny, 1934.

Dick Costello, in the Golden Eagle, was a student with Bobbi at Burdett's airport in 1928.

Bobbi won several air races, including the Women's Air Race at the official opening of United Airport, now named Burbank Airport, May 30-31, 1930. Pratt-Whitney sponsored the Air Race. Bobbi won the closed-course race around pylons that day, flying a Kinner Fleet. Mrs. Thomas Hamilton of Hamilton Aero Manufacturing Company presented her with a silver cup for winning.

Bobbi continued to enter races at air meets and airport openings. She was an entrant in the meets Cliff Henderson was masterminding to help unemployed aviators and to promote aviation. Through Edna May Cooper, a young starlet who had just earned her private pilot's license, Bobbi met Joseph Martin, an investment broker, who was interested in advertising to promote his new office.

Edna May had suggested that she and another woman make a women's refueling endurance flight, a sure way to gain publicity for Martin. This was a great idea to Martin, who told Edna May that if she could get another woman with more experience to go up with her, he would put up the money to pay for the flight. Martin suggested she contact Bobbi Trout.

Edna May contacted Bobbi by phone. It did not take Bobbi long to decide to participate. Martin, upon receiving confirmation that Bobbi had agreed to do the flight with Edna May, contacted Major Corliss C. Mosley, manager of Grand Central Airport, and purchased a used Challenger Curtiss Robin monoplane. He named the aircraft Lady Rolph, in honor of the California governor's wife. He assumed, and rightly so, that this would add to the news coverage.

Martin hired the Timm brothers, Otto and Wally, to do the necessary work on the airplane. They installed a large gasoline tank in the cabin with proper filling tubes and a hatch in the fuselage for Edna May to put her head and torso through to receive the gasoline and bags containing food, oil, and messages. They installed a good wind-driven gasoline pump for pumping the fuel from the large tank into the regular fuel tanks in the wings. They also installed engine rocker oiling lines that oiled the valve rocker arms and filler pipe into which the women could pour oil from the pilot's seat, enabling them to add oil to the crankcase.

May 31, 1930—Bobbi receives congratulations from Mrs. Hamilton after Bobbi won the woman's race at the opening of United Airport (now Burbank Airport).

Bobbi shows the trophy Mrs. Hamilton presented to her.

Dedication of the plane used by Miss Bobby Trout and Edna May Cooper in their record-breaking endurance flight. Left to right: Bobbie Trout, Louis Mayer (motion picture magnate), Mrs. Jos. Martin, Miss Mary Virginia Hess, Jos. Martin (sponsor of the flight), Edna May Cooper and Anita Page.

Bobbi's second refueling endurance flight well wishers and press prior to take off, Jan.1, 1931.

The Timms added a special petcock at the bottom of the crankcase for draining out the used oil. However, Martin failed to have the engine itself thoroughly checked. This oversight cost them dearly.

Martin arranged with Louis B. Mayer of MGM Pictures to have actors, actresses, and all of their families and friends at the airport when Bobbi and Edna May took off. There were many gifts of flowers, and champagne, at the field. All the press and media around the Los Angeles area attended to magnify the importance of the event. Takeoff was scheduled for four o'clock in the afternoon on January 1, 1931.

Bobbi and Edna May left the runway with very little gas in their tanks because the refueling ship was supposed to come up right after the takeoff to give them their night's supplies and to make their first refueling contact. Martin rented the old Curtiss Carrier Pigeon—the same one that had let Bobbi and Elinor down on the first refueling flight. It had been rebuilt and was supposed to be in perfect condition. After they took off, Bobbi and Edna May circled over Mines Field, where the ground crew was trying to get the refueling ship's engine started. The mechanics ran the prop through again and again. They added more men to help pull the huge prop through, only to be unsuccessful time after time, continuing into the dark of night. Bobbi and Edna May circled above until after dark, waiting and wondering what was happening below.

Darkness fell and still the refueling had not been accomplished. Bobbi decided there was no logical reason to stay up any longer and extend the risk of running out of gas completely. Bobbi finally decided she was going to land the airplane. Making contact in the dark was risky, even if the ground crew had been able to start the Pigeon's engine.

Girl Flyers Try Again for New Endurance Record

Bobbie and Edna Soar Again Today

Bobbie Trout and Edna Mae Cooper will make another start in their attempt at an endurance flight record today at 1 o'clock when they will take off in Miss Trout's ship at the Municipal Airport. Their first attempt, New Year's Day, lasted only two hours and forty minutes when they were forced to land because of refueling difficulties.

Bobbi and Edna May in the news.

—Daily News Photo.
UP THERE AGAIN — Monoplane Lady Rolph, shown above, as it took off from Los Angeles municipal airport yesterday as Edna May Cooper (left) and Bobbie Trout made new attempt to set women's endurance flight record.

GIRL REFUELING FLYERS HOP OFF

In a new attempt to shatter the world's air endurance record for women, Bobbie Trout and Edna May Cooper hopped off from the Los Angeles Municipal Airport at 2:30 o'clock yesterday afternoon.

The two women were forced to abandon their first record try on New Year's Day through failure of their refueling plane after they had remained aloft for about two and a half hours.

Upper photo shows the Lady Rolph, Curtiss plane in which Miss Bobby Trout and Miss Edna May Cooper hope to set a new endurance record. They will take off at the Los Angeles Municipal Airport tomorrow. Below, left to right, Edna May Cooper, Joseph Martin, sponsor of the flight, and Bobby Trout.

Girls Seek Endurance Mark

A few moments after this picture had been taken, Edna May Cooper and Bobbie Trout took to the air over Los Angeles in their plane, "Lady Rolph," in an effort to stay aloft several weeks and set an endurance flight record for women that would stand for years to come. This picture

Articles and pictures of Bobbi and Edna May Cooper as they set out after a new refueling record—January 4, 1931.

Angry and swearing, Martin stormed up to the Lady Rolph as it rolled to a stop. He could not understand why they had landed. "I was just about to send someone up with five-gallon cans of gasoline," Martin said.

Bobbi almost exploded. "Cans of gasoline? Of all the idiotic ideas. You trying to kill us?" Bobbi could not believe he considered such a thing. It was too hazardous. She knew she was not that crazy. Martin intended to keep them up once the flight began and was furious with Bobbi for spoiling his plans. He put forth the idea that they lower five-gallon cans of gasoline by rope with a lighted lantern attached to the end of it. The only trouble was, he couldn't find any pilots who were willing to take on the job.

Four days went by and Martin rented another ship and remodeled it into the refueling ship. He then hired Bud Hussey and Ralph DeRose to do the flying and refueling.

On January 4, 1931, Bobbi and Edna May took off again, hoping to stay up for at least a month. Contact was made with the refueling ship and the operation went along perfectly. It

was late in the day, the sun was setting and they had plenty of gasoline for the night. Edna May opened the bag of goodies they received from the first refueling. It contained oil cans, mail, and food. Attached to the oil cans was a note and a ten foot diameter parachute. The note directed Edna May to put the empty oil cans in the bag, attach it to the chute and drop them over the field, together with any messages they might have.

Bobbi read the instructions and shook her head in disbelief. She told Edna May to do what it said. But, she said to be sure to wrap the bag of cans in the chute tightly. There could not be any chance of it opening immediately, or it might get caught in the tail assembly. She told Edna May to throw it away from the airplane with all her might.

Edna May prepared the chute bag as told, not really realizing the imminent danger. Bobbi flew the plane about twenty-five feet off the ground, close to the hangars, so that the crew would not have to go far to retrieve the cans. Edna May's first throw sent the chute right

GIRL ENDURANCE FLYER PREVENTS CRASH OF PLANE

Only the cool headwork of Edna May Cooper, co-pilot of the Lady Rolph, which took off yesterday afternoon at 2:30 o'clock in a second attempt to shatter the women's endurance flight record, prevented a serious accident over the municipal airport shortly after the takeoff.

While Bobbie Trout was piloting the ship, Miss Cooper was receiving supplies from the refueling ship, piloted by Bud Hussey and Ralph De Rose, when a rope from the latter ship became entangled in the tail structure of the endurance plane. Miss Cooper and untangled the rope.

THREE REFUELINGS

Three refuelings were made before night, during which 170 gallons of gas were placed aboard the Lady Rolph. The 5 p. m. refueling was accomplished in 15 minutes, which is believed to be a world's record for such an event.

Dr. Joseph L. Martin announced that the Lady Rolph will fly through the night without again refueling, the next contact being scheduled for 6 a. m. today. Three refuelings a day are scheduled throughout the flight.

AFTER BIG RECORD

Dr. Max Kaplan has been retained as dietitian for the flyers, preparing nourishing dishes at the airport.

After the ill-fated attempt New Year's day, when the Lady Rolph was forced to land because of the inability of the refueling ship to take off, the pilots will attempt to shatter not only the women's record of 42 hours and 16 minutes, but also the men's international record of 645 hours and 28 minutes.

Bud Hussey and Ralph De Rose were the crew of the refueling support plane.

In the meantime, the refueling crew on the ground saw their plight. Someone located a long bamboo pole, to which they tied a sharp knife. This pole was taken up and contact was made just before darkness fell. It was handed very carefully to Edna May.

Leaning halfway through the trap door, Edna May sawed at the cords caught in the tail controls, trying not to penetrate the plane's fabric with the knife. With only the moon to give her light, it seemed like it took an hour for her to cut the lines.

Suddenly the ship gave a great lunge forward. The chute dropped, and Bobbi wiped her brow with relief, her hands still shaking. She had envisioned the sharp knife penetrating the skin of the plane instead of the cords.

An hour later it was Edna May's turn at the controls and Bobbi gladly handed them over to her. Lying on top of the large gas tank with a down comforter, she closed her eyes and started to relax when she realized the ship was starting to dive. "Edna May! Pull back on the stick. We're going into a dive," Bobbi yelled.

Edna May pulled back on the stick, as instructed, but kept pulling back until they were going too slow and at such an angle upward that Bobbi had to yell again, "Push on the stick. We're going to stall."

back into the tail, where it caught and opened, acting like a brake. Bobbi was terrified, for the chute kept dragging and the gas tanks were full. If they should crash they would become a huge fireball.

The plane wanted to flip over and go down. Bobbi used all of her knowledge and ability to keep the airplane airborne. She also had to get the plane to clear the high-tension lines at the west end of the field. With her heart beating furiously, she kept a clear head and they miraculously began a slow climb. They cleared the wires and as the chute's shroud lines slowly twisted around each other, the chute began slowly to close. The drag began to lessen, and at last they gained some altitude.

GIRL FLYERS SET RECORD AND AIM AT MEN'S GOAL

Two Los Angeles women pilots, Edna May Cooper and Bobbie Trout, completed their fifty-eighth hour of continuous flight at 12:30 a.m. today after piloting their endurance monoplane past the world's air endurance record for women yesterday morning. They were circling Los Angeles Municipal Airport during the early morning hours piling up hours in pursuit of the world's record for men.

The two plucky women equaled the former record of 42h. 16m. at 8:48 a.m., drove their ship, the Lady Rolph, low over Municipal Airport, base of the flight, and pulled up again to settle down in pursuit of the world's record for men—645h. 28m. 30s.

MISS COOPER BURNED

Less than three hours later during a refueling contact with the Carrier Pigeon, manned by Bud Hussey and Ralph De Rose, Miss Cooper received gasoline burns that for a time threatened to force the victorious ship to the ground.

The air was unusually bumpy. While the Carrier Pigeon rode less than 100 feet above and gasoline streamed downward through the contact hose, a sudden air bump tore the hose from Miss Cooper's grasp.

High-test gasoline deluged her as she stood up in the refueling hatch toward the rear of the ship. The hose swung free and the supply was cut off from above, but not quick enough to prevent a quantity from saturating Miss Cooper's clothing. She sank to the floor of the endurance craft, Miss Trout unable to aid her because the former had to stick to the controls in the pilot's seat at the ship's nose.

TAKE SALVE ALOFT

Hussey and De Rose realized what had happened and dived earthward to the port. They obtained some salve and bandages and raced aloft again to deliver them to the suffering woman.

It was nearly four hours before Miss Cooper was able to handle the gasoline hose to complete the interrupted refueling, but contact was made with forty-two gallons of gasoline and four gallons of oil lowered without further mishap.

The woman pilot dropped a note stating that the salve had taken the sting out of her burns and that she would be able to continue.

Evidently still in a high state of excitement following a battle in the darkness with a fifty-mile-an-hour gale and driving rain the night before, the two flyers sent back the breakfast lowered to them yesterday morning.

During the afternoon, however,

(Continued on Page 2, Column 4)

FLYERS AFTER MEN'S RECORD

(Continued from First Page)

their appetites had returned an they accepted some tomato juic oranges, baked apples, celery, chick en sandwiches and candy.

Men flyers at the port were lou in their praise for the aviatrices i sticking out the night in the fac of the storm that harassed them.

WOMEN TAKE TURNS

The women were taking turns a the single set of controls, supposedl in four-hour shifts, but they report ed one would fly when the othe showed any signs of drowsiness t prevent possibility of going to slee while guiding the plane.

They catch what rest they ca on an air mattress atop the 116 gallon gasoline tank that takes u most of the room in the tiny cabin

As the endurance Curtiss Robi high-winged cabin monoplane, pow ered by a 170-horsepower Challenge engine, swooped down to break th women's record—held by Miss Trou and Elinor Smith, New York flyer a crowd of nearly 500 persons raise a cheer and hats were tossed at th black-and-orange ship as it zoome the field, the two girl pilots wav ing from a cabin window.

Aviation heads interested in th flight who gathered to witness the record breaking included Joe Ni krent, official timer of the Nationa Aeronautic Association; Joseph L Martin, sponsor of the flight; W. H Hitchman, Shell Oil official; Col Richard Barnitz, director of the mu nicipal field.

Plans were being made last nigh to send up a birthday cake toda for Miss Trout. It was learned tha she will pass her twenty-fifth birth day in the ship and a special mea will go along with the cake—groun officials hoping she will be able t take other than liquid foods today

Pilots pointed out that if the physical condition of the two wome remains good the feminine skipper stand a chance to break the men' record—the motor of the enduranc ship ticking off miles in perfec running order in a wide circle abov the field.

The equipment is the same-typ plane and engine used by Fores O'Brine and Dale Jackson whe they set the men's mark last sum mer over St. Louis, Mo.

Women's Endurance Record Is Smashed by Girl Fliers

Own Mark Passed by Bobby Trout With New Flying Companion; Pair Are Now Going After Honors Held by Men.

LOS ANGELES, Jan. 6. — (P) — Bobby Trout, with a new girl flying partner, Edna May Cooper, actress and aviatrix, set a new women's endurance flight record today. At 9:47 a. m. she piloted the Lady Rolph an hour past the previous record of 42 hours and 16 minutes set by herself and Elinor Smith, New York aviatrix, some months ago.

Soaring on beyond the new feminine mark, the two swung around another milestone in their flight this afternoon. At 2:30 p. m. the trim monoplane had been in the air 48 hours. The girl fliers declare they aim to crack, if possible, the present men's mark of 645 hours, held by Dale Jackson and Forest O'Brine of St. Louis.

Rough air, from a choppy wind which followed last night's rainstorm, upset the noon refueling. Miss Cooper got a shower bath of gasoline and the Lady Rolph obtained but 38 gallons of fuel. An emergency refueling was made at mid-afternoon, when the air was comparatively quiet.

Tomorrow Miss Trout will celebrate her twenty-fifth birthday.

GIRLS ALOFT FOR PLANE RECORD

New world records were the only birthday presents Miss Bobbie Trout expected today as she and her co-pilot, Edna May Cooper, soared over Municipal airport in the monoplane "Lady Rolph," adding hour after hour to their new refueling endurance record for women.

Miss Trout was 25 years old today. A birthday cake was promised her by the ground crew, but she and Miss Cooper said they would only look at it.

A strict diet outlined by a physician at the field would not permit them to bite even into the frosting and the cake, he said, must remain uneaten until they return to earth.

If the girls attain complete success, the cake would be rather stale by the time they are allowed to eat it, for they were intent upon eclipsing the world's mark of 647 hours, 28 minutes, 30 seconds, set last summer by Forrest O'Brine and Dale Jackson in St. Louis. Thirty minutes more than 27 days was their objective, and possibly as much as a month.

One of the most interested spectators at the field yesterday when the two girls equalled the former unofficial mark for women of 42 hours, 16 minutes, was Carl Cooper, nine-year-old son of Miss Cooper.

Even close friends of the former motion picture actress were unaware that she had been married, and airport officials professed no knoledge of the name of her former husband, other than that he was a Texas man.

WOMEN PILOTS BATTLE STORM

Endurance Flyers Narrowly Escape Disaster

Parachute Becomes Tangled in Plane's Tail

Miss Trout and Miss Cooper Pass Halfway Point

Narrowly escaping disaster for the second time since they left Los Angeles Municipal Airport at 2:30 p.m.

EDNA MAY COOPER.

Sunday, Edna May Cooper and Bobbie Trout, local pilots, flew past the halfway point yesterday en route to a new world's air endurance record and were riding out a wind and rainstorm last night in their light cabin monoplane.

At 12:30 a.m. they had been in the air thirty-four hours hopeful that they could pass the present women's record of 42h. 16m., held by Miss Trout and Elinor Smith, and go on to pile up hours on the men's record of more than 600 hours.

In getting out of a harrowing situation yesterday Miss Cooper was forced to lean far out of the hatch in the top of the fuselage of the ship and cut loose a small parachute that had fouled the tail surfaces. On their first day aloft, the women pilots were nearly forced down when a rope from the refueling ship also tangled in the tail assembly.

KNIFE ON POLE USED

Yesterday's danger came about when Miss Cooper released the small 'chute, carried to drop small articles to the port, and its shrouds stuck on the tail.

For two hours the women flew around, unable to gain altitude because of the parachute jamming the tail elevator.

Meanwhile members of the ground crew fashioned a knife, attached it to the end of a bamboo pole and lowered it to the women. Miss Cooper cut the tangled lines with this and the danger was over.

BOBBY TROUT.

As the refueling ship, Carrier Pigeon, manned by Bud Hussey and Ralph DeRose, went aloft at dusk to replenish the endurance plane's tanks, a heavy rain pelted the two ships.

The craft were able to swing into position—100 feet apart, with the refueling ship above and a little ahead—and seventy gallons of gasoline slid down the hose to fill the endurance ship's 166-gallon capacity tanks.

Women Endurance Fliers Flee as Storm Threatens

Bobbie Trout and Edna Cooper Seek Better Weather Over Imperial Valley Desert in Attempt To Set New Record.

LOS ANGELES, Jan. 7.—(AP)—A storm brewing off the Pacific coast sent the endurance plane, Lady Rolph, and its two fliers, Bobbie Trout and Edna May Cooper, in full flight for better weather late today.

With their refueling ship, they beat a hasty retreat to Imperial Valley, planning to spend the night soaring over the desert near El Centro.

When they left Los Angeles at 2:30 o'clock this afternoon they had passed the seventy-second hour of their attempt to break the endurance refueling record of 645 hours.

If they are forced down at any point other than the airport here, their flight will have been for naught and the women's endurance refueling record which they exceeded on the second day will stand.

Rules of the flight provide the plane must be landed at the same port of take off to claim the record. The women's record of 42 hours was set some time ago by Miss Trout and Elinor Smith of New York.

GIRLS IN AIR EIGHTY HOURS

Edna May Cooper and Bobbie Trout Flee Before Storm to Imperial Valley's Clear Skies

Chased by storms nearly 200 miles from their flight base, Edna May Cooper and Bobbie Trout, who already have nearly doubled the former world's air endurance record for women, had been aloft in their little monoplane eighty-two hours at midnight, spending the night cruising at 2500 feet over Imperial Valley.

Officials at Imperial County Airport reported last night the aviatrices were killing time by flying giant circles through the clear skies above the field, waiting for daylight, more gasoline and a chance to get back to Los Angeles.

The two plucky women air skippers stuck it out as long as possible yesterday afternoon over Municipal Airport, base of their flight, but clouds closed down on them until they were "hedge hopping" at only a 100-foot altitude.

They turned suddenly and headed eastward, searching for clearer weather. Their Curtiss Thrush, refueling ship, piloted by Bud Hussey, with Ralph DeRose as supply man, took on a full load of gasoline and set out in pursuit of the endurance Curtiss Robin.

the local metropolitan area the aviators found a 2000-foot ceiling over March Field, Riverside.

Hussey located them there, circling, hoping the storm would not catch up and force them on to El Centro.

The refueling ship dropped its hose, made contact at 4 p.m. and settled at March Field to take on fuel in case the women asked for more to last them overnight.

The weather closed in two hours after the refueling and the girls flew 100 miles to find clearer skies over El Centro.

If they should be forced down at any point other than the Los Angeles field—start of their flight—their record would not be accepted by the National Aeronautic Association.

Because of this the girls planned to nose their little ship back to Los Angeles at the first sign of a break in the rain-laden skies, but ar-

Edna May complied immediately, but kept going in the direction ordered instead of leveling off at a cruising angle. Bobbi then realized that Edna May was a green pilot and had no feel for the horizon. Bobbi had never met anyone who had this particular difficulty before. Most pilots have a natural feel for where the horizon is, even though they cannot see it in the dark. Edna May was one of the few who had to learn the hard way.

Edna May continued seesawing for some time, until finally she began to get a fair feeling for the horizon and a cruising position. By this time Bobbi was exhausted.

The next two days and nights went along rather smoothly. After they had broken Bobbi's first refueling record of forty-two hours, three and one-half minutes, the sky was filled with planes coming up to congratulate and photograph the Lady Rolph. Some of the ships were emblazoned with messages on their sides and wings. The heartwarming spectacle was just the impetus the tired aviators needed to carry on.

On January 7, Bobbi's twenty-fifth birthday, her good friend Marie Kelly Sponholz sent up a large chocolate birthday cake, minus candles. This, with many birthday cards and a lot of good wishes for their success, made it a memorable birthday.

Marie had been a long-time friend of Bobbi's and was always doing clever and interesting things. She was the first woman hired by Lockheed Aircraft, in 1928, to take charge of the office. Bobbi ate a piece of the cake for breakfast. She then passed the time by writing a letter to their crew on the ground and in the refueling plane. It was dated 1:45 a.m., January 7, 1931, and read:

Well, we have been here approximately 60 hours. And, all's O.K. except we are still weak from our engine cutting out.

It was this way—I decided to follow instructions and shut off the left tank for our last resort—I told Edna about it and to be sure and fill the right tank at 10:00 p.m. (You see we found that we were losing gas from the new vent so we just pump gasoline until it starts to overflow and shut off gas through air pump). Until that time–10 a.m.—we were cruising at 55 and 1,425 rpm's. Our tank ran out a few minutes before 10. Edna started for the field

and I almost jumped out of my skin, and tried to think what awakened me. Edna about that time, decided it was gas and turned on the emergency, right or left, tank. We think we shall use from both, as it seems to work out better.

I don't suppose you'll be able to read this, as I am flying with my right foot only—cruising at 50 mph and running 1,350 rpm, 2,200 feet. I am using the moon above to try to space these lines—I can not read much of what I am scribbling tho . . .

The millions of lights from L.A. and the beaches and Inglewood are twinkling and blinking until I begin to wonder if I'm really awake or just dreaming . . . until the cramp in my leg or the indentation made by a snap into my sitter and the hardness of the chute (which I have been using as a cushion) let me know that I am not dreaming but getting sorer and sorer.

My oil pressure is 100 and temperature is now approximately 62 degrees. I change oil morning and night by letting enough old oil drain out to make the pressure gauge start to lose and shut off and pour in new oil immediately, so that the temperature never drops much—I told you about the left magneto cutting out? Well, it did it again yesterday a little and then the next time I tried it, it was O.K. Same plug must have wanted a vacation for a short time—yes?

Talk about rain storm yesterday. Well the rain wasn't so bad, but that wind almost turned me gray. I had that full load and gosh, some of the bumps would turn me over and leave me there—the ailerons might as well have been just plain wing.

I can use about three gallons of oil in the morning and evening (4:30). That gives me time in daylight to drain and fill, before full load too.

I must re-fill grease gun before morning—it will be the first time. Our Hot Shot played out first night.

I just shut off wing tanks pump, cause they are both full according to the main tank gauge. I have 25 more gallons here and 50 in wing. I believe it is 3:00 a.m. now, and at ten gallons per hour I would last until 10:00 a.m., but let's not try–I usually have between one-half to one-quarter at morning contact. I thought you motioned me away last evening before we were full, but I read the gauge then and when I held the ship's nose down to 60 mph, it

GIRL OBSERVES BIRTHDAY IN AIR

Through scattered billowy clouds the monoplane Lady Rolph today soared above the Los Angeles Municipal Airport, each hour bringing it closer to the world's endurance flight record for men, set as the goal by its intrepid girl pilots, Edna May Cooper and Bobbie Trout.

With the endurance flight record for women already safely tucked away, for the present at least, the two dauntless young women pressed onward toward the international mark, which yet is weeks away. At 12 m. the Lady Rolph had been aloft 69 hours and 30 minutes.

And today is a memorable one for Bobbie Trout.

It is her twenty-fifth birthday.

DINES ALONE

Instead of an elaborate birthday table surrounded by groups of friends Miss Trout will sit down to a dinner laid out on the top of the fuselage gasoline tank, alone, while Miss Cooper keeps the endurance plane on its course.

A real, old-fashioned turkey dinner with all the trimmin's plus a huge birthday cake was sent up to Miss Trout at noon today, which made her natal day anniversary in the air quite unique. Scores of presents were received at the airport today, but as there is no room in the plane Miss Trout will have to wait until the flight is over before seeing them.

showed 90 gallons—which should have carried us through until morn.

Edna is "sawing logs" and is plenty game —she keeps me busy too. She will be lying down and my stabilizer will be set fine, when all of a sudden the nose goes up into almost a stall—at first I would think some air draft had done it and I would use the stick. But now I just reach for the stabilizer and use it—I don't even have to look around to keep track of her—she is offering me a sandwich, tea, orange juice or something all the time, but I believe it not best to keep one's stomach full up here—we have not been sick and don't want to either—being sore is enough!

Gee, I hope the weather stays this way!

Everything seems to be asleep except this engine and me. I can't see an automobile out —not a one in Inglewood or around the field either. Oh yes—I just saw one—someone going to work I guess.

Say, it wouldn't hurt to send up 2 or 3 batteriesfor this flash light for when it goes out —no hurry. We have the other one if it can be found among the oil, water, rags, grease, clothes, food, etc. Aisles weren't made to walk in endurance ships. It won't be long until we'll prove Darwin's theory—and how!

We certainly enjoy our messages from all of you. It is a real treat to know there are so many friends pulling for us. We can use it too, cause no one knows how much work is needed to keep this engine purring and an endurance ship in the air until one tries it. We must stay in the air and make a full month's record.

Tell Dorothy and Charley that the turkey was good and we won't worry about starving with all the food they send up. Please send no toasted sandwiches to me. I love the orange juice, buttermilk, grapefruit juice too—but like the thin tomato juice better.

On Bobbi and Edna's third day, when they made their evening contact with the refueling ship, they received a note telling them that a big storm was coming and that they had better go down to Imperial Airport about two hundred miles away, where they would be met in the morning for contact. They had finished eating and taken care of all their other chores when darkness descended. Soon after, the worst storm in years, with howling winds and heavy rain, struck with such force that the sound of the engine was drowned out. They wasted no time heading to Imperial Valley Airport.

GIRL FLYERS SOAR ON TOWARD A NEW ENDURANCE MARK

By keeping their airplane "Lady Rolph" in the air for more than 42 hours and 16 minutes, Bobbie Trout and Edna May Cooper, of Los Angeles, have set a new refueling air endurance record for women. Circling high over the countryside near Los Angeles, they say they now want to break the men's record of 645 hours. These photographs show Miss Trout, upper left, and Miss Cooper, below. At the right Miss Trout is shown with the gasoline hose from the refueling plane.

GIRL ENDURANCE TEAM ELUDES GALE IN VALLEY

IMPERIAL, Jan. 7 (A.P.)—Hounded 150 miles away from their base by a drenching rain, the persistent girl endurance team, Bobbie Trout and Edna May Cooper, arrived over Imperial Valley airport here tonight.

They were forced to break the circle, in which they had flown about the Los Angeles municipal airport for 72 hours, when the storm made refueling impossible and flying dangerous at 2:30 p. m.

With the refueling ship fully loaded and in pursuit, Miss Trout, who was at the controls, turned the Lady Rolph toward the southeast in search of a clear patch of sky under which much needed gasoline might be taken aboard.

The sky was cloudless over March field, Riverside, and a contact was made, but scarcely had the refueling plane landed at the army air school there and taken on more gasoline when the storm closed in.

Again taking to the air lanes, the girls pushed through the hazardous San Gorgonio pass and another refueling contact was made over Palm Springs, in the upper reaches of the desert, guarded from storms by high mountains.

The refueling plane landed here 15 minutes before the Lady Rolph appeared and signalled everything was all right.

GIRLS, ALOFT 23 HRS., IRKED BY SHINY NOSES

After 23 hours in the air at 1:30 p. m. today, the endurance fliers, Edna May Cooper and Bobby Trout, pilots of the endurance ship "Lady Rolph," were more concerned about their shiny noses than they were over the flight.

Early today the endurance plane "Lady Rolph" dipped low over the Los Angeles Municipal airport, where it had been hovering all night, and dropped a note to the ground which proved that the eternal feminine was not entirely lacking in the flight.

The note read:

"We don't mind the grease and rattle and bang up here. We can take it and intend to for a long time. But we'll be doggoned if we'll go round and round with shiny noses. We have no mirror up here. We tried the metal on the instrument board, the bottom of the thermos jug and everything else that shines, but nothing works. So send up a small mirror with the grapefruit and toast. It will be O. K. if you forget the toast, but don't forget the mirror."

Four contacts between the refueling ship, piloted by Bud Hussey and Ralph De Rose, and the endurance ship were made this morning. Food, oil, gasoline, a parachute to replace the one which became unpacked yesterday, and the mirror were dropped to the girl fliers. who are attempting to surpass both the women's and men's records for sustained flight. An elapsed time of only 40 minutes was required for the four contacts.

ENDURANCE PLANE GETS GAS

The Lady Rolph, in which Edna May Cooper and Bobby Trout (right) are making records for women fliers, is shown taking nourishment of gasoline and oil from the Carrier Pigeon, refueling plane, over Los Angeles Municipal airport. Miss Trout celebrated her twenty-fifth birthday today.

—Stockton Photo.

On Goes Wee Monoplane Toward Men's Mark for Time Flight

With the motor of their plane purring smoothly, Edna May Cooper and Bobby Trout chalked up 71 hours and 45 minutes at 2:15 o'clock this afternoon.

A small leak in the left wing gasoline tank of the monoplane, Lady Rolph, was an uninvited guest at the birthday party which Bobby Trout and Edna May Cooper were celebrating today over the Los Angeles Municipal airport in their record-breaking woman's endurance flight.

Miss Trout, who was 25 years old today, told of the misfortune in a note to the ground crew, but said the leak was not serious.

70 Hours in Air

The leak and the gathering clouds which threatened to give the Lady Rolph a drenching were the only thorns in the birthday celebration. The seventieth hour in the air was passed at 12:30 o'clock and the three-day mark was to be crossed at 2:30 o'clock this afternoon.

A turkey dinner and an angel food cake, baked by Miss Trout's mother, were offered as solace to the fliers for the leaky tank. Although the cake held the traditional birthday candles, these were not lighted. Lighting them would have ended the flight then and there.

Leak of Little Concern

The gas leak was caused by pressure on the vent of the left wing tank. This tank has been cut off from the gasoline circulatory system and members of the ground crew said that except for the loss of a small amount of gasoline through the vent, the flight should not be otherwise impaired.

The two aviatrices, who have pointed the nose of their small monoplane toward records held by their brothers of the air, today had settled down to the long grind of droning through the hours. The first objective is the 150-hour endurance flight record for transport planes, set by the Question Mark in January, 1929.

Get Birthday Meal

But the prize that most lures them on is the breaking of the world endurance flight record of 645 hours, 28 minutes and 30 seconds, held by Forest O'Brine and Dale Jackson of St. Louis.

The Carrier Pigeon, refueling plane, piloted by Bud Hussey and Ralph de Rose, arose aloft at noon with the birthday meal and a cargo of gasoline and oil. Ten refuelings have been made and 845 gallons of the devil's torment, and it's grand to be back among the living, toiling, bright-eyed, gallivanting humans who make up this workaday world. Even the jangle of the nine telephones in this office is music to one who has discovered that hands, after all, are not made to talk with, unless you're a Sioux.

* * *

On the pillows, however, the old think-tank roamed more than a column a day. It went soaring with the two Girl Friends, Edna May Cooper and Bobbie Trout, trying to establish the refueling endurance flight record for the world. Each time a droning plane zoomed "right over my roof," it was they, and I was with them. These girls seem to have the earnest good wishes of everybody in their brave attempt.

* * *

And as the engine whined past, a fleeting memory of the girls' mothers took form. Bobbie's mother, the sweet thing, is the most understanding person a girl flier could possibly have. But she looks at things reasonably, and wishes her little girl's enthusiasm could be tempered with restraint, at least during these uneasy times, for Bobbie has a decided flair for business judgment and could make a splendid business swoman. Edna May's mother is wrapped up in her daughter's aerial career, and follows her, at least in spirit, on every flight.

* * *

GIRL FLIERS PASS 100 HOUR MARK

Well started towards its second hundred hours in the air, the plane Lady Rolph was cruising slowly over the municipal airport here today, with the world's refueling endurance mark as its aim.

At 8:30 a. m., the ship, piloted by Bobbie Trout and Edna Mae Cooper had passed the 114 hour mark, with fair weather continuing to aid their efforts to stay aloft.

After being forced to fly to Imperial valley to avoid a storm here, the girls returned to their home port shortly after noon yesterday, and continued to fly through the daylight hours in a light rain. When the weather cleared, it turned cold, but this did not hinder them in the least.

Shortly after 11 o'clock last night, a bright moon rose and the high visibility brought the countryside out in clear relief, making blind flying unnecessary for the young fliers. Twenty miles away they could see the Sierra Madres blanketed in snow, adding a winter touch to the picture.

The advance of aviation in two short years was pointed out by flight attaches today when it was noted that the world endurance mark set here in January, 1929, by the army plane, Question Mark, was only 150 hours 40 minutes 16 seconds, and that with a tri-motored plane.

The present record which the girls seek to better is 647 hours 27 minutes 30 seconds, held by Forrest O'Brine and Dale Jackson of St. Louis.

100-Hour Mark Is Passed By Girl Endurance Fliers

Plane Brought Back to Los Angeles After Clouds Envelop It Over Imperial Valley; Pilots Resigned to Flying in Storm.

LOS ANGELES, Jan. 8.— (AP) —A rain soaked monoplane, carrying Bobbie Trout and Edna May Cooper, girl endurance fliers, rounded out its one hundredth hour in the air tonight at 6:30 o'clock.

Resigned to flying through the storm after clouds enveloped them in the Imperial Valley where, they sought clear skies last night, the girls brought the Lady Rolph back to its circle over the municipal airport here.

None of the bright little messages the girls dropped during the early part of the flight came down today. "We want to beat the Question Mark," one of the two notes said. The other was in a grimmer vein, "Send up a bottle of wing dope and a small brush."

The latter, managers pointed out, indicated the girls had discovered a rip in the fuselage of the plane. The materials requested are used in patching plane fabric.

The Question Mark, the army's contribution to endurance flying, set the first refueling mark here just two years ago. It was aloft a little more than 150 hours

Under a sodden sky the Lady Rolph was refueled at twilight for the nineteenth time since its take-off at 2:30 o'clock, Sunday afternoon. With its tanks full the plane was prepared to fly through a dreary night. The girls exceeded the old 42-hour mark Tuesday.

GIRL FLIERS UP 115 HOURS; GOOD WEATHER AHEAD

Bobbie Trout, Edna Cooper Welcome End of Struggle With Storms

Los Angeles, Jan. 9.—(AP)—Clear skies and a promise of good weather greeted Bobbie Trout and Edna May Cooper today as a welcome relief from a three-day struggle with rains and wind in their monoplane, Lady Rolph, which passed the 115th hour of sustained flight at 9:30 A. M. (1:30 P. M.. Philadelphia time).

The twentieth refueling was made at dawn. While the two young women dropped no messages, they waved gayly to the ground crew. They were holding the course of their ship close over the airport.

GIRL FLIERS WINGING WAY TO RECORD

In Air 116 Hours This Morning; Nearing Record of Old Question Mark; Storm Changes Course

LOS ANGELES, Jan. 9.—(United Press)—Well started towards its second hundred hours in the air, the plane Lady Rolph was cruising slowly over the municipal airport here today, with the world's refueling endurance mark as its aim.

At 2:30 a. m., the ship, piloted by Bobbie Trout and Edna Mae Cooper, had passed the 108-hour mark, with fair weather continuing to aid their efforts to stay aloft.

After being forced to fly to Imperial valley to avoid a storm here, the girls returned to their home port shortly after noon yesterday, and continued to fly through the daylight hours in a light rain. When the weather cleared, it turned cold, but this did not hinder them in the least.

Shortly after 11 o'clock last night, a bright moon rose and the high visibility brought the countryside out in clear relief, making blind flying unnecessary for the young fliers. Twenty miles away they could see the Sierra Madre mountains blanketed in snow, adding a winter touch to the picture.

As planned, the refueling ship was there at daybreak, waiting to refuel them with the usual necessities and food. The weather at Imperial Airport was perfect and ideal for flying. Late in the afternoon they returned to Mines Field as the weather over Los Angeles cleared. It was important for them to be within landing distance of the field where they had taken off, or their endurance record would not be official.

At daybreak on January 9, Bobbi took over the controls. She settled down to check the oil, grease the rocker arms, and await the arrival of the refueling ship. "What a beautiful day it's going to be," she thought. Then, the tranquility of early morning was shattered by the sound of the engine emitting a terrifying cough. It simultaneously began to spit oil out of the filler tube inside and onto the windshield. The rhythm of the revs began fluctuating wildly, going way down, then speeding up again. With each peaking of the revs, the engine coughed again and spit more oil.

Shortly after the engine began to spew oil, the refueling ship arrived to made contact, but they could see something was wrong with the Lady Rolph. Within an hour the windshield was covered with oil so that nothing could be seen through it. Bobbi became an oily mess as the oil spurted at her from the oil filler tube in front of the stick.

About one o'clock in the afternoon the refueling ship came into position and could see their plight, but there was nothing they could do to alleviate the problem. The synchronized flight of the two aircraft for refueling had to be managed by the refueling ship alone. Bobbi could see only a slight shadow above, which was not enough to maintain the refueling position. With precision the refueling crew did well with this extra contact.

She stayed at the controls all day and, often adding oil, made the last refueling contact about three o'clock in the afternoon. By now Bobbi was doing her best to keep the Lady Rolph in the air. She knew that it was only a matter of time before they would be forced to land.

After the last refueling contact, Bobbi asked Edna May to take over the controls while she visited the rear of the cabin where the toilet facilities were located. As Bobbi sat down, the ship began to dive, and there she was again, yelling to Edna May, "Pull back, we're going into a dive."

Edna May obeyed, but kept on pulling the stick back until Bobbi had to yell again, "Edna May, push it forward, we're going to stall." Edna May continued to try to keep the aircraft in level flight. The ludicrous aspect of the whole thing struck Bobbi, and she began to laugh, until shortly her laughter became so uncontrolled that she was hysterical. She thought she would never be able to stop because the situation was so funny. When she finally regained control of her laughter, her sides were aching. Edna May could not see through the oil on the windshield, and she still hadn't learned to fly by the seat of her pants. Bobbi hurried forward to take over and extend all the time possible before having to land.

Later Bobbi told Edna May that they would be landing soon, so if she wanted to get cleaned up and put on her make-up, now was the time.

Edna May carefully cleaned her face and begin to apply her make-up. She had a good disposition and never complained.

When the night set in, their altitude became precariously low from loss of power. Bobbi was forced to land. They did however, gain a new women's refueling record.

News cameras, reporters, and a large crowd were waiting to greet them when they touched down. Edna May was first out, all shiny clean and tidy, and delightedly posed for pictures. Bobbi, on the other hand, emerged from the cockpit with oil spattered all over her face and clothing. Her grimy state was no deterrent to her mother, however, who greeted her with the usual big hug and kiss. When they had been photographed and thoroughly interviewed, Martin had an ambulance ready to take them to the California Lutheran Hospital. "I feel fine." Bobbi protested, but she gave up the argument when Martin mentioned a warm bath and good, hot food.

ENDURANCE-FLIGHT GIRLS LAND AFTER 122 HOURS

Descent Forced by Motor Troubles; Five Hundred Greet Plucky Pair at Municipal Port

Having remained aloft in an airplane on continuous flight longer than any other women in the world, Edna May Cooper and Bobbie Trout, Los Angeles pilots, landed safely at 5:20 p.m. yesterday on Los Angeles Municipal Airport after 122 hours and 50 minutes in the air—a new endurance record for women.

Motor trouble, believed by pilots to have been caused by a cracked piston, had sprayed their little Curtiss Robin monoplane with oil and filled the cabin with exhaust fumes for several hours before the end and forced them down.

Flight directors declared the women were ordered to the ground because of complaints by Inglewood residents and possible interference by the United States Department of Commerce.

"Guess we have lost a little weight, but we feel fine," Miss Cooper told the crowd of nearly 500 persons gathered at the port when the orange-and-black plane settled to an after-dark landing.

"No, I wouldn't want to go up tomorrow," said Miss Trout, one of the few women transport pilots in the nation.

"I hated like the deuce to have to come down, though. There wasn't anything particularly hard about the flight. Never felt better.

TAKEN TO HOSPITAL

Despite their cheery mood and evident physical fitness, the two aviatrices were taken to the California Hospital shortly after they landed—there to catch up on their sleep and partake of the first solid food since they took off from the municipal field at 2:30 p.m. last Sunday.

During their stay aloft the girl flyers covered 7370 miles at an average speed of sixty miles an hour, took on a total of 1138 gallons of gasoline and thirty-four gallons of oil for their motor and received supplies and food in sacks during twenty-two contacts with their Curtiss Thrush refueling ship, manned by Pilot Bud Hussey and Ralph De Rose.

Several hours before the end airmen at the port concluded that it would not be long before the ship would land — puffs of smoke were coming from the 170-horsepower Curtiss Challenger engine.

FUMES FILL CABIN

"Apparently you have a cracked piston which should last fifty or more hours, before giving way." De Rose told the girls in a note lowered from the supply craft yesterday morning.

Inside the cabin, however, the failing motor was causing the pilots great discomfort, it was learned from Miss Cooper. Fumes that prevented sleep filled the tiny control room, oil splashed from the engine every time the girls attempted to put in a fresh supply, and oil was plastered on the windshield so that the pilots could see from only one side.

Joe Nikrent, official timer of the National Aeronautic Association, said last night the barograph, an instrument which records altitude and time, was in good shape when removed from the plane, where it has rested during the flight. It will be forwarded to Washington for calibration to make the mark official.

Just before the record was set the monoplane circled the port in a lazy circle at an altitude of about 2000 feet. It dropped lower and lower until, approaching from the east, it came down on a landing angle—the motor still running at fair speed.

Engine Fails Long Before Their Courage Wanes

LANDED AT MUNICIPAL AIRPORT 5:20 P.M. FRIDAY JAN 9

TAKE-OFF MUNICIPAL AIRPORT 2:30 P.M. SUN. JAN. 4.

TOTAL MILEAGE 7370 MI.

122-HOURS 50-MINUTES IN AIR

22-REFUELING CONTACTS

SALTON SEA

IMPERIAL VALLEY

EL CENTRO

CALEXICO

MEXICALI

ENDURANCE PLANE USED 1158 GALLONS OF GASOLINE AND 34 GALLONS OF OIL

When Endurance Ship Came Down

Happy over landing safely with a failing motor Edna May Cooper, left, and Bobbie Trout, greet throng at ending of world-record flight. In surrounding sketches by Staff Artist Phil Leonard, pertinent facts of endurance hop are graphically presented.

GIRL PILOT DESCRIBES LAST HOURS OF FLIGHT

Excepting for oil-stained clothing the women showed little evidence of their battle with the elements over Southern California during the six days aloft. Neither had shiny noses—both evidently having found time to apply a dash of powder before the climb from the little ship that had been "home" to them for so many hours.

SURVIVED STORMS

They were escorted from their stalled plane to a spot in front of the port hangars where they posed for pictures and received the congratulations of relatives, friends and men pilots.

"Nice work," was the prevailing comment of airmen—flyers who knew what the two women had been through in fighting to stay off the ground in face of winds, rain and fog.

It seemed ironical, pilots agreed, that after battling through storms that had beset them practically from the time they took off, the first day of good flying weather should be the one on which they had to be grounded. They had intended to whiz along at least to the 150-hour mark and shatter the first refueling mark ever set—made by the Army's Question Mark in a trimotored airliner here with a crew of five men.

"HOME" CLUTTERED

Although they had "kept house" to the best of their ability inside the little cabin of the Lady Rolph, the interior was oil streaked and cluttered up with supplies. It was placed in a guarded hangar while one assistant flight manager offered a $10,000 wager on behalf of the flight sponsors that the ship could be taken aloft without a motor adjustment and flown for 200 hours more. There were no takers.

BY EDNA MAY COOPER

LOS ANGELES MUNICIPAL AIRPORT, Jan. 9.—Cheerio! Here we are on the ground again, champions of the world with a new record for women of 122h. and 50m.

This morning our cabin became full of smoke, windshield covered with oil. Our top left cylinder has been smoking for the past two days. We used plenty of oil and stayed within gliding distance of the field.

At 7:15 a.m. we refueled. We could not go on much longer. Our cabin was filled with smoke and we were leaving a long trail of smudge in the skies behind us. The refueling boys looked the situation over and told us our piston was cracked. We knew we would be forced down now any minute and we were greatly disappointed. We

were too troubled to eat. We were wearing our parachutes all the time. Undaunted, Bobbie Trout was sitting at the controls reading the paper. The oil on the windshield had completely cut off our view but nevertheless at 8:10 o'clock I took my bath and hoped we would not land until I got dressed again.

ALL DRESSED UP

I got all dressed up with my parachute and waited for something to happen. I was dead tired and the cabin was filled with acrid fumes from the engine. We did not have room enough to lie down with parachutes on, so I squatted in the little refueling compartment. I moved my chute and tried to get some sleep but the cabin filled with smoke and it was impossible to rest. We made contact at 10:20 o'clock and got more oil. We received a note signed by Ralph De Rose and he told us apparently we had a cracked piston which should last fifty or more hours before giving away. They gave us detailed instructions on how to circle the field while refueling so that if the motor should suddenly stop we would be within gliding distance.

Air Champions In Show

BOBBIE TROUT
EDNA MAY COOPER

EDNA MAY COOPER and Bobbie Trout, intrepid women aviators who recently established a new world's record for endurance flying, will make the first of four nightly appearances tonight at the United Artists theater, in conjunction with the mighty epic of the air, "Hell's Angels." The daring girl pilots, who are appearing through the courtesy of Joseph Martin, sponsor of the record-breaking flight, will relate highlights of their experiences at nine o'clock each evening.

"Hell's Angels," which is having its first showings at popular prices in downtown Los Angeles, is proving one of the finest attractions the United Artists has played in several months, according to the management. Jean Harlow, James Hall and Ben Lyon are starred in this great aviation production.

Officially, they had been aloft one hundred seventy-two hours, fifty minutes; covered seven thousand three hundred-seventy miles at an average speed of sixty miles per hour; taken on a total of one thousand one hundred thirty-eight gallons of gasoline and thirty-four gallons of oil; and received food and supplies during twenty-two contacts with the refueling ship.

When the repair crew opened up the engine of the Lady Rolph, they found the problem to be a large hole, the size of a silver dollar, in the top of the number one piston. It was this hole that caused the oil to squirt on the windshield and up the oil filler pipe. Bobbi and Edna May were heartsick not to have made a record of at least one month in the air.

One month after the flight ended, Martin told them he had arranged for them to fly the Lady Rolph to Sacramento for the State Fair. They would display the aircraft there and be on hand for a week to sign autographs. They would leave the plane on the fairgrounds and return to Los Angeles by train four days later. As they came into the Los Angeles station, Edna May turned to Bobbi and said that even though they didn't stay up a whole month, it was worth it. The two parted good friends.

Two years after the flight, King Carol of Rumania sent Bobbi an Aviation Cross which he had designed for pilots who made record flights. The Cross, and its special plaque, was presented to Bobbi at a reception in her honor at the home of Pancho Barnes in San Marino. King Carol gave out only three of these awards to Americans—the other two went to Lindbergh and Amelia Earhart.

2 GIRL FLYERS TO TRY AGAIN

Bobbie Trout and Edna Cooper Aloft For 122 Hours 50 Minutes

Already the holders of a record for endurance flying three times as great as that possessed by any other women of the world, Bobbie Trout and Edna May Cooper, intrepid young air conquerors, today were planning a new attack upon the mark set by Forest O'Brine and Dale Jackson.

After 122 hours and 50 minutes in the air, the two girl champions landed at 5:20 o'clock last evening at Municipal Airport.

Motor trouble, which developed because of a cracked cylinder, could have been conquered and the flight continued, sponsors of the record attempt stated, but complaints registered by citizens of Inglewood against noise of the plane at night hastened the descent.

Both young women were in high spirits and were "fit as fiddles" physically when their trim plane, the "Lady Rolph," was brought to earth, despite the long grind and hectic battles with storms.

GIRLS FORCED TO LAND BUT SET NEW AIR RECORD

The new world's endurance airplane refueling flight record for women is 122 hours, 50 minutes, and was set by Miss Bobbie Trout and Mrs. Edna Mae Cooper.

After landing their Curtis Robin plane, the Lady Rolph, at 5:20 p.m. yesterday, the girl fliers estimated they could have gone on for many more hours had not their backer, Joseph L. Martin, ordered them to stop because residents near the airport complained about the incessant roaring of the airplane motor overhead.

The new record is almost three times as great as the former record of 42 hours, 16 minutes, set last summer by Miss Trout and Elinor Smith of New York. It is, however, only a little more than one-fifth as great as the men's record set by Forest O'Brine and Dale Jackson of St. Louis.

"We were just getting started," said Miss Trout after the Lady Rolph touched ground for the first time since 2:30 p. m. last Sunday. "Naturally we are not the least bit disappointed as the result of the flight, but I feel that we could have

gone on for a long time yet," she continued.

"We're just a little ground-shy," Mrs. Cooper, formerly an actress, said as she embraced her mother, Mrs. Mary May Cooper, upon landing.

Martin declared that the motor of the plane was in excellent condition. Trouble which threatened yesterday when smoke was seen pouring from the exhaust had entirely disappeared, he said.

With the exception of one stormy day, the fliers enjoyed almost perfect weather during their long stay in the air. The storm broke Wednesday, but they escaped it by flying to the Imperial valley and remaining until the weather cleared again here.

During the flight, the girls completed 22 refueling contacts, with Mrs. Cooper handling all refueling operations. They took aboard 1138 gallons of gasoline and 34 gallons of oil. They flew approximately 7400 miles at an average speed of 60 miles per hour. They alternated at the controls.

SEEKING AIR RECORD

Bobbi, Ralph De Rose, Edna May and Fred Hattoom.

Bud Hussey, Margaret Perry and Ralph De Rose take a break while Bobbi and Edna May are adding hours in the air to their endurance record.

Jan 4–9, 1931—A copy of the actual barograph reading from the endurance plane, proving they were airborne all the time on the flight.

NEW YORK HERALD TRIBUNE, SUNDAY, JANUARY 18, 1931

LADY ROL

Close up of the Lady Rolph taking on supplies and receiving gasoline, when the nozzle got down to the ship, from the refueling crew above. Ralph De Rose handled the refueling hose and guided Bobbi (by hand motions) in making good connections.

A World's Record
Bobby Trout and Edna May Cooper set a new women's mark for continuous flying—122 hours and 50 minutes, as opposed to the old record of 42 hours and 16 minutes. Above — Their plane, "Lady Rolph," is being refueled over Los Angeles airport. Right — The two flyers after landing.
Herald Tribune—Acme

Rest After Setting Flight Record

Photo shows Edna May Cooper, left, and Bobbie Trout, Los Angeles aviatrices, resting up in a hospital today after a flight of 122 hours, 50 minutes in which they bettered the women's refueling endurance record by 80 hours, 32 minutes. They are shown reading congratulatory "fan mail," telegrams and contracts.

122-HOUR FLIGHT ENDED; GIRLS SLEEP

Endurance flying is one thing, but sleeping — well, that's something else again.

So declared Bobbie Trout and Edna May Cooper, the two daring girl pilots, today in their room at the California Lutheran hospital, where they were taken after breaking the women's world's refueling endurance record by flying 122 hours and 50 minutes through wind and rain.

Edna May and Bobbi, after their flight and a good warm bath, while they relax and read some congratulatory mail.

Ralph De Rose, Bobbi's good friend, who did the hard work of handling of the supplies and gasoline.

L. A. Girls In Sky Marathon

In an effort to bring to women the record for sustained flight Bobby Trout and Edna May Cooper, note aviatrixes, today will take off from the Los Angeles Municipal Airport with the intention of staying aloft in an airplane until mechanical or physical troubles bring them to earth.

A few moments before the intrepid young women take to the air their plane will be christened 'Lady Rolph' in honor of Governor-elect James Rolph, jr.'s, wife, who will officiate at the ceremonies.

As soon as the plane takes to the air it will be directed by its pilots toward the Rose Bowl in Pasadena, where Alabama and Washington State universities are struggling for football supremacy. The plane will circle the field and then return to the point from where it started to receive its first refueling contact, about dusk.

Newsletter of the National Aeronautic Association, Jan. 1931.

THE AILERON

Official Publication of The Southern California Chapter
National Aeronautic Association

Vol. 2	January 27, 1931	No. 1

PROGRAM for JANUARY MEETING
AIR MAIL AND WOMEN PILOTS NÌTE

TUESDAY, JANUARY 27, 1931 — 6:30 P. M. — ALEXANDRIA HOTEL

THE program for this interesting meeting is so full that we can not go into details about each speaker here but urge that you turn out for this meeting, and give the little girls a big hand, and learn about Air Mail from those who know.

BOBBY TROUT and EDNA MAY COOPER—The girls who just came down after spending 123 hours in the air will be presented with trophies by the N. A. A., contributed by the Aviation Dept. of the Union Oil Company.

GLADYS O'DONNELL—The crack woman pilot of the 1930 National Air Races will be presented with the $3,000.00 Cleveland Pneumatic Aerol Trophy by Mr. F. H. Burr of the Cleveland Pneumatic Tool Company.

❖❖❖❖❖❖❖❖❖❖❖❖

H. W. BECK—Traffic Manager, Transcontinental Western Air Line Inc.
"Traffic Management on the CAM4 and CAM34 Air Mail Lines."

E. L. REMLIN—Veteran pilot of the Boeing Systems.
"From the pilots viewpoint on the CAM8 Air Mail Line."

J. B. ALEXANDER—Southwest Air Fast Express, Div. of American Airways.
"Ground operations on the CAM33 Air Mail Lines."

❖❖❖❖❖❖❖❖❖❖❖❖

ENTERTAINMENT—"Just a bit of Paris," sponsored by Bert Rovere of the Paris Inn Cafe.

PLEASE MAKE RESERVATIONS NOW — CALL WESTMORE 1436 or SEND IN YOUR NAME AND ADDRESS, WITH YOUR CHECK, IF CONVENIENT, TO

.... 'll Street.

.... Address.

Union Oil Company presents a trophy to Bobbi and Edna May as other Union Oil officials look on.

Two — The AILERON

The National Aeronautic Association
Southern California Chapter
Headquarters—1168 South Hill Street, Los Angeles
Phone WEstmore 1436

OFFICERS
W. E. "Tommy" Thomas, President
Frank Bireley, Vice President — W. P. Balderston, Secretary
Robert Porter, Treasurer — Anona D. Hansen, Executive Secretary

DIRECTORS
Waldo Waterman — Thomas F. Hamilton — Larry Therkelson
Richard B. Barnitz — Dudley M. Steele — Clifford Mutchler
Walter Parkin — C. A. Elliot

ADVISORY BOARD
Robert J. Pritchard, Vice-President N. A. A.
C. F. Lienesch, N. A. A. Governor State of California
D. E. McDaneld — Joe Nikrent — C. F. Willard
Dr. T. C. Young — H. H. Wetzel — Will G. Bonelli

CLEVELAND AND THE NATIONAL AIR RACES--(10 YEARS)?

SENATOR HIRAM BINGHAM of Connecticut, who is National President of the N. A. A., recently issued a statement announcing that he had awarded the National Air Races to the city of Cleveland for ten years. This action was taken without the knowledge of any of the officers of the N. A. A. or members of the Board of Governors residing in the Western States. Immediately after the receipt of this announcement a meeting of prominent members of the N. A. A., including two national officers and two members of the board of Governors, and a number of men prominent in the aviation industry, was called in Los Angeles to consider the matter.

The sentiment of this meeting was unanimous in condemning the arbitrary and high-handed action of Senator Bingham, and a committee was appointed to organize a campaign to urge the abrogation of the ten year contract with Cleveland.

The members of this committee are Robert J. Pritchard, National Vice President, Chairman of the committee, Rufus J. Pilcher, National contest committee member, C. F. Lienesch, Governor for California, Russell Lawson, Governor for Oregon, G. H. Benefiel, Governor for Arizona, and W. E. Thomas, President Southern California Chapter, N. A. A. The committee immediately drafted a letter to tor Bingham demanding the abrogation of the contract and a move to organize the sentiment of the N. A. A. Governors of the vi states was launched.

Emory Bronte, President of the San Francisco Chapter, was u to attend the meeting but when notified regarding the action committee by phone expressed his hearty endorsement. The foll statement is the expression of the committee:

"There is general resentment among the various N. A. A. Chi of the West over the arbitrary awarding of the Races to Clev without previous consideration of the Western officers or We members of the board of Governors. Several Western states expressed a desire to entertain the National Air Races within the few years. Spokane, the scene of the 1927 National Air Races, the most successful meets on record, wants the races again. Los les has committed itself to the holding of the National Air Rac this city in 1933. These facts were known to Senator Bingham to National headquarters of the N. A. A. but apparently were absolut disregarded in awarding Cleveland the ten year contract. The committee has serious doubts as to the legality of the contract with Clev and proposes to leave no stone unturned to have this contract celled."

ROBERT J. PRITCHARD,
Chairman of the Committee

The Secretary Says--

WE know that times are not what they used to be but business, aviation, and the N. A. A. must go on, we can't weaken now, so when you get those little yellow slips notifying you that it is time to pay your 1931 dues just remember that we started this, and we have to go on and finish it in a BIG WAY. Not only that, if aviation ever needed a good live and loyal organization it is now, so why not all stick together and put it over the top. Send in your check now!

The month of December saw two very interesting meetings. On December 9th the membership meeting was held at the Flying Club of California. There were over fifty present, this was pretty good turnout but when you figure this Chapter has 350 members it does not show a great deal of active interest on the part of the members. The ones that did attend enjoyed a very interesting meeting. William Clover, meteorologist for Transcontinental Western Air, gave a very enlightening talk on meteorology. A discussion on "What isn't the matter with aviation" was also an interesting topic, and it was very satisfactorily decided that there is nothing the matter with aviation, all it needs is just time, just like any other growing industry.

On December 18th the Glider Section of the Chapter had their monthly meeting in a somewhat different fashion. The Club house of the Cal...

The AILERON — Three

Air Mail Statistics

THE FIRST United States Air Mail route was established September 23, 1911 between Boulevard, L. I. flying field, and the Mineola Post office. For a period of nine days Earle Ovington flew a Queen monoplane at regular intervals, dropping the mail bags at Mineola for the postmaster there to pick up. The first air mail contract offer given by the post office department was February 12, 1916, for an air mail line from New Bedford to Nantucket, Mass., and a certain route in Alaska. The Mass. route was not ever bid on, and there was only one bidder on the Alaska route and that bid was not accepted.

During the years between 1911 and 1913 a few air mail routes were operated by the post office department for short times for experimental purposes. The first scheduled route, which really was the beginning of air mail service in the United States, was established May 15, 1918, between New York and Washington. The pilots and ships first used on this route were from the Army but after a few months it was turned over for civilian operation. From 1918 to the present day the transportation of mail by air has become one of the most important factors in the progress of the United States. From 1918 to 1925 there were no special air mail fees, the post office department sent first class mail by air up to the capacity of the ships under contract. In the latter part of 1924 and the beginning of 1925 a fee of ten cents was charged for every ounce of mail going by air, that fee being later changed to five cents for the first ounce and ten cents for every ounce thereafter. You will note by looking at the table below that in the years 1924 and 1925, due to the air mail fee, the poundage of mail dropped a good deal. The following table gives an accurate and interesting report on the development of air mail for the past twelve years it has been in use by the people of this country:

Year	Airmail mileage scheduled	Airmail mileage flown	Per cent of scheduled flown	Pound of mail
1918	18,000	16,009	88.94	17,831
1919	166,843	160,066	95.92	230,251
1920	653,764	549,244	84.00	526,573
1921	1,819,975	1,554,985	85.45	1,120,852
1922	1,629,256	1,537,927	94.41	1,224,723
1923	1,644,457	1,590,637	96.71	1,696,896
1924	1,599,425	1,522,763	95.12	1,500,034
1925	2,160,022	2,076,764	96.15	232,513
1926	4,447,013	4,133,478	92.93	850,931
1927	5,541,973	5,041,659	90.97	1,452,426
1928	8,201,036	7,673,186	93.56	3,542,074
1929	14,217,557	13,052,507	91.80	7,100,027

For the first nine months of 1930, 19,838,527 miles were scheduled, 18,808,425 miles were flown with a percentage of 98.02, and 5,043,074 pounds of mail were carried. It can easily be seen from the above figures that there has been a steady increase in the use of air mail. The 1929 and 1930 figures include mileage and air mail of the foreign air mail lines, that is lines originating in the United States and carrying mail to Canada, Mexico and South America.

There are six foreign air mail lines, contracted by the Colonial Division of the American Airways, and the Pan American Airways Inc., and the Pan American Grace Airways, Inc. One line goes into Canada, and the other five into Mexico, South America and Cuba.

Los Angeles has four U. S. air mail lines, two trans-continental, one to Salt Lake City, and one up and down the Pacific Coast. The first line to begin in Los Angeles was the CAM4, Western Air Express in April 1926, the following September the Pacific Air Transport, CAM8, line came down from Seattle, Wash., to Los Angeles. In October 1930 the two transcontinental lines were inaugurated, the Trans-continental Western Air, CAM34, and the Southwest Air Fast Express or American Airways, CAM33. It has been estimated that Southern California has from 21 to 33 per cent of the air mail poundage of the U. S.

EDNA MAY AND BOBBY

TWO guests of honor at the January meeting will be Edna May Cooper and Bobbie Trout who have recently commanded the admiration of the aviation industry by establishing a new world's endurance record for women flyers.

Without a single detail unattended by Joseph Martin, president of the Joseph Martin Company and sponsor of the flight, Miss Cooper and Miss Trout took-off from the Los Angeles Municipal Airport on January 4th to establish a new record which will stand for some time to come.

While these two intrepid girl fliers remained aloft for 122 hours and 50 minutes they continually demonstrated skill which included 22 different refueling contacts and the exchange of over 1,100 gallons of gasoline.

As an expression of the appreciation of the local aviation industry for their admirable achievement trophies donated by the aviation department of the Union Oil Company will be presented Edna May Cooper and Bobbie Trout by the Southern California Chapter of the N. A. A.

Cleveland Pneumatic Aerol Trophy to be Awarded to Gladys O'Donnell.

AN interesting guest, who will be present at our January meeting, will be Gladys O'Donnell, the well known Long Beach aviatrix, who will be presented with the Cleveland Pneumatic Aerol Trophy by Mr. Frank R. Burr and W. F. "Pop" Cleveland of the Cleveland Pneumatic Tool Company, who have flown to Los Angeles especially for this event. This trophy is worth $3,000.00 and is awarded each year to the woman who has the best record for performance during the National Air Races. At the 1930 National Air Races in Chicago Gladys was chosen as the winner from the many fair participants.

Union Oil publication, February, 1931.   11

Scenes at Lindsay, California, Where Union Heater Oil Saved Valencias

Upper left, tank trucks awaiting supply of fuel. Upper right, Roland Fitton, left, agent at Lindsay, checking tank car deliveries with Otto Nissen, center, assistant district manager at Fresno, and C. S. Myer, manager of the district. Center, special train of Union Diesol arriving at Lindsay. The pall of smudge smoke hanging over the country gives this photograph, taken at 10 o'clock in the morning, the appearance of having been taken in a fog. The arrival of this train brought a sigh of relief from the growers, as it looked at the time as though the supply of fuel on hand would be insufficient to carry them through the night. At the bottom are two daytime views of the orchard heaters which hold ten gallons of fuel. On cold nights they consume oil at the rate of one gallon per hour.

California Aviatrices Win New Place in Air

WOMEN flyers have been steadily encroaching upon the records of the male birdmen, and Bobbie Trout and Edna May Cooper, early in January, besides setting a new world's refueling record of 122 hours and 50 minutes for women, came dangerously near the first men's refueling record established by the Question Mark. The previous women's endurance record, of which Bobbie Trout was a co-holder, was 42 hours.

The flight by Miss Trout and Miss Cooper was far from a pink tea affair. For three of the five days they remained aloft they battled rain storms and were once forced to run to Imperial Valley to keep from being forced down by the thick weather.

During the 122 hours and 50 minutes the women flyers kept their endurance plane, "Lady Rolph," in the air they made 22 contacts, took on 1138 gallons of Union aviation gas and oil, and traveled nearly 7500 miles. During the refueling con-

12   UNION OIL BULLETIN for FEBRUARY, 1931

No. 1—Bobbie Trout, left, and Edna May Cooper, who remained in air 122 hours 50 minutes to establish new world's refueling record for women.   No. 2—Ralph De Rose, left, and Bud Hussey, the refueling crew.   No. 3.—The "Lady Rolph" taking on supply of Union gasoline over Los Angeles.   No. 4—Roy Harding taking news photographer aloft to photograph endurance plane.   No. 5—The success of the refueling contacts depended to a considerable extent on the skill with which De Rose handled the 50-foot gasoline hose. He is shown here lowering the hose to the "Lady Rolph."

tacts the ships were never more than thirty feet apart, and frequently they were as close as fifteen feet.

There was no doubt in the minds of the observers of the flight but what the women would have remained in the air several days longer had their engine not developed a cracked piston which forced them to land.

The flight was backed by Joseph Martin of the Joseph Martin Company, general brokers, Los Angeles.

February 14, 1931

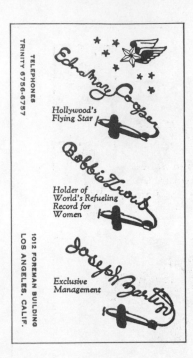

One of Bobbi's business cards.

Miss Bobbie Trout
418 South Soto Street
Los Angeles, California

Dear Miss Trout:

Your itinerary for the coming week beginning tomorrow, calls for your appearance at the Sacramento Auto Show for four days, beginning February 17th in connection with the display there of the Endurance Plane, LADY ROLPH. The show is to last four days from the 17th to the 20th inclusive. In making your personal appearance at the show, you are to attend the display and personally contact people, answer questions, and give out souvenir post cards as you did at the Los Angeles Auto Show.

However, please remember from your experience at the Los Angeles Auto Show not to spend too much time talking with one person or with anyone group. You can excuse yourself from the clinging type by politely explaining that many others would like to ask some questions and leave them with a smile and a souvenir card.

During your appearance in connection with the LADY ROLPH exhibit at Sacramento you are to appear in your flying togs as you did here in Los Angeles. Also, please note, that you are to wear your flying togs on all occasions in Sacramento whether the occasion be formal or informal.

Your salary will be Fifty Dollars ($50.00) per week, this to be exclusive of your expenses which is being handled through this office. We ask of you, however, to please cooperate with us in keeping your daily expense for incidentals to a minimum. Transportation will be supplied you between the hotel and the show.

Yours very truly,

JOSEPH MARTIN COMPANY

FRED L. HATTOOM
Director of Publicity

One of many letters sent by Joseph Martin's Publicity director, Fred Hattoon, giving Bobbi her itinerary after the second refueling endurance flight record.

Bobbi advertising for the Union Oil Company, 1931.

UP FOR LOST

Article on Edna May's temporary disappearance. Everything was fine when Bobbi last saw her at the depot after coming home from Sacramento.

Upper right: Edna May Cooper, left, and Bobbie Trout came back to earth at Los Angeles January 9, after five days in the air, bringing a women's sustained flight record of 122 hours, 50 minutes with them. Miss Trout, with Elinor Smith of New York, established the original mark of 42 hours, 16 minutes. Motor trouble forced the monoplane Lady Rolph down after Misses Cooper and Trout had weathered two rainstorms.

AVIATRIX STILL MYSTIFIED

Cooper Lays Memory Loss to Flight; She's Sure There's No Scandal Involved

MONTEREY, March 3. (Exclusive)—Edna May Cooper, actress and aviatrix, located here after being missing from her Los Angeles home for six days, today attributed her seeming amnesia to the strain of financial difficulties and her endurance flight with Bobbie Trout for t women's record. She said she was trying to think what happened to he. and how she got to Monterey but appeared not very successful.

Her mother and son arrived during the day and went at once to the hospital where Miss Cooper was persuaded to go for examination by the wife of Gouverneur Morris, who knew Miss Cooper in motion pictures.

To her mother, Miss Cooper said: "I remember I had a splitting headache. I think the strain of continual flying and financial disappointments snapped some chord of my memory and I just wandered about in a daze.

"I'm sure, though, that there was no scandal connected with my disappearance. I did not elope with any man and I have not quarreled with Trout. She's still the in the world."

actress also said she would think her ex- a publicity stunt.

All she can remember to the present, she said, is that she started for Santa Monica to rest. She declared she remembers getting on a street car, but cannot recall anything else. She was astonished, she said, when she discovered she was in Monterey, having thought she was in a hotel in Santa Monica. The name "Caroline Hope," under which she was registered at the San Carlos Hotel here, was assumed, she said, as part of her plan to secrete herself so she could obtain complete rest and relaxation and not be annoyed. It was the name she intended to use in Santa Monica, Miss Cooper averred.

Remaining unexplained, among several other things, is the manner in which Miss Cooper received numerous bruises about the body and the source of the injury at the base of her skull.

Bobbi Trout, Jan 1931.

Bobbi's official letter from President of National Aeronautic Association, N.A.A., and flight certificate. The certificate was notarized January 20, 1931.

NATIONAL AERONAUTIC ASSOCIATION
WASHINGTON

HIRAM BINGHAM
PRESIDENT

February 4, 1932

Dear Miss Trout:

It gives me pleasure to send you, under separate cover, a certificate in recognition of your establishment of an international feminine duration with refueling in flight record for "Airplanes" (Class C) of 123 hours at Los Angeles, January 4-9, flying a Curtiss Robin monoplane powered with a Challenger 170 h.p. engine.

I was sorry that you were unable to be present at the Reception and Ball given by the Aero Club of Washington and to receive your certificate in person.

May I take this opportunity to congratulate you upon your splendid achievement and to assure you that the National Aeronautic Association deeply appreciates your contribution to the development of aviation.

Sincerely yours,

[signature]

President

Miss Evelyn Trout,
418 S. Soto Street,
Los Angeles, California

To: Contest Committee, National Aeronautic Assoc
Dupont Circle, Washington, D. C.

DIRECTING OFFICIAL'S R
on Record Trial und
F.A.I. regulation

Record Classification:

Duration _X_ *Refueling* Distance _ _ _ _ _ _ _

Date January 4, 1931 - Place Los Angeles

1st Evelyn (Bobby) Trout F.A.I. Certificate

Pilot Edna Mae Cooper F.A.I. Certificate

Crew Refuelers Bud Hussey Ralph

Plane Curtiss Robin Mfr. Curtiss-Wright

Engine Challenger Mfr. Curtiss-Wright

Course _ _ _ _ _ _ _ _ Laps _ _ _ _ _ _ _ _ _ Distance _ _ _ _ _

Course Description _ _ _ _ _ _ _ _ _ _ _ _ _ _ _

_ _ _ _ _ _ _ _ _ _ _ _ _ _ Certified by _ _ _ _ _ _ _ _ _ _

Payload _ _ _ _ _ _ _ _ _ _ _ _ Weighed by _ _ _ _ _ _ _ _ _

Barograph Jules Richard 083470 Sealed by J. W. Nikrent _ _ _ _ _ _

Remarks _ _ _ _ _ _ _ _ _ _ _ _ _ _ _ _ _ _ _

I hereby certify that as Directing Official of this record trial I prepared and installed the barograph in the plane and immediately after the flight removed it from the plane and shipped it with seals intact to the Contest Committee of the National Aeronautic Association for calibration at the Bureau of Standards, Washington, D. C.

Ray Nikrent
Official Observer

Fred Blaurelt
Official Observer

E. L. May
Official Observer

_ _ _ _ _ _ _ _ _ _ _ _
Official Observer.

Joe Nikrent
Directing Official.

Joe Nikrent
Official Timer

This report must be notarized and forwarded in triplicate with photographs and certified map of course.

Bobbi, March 26, 1932.

Ramblings
— by —
The Rambler

Today's Hand

Who gets the big hand today?

Why, of course....

THE STOCKTON CHAPTER OF THE NATIONAL AERONAUTICAL ASSOCIATION

who were presented last night with a charter, making Stockton aviators and airports a part of the greatest organization in the United States for the development of aviation.

Now, all together!

Miss Bobbie Trout . . . nationally known aviatrix . . . and the especial pride of the Pacific Coast . . . Rambler's been thinking . . . about you and your profession . . . ever since he . . . had the good fortune . . . to meet you in person . . . yesterday afternoon. . . .

Of course . . . Bobbie . . . Rambler's met you many times . . . through the medium . . . of newspaper print . . . but then he was not prepared . . . to see so young . . . so feminine . . . a college girl type . . . as you . . . Bobbie . . . already an experienced . . . and seasoned aviatrix. . . .

But Bobbie . . . Rambler thrilled to all you said . . . for even though some . . . of the technical terms . . . were as high over his head . . . as you sail in your gallant plane. . . . Bobbie . . . Rambler caught . . . and understood every single syllable . . . of your earnestness . . . your pride . . . in your profession . . . which shone through . . . your dignity and poise . . . and he saw in you . . . Bobbie . . . the personification of the "new woman" . . . a pioneer . . . in the field of aviation. . . .

And the thing . . . Bobbie . . . that made Rambler . . . old codger that he is . . . feel so much at home with you . . . was that while . . . you symbolize . . . the magic of the modern world of today . . . you also breathe . . . the eternal feminine . . . your voice . . . your manner . . . your whole personality . . . have the womanly charm . . . that is timeless . . . and belongs . . . to certain women . . . of all ages . . . all races. . . .

And Bobbie . . . Rambler saw in you . . . the reflection . . . of the courage . . . the strength . . . and the underlying sense of humor . . . that have been . . . the gifts the gods . . . vouchsafe pioneer woman . . . whether her path . . . lay over . . . the "Covered Wagon" Trail . . . helping to clear the wilderness . . . or traveling . . . across the seas . . . to cast her fortunes . . . in a new and unknown country. . . .

Your steady glance . . . the strength of your capable hands . . . your indomitable will to dare and do . . . Bobbie . . . sheathed in modesty . . . and feminine grace . . . Rambler thinks . . . are probably the heritage . . . from some forebear . . . who pioneered . . . in a different . . . way . . . in a different time. . . .

JANUARY 14, 1932

HONOR BOBBIE TROUT

Woman Flier To Be Given Medal For Air Exploits

Upon the close-cropped head of Bobbie Trout, woman flier, there rested today one of the highest honors possible for an aviatrix to obtain.

It was the medallion of the Federation Aeronautique Internationale, world honorary flying organization, which is bestowed annually upon fliers who have established outstanding records during the previous year.

Presentation of the medallion will be made January 30 at the annual banquet of the Aero club of Washington, with Hiram Bingham, president of the Federation Aeronautique making the presentation.

Bobbi poses with King Carol's Cross in front of gasoline pumps at Trout's Service station, 1933.

(left to right) Joe Nikrent, Bud Hussey, Ralph De Rose, and crew. (lower row from left) Lola Trout, Bobbi, Edna's son, Edna, Edna's parents.

Bobbi's Certificate from National Aeronautic Association. N.A.A.

Uncle Sam's far-flung airmail system now begins its 21st year and this is the little-known story of Earle Ovington, who piloted the first mail plane in 1911, and is still flying

The Airmail Comes of Age

First of all airmail planes. . . . Earle Ovington flying the Bleriot monoplane in which he made his historic flight in 1911 . . . carrying his cargo in his lap.

The first bag of airmail goes aloft. . . . This historic picture, taken in 1911, shows Postmaster General Frank H. Hitchcock handing to Pilot Earle Ovington the first sack of mail ever carried by plane.

Ovington's mascot on the first airmail flight . . . a little French policeman, "Trieze," which perched in the plane's framework.

The progress of 20 years. . . . A modern tri-motor airmail plane being loaded in wing compartments at Bolling Field, Washington . . . so that the pilot no longer has to carry the mail in his lap.

By ISRAEL KLEIN

IT'S a daily grind now, flying the airmail. Some 300 bored pilots are doing it today, speeding in several directions across the country, day and night, over 24 routes, carrying thousands of pounds of Uncle Sam's mail as unassumingly as though they were working on a rural free delivery route.

Each day thousands of letters and packages, carrying the special long airmail stamps, are being posted throughout the country with the same degree of indifference with which any ordinary mail is being dispatched.

The other day, the Post Office Department celebrated, with special ceremonies, the twentieth anniversary of the first airmail flight. It was a stirring and memorable event—to those who understood its significance. But at the time this was going on, more airmail letters were being dispatched and pilots took the air just as nonchalantly as they had been doing day after day.

Yet that first airmail delivery, on September 23, 1911, is a historic event in the annals of the United States Post Office Department. It marked not only the first attempt on the part of this country to make use of the airplane for speedier delivery of mail, but, even more important, it was the first move on the part of the United States to encourage aviation in other than a military way.

Comparatively recent as this event was, it was a bold and crazy venture. Frank H. Hitchcock was postmaster general at the time. A 10-day "international" aviation meet was in progress in an "aerodrome" on Long Island. Timothy L. Woodruff, Lieutenant Governor of New York, lent an official atmosphere to the occasion by his daily appearances. He was the pioneer airport manager and airmeet director.

On the field, George Beatty, one of the first aviators in the country, was warming up his white-winged Wright biplane. Not far from him were Captain Tom Baldwin and his "Red Devil," Tom Sopwith and his great, gray "family bus," and Earle Ovington, with his cream-colored Bleriot monoplane.

IT was a colorful and curious flock of flying machines. The most daring pilot today would hardly think of taking the air with one of these. For they were slim, scraggly structures compared with the machines of today.

Yet here was the start of the American airmail, of modern commercial aviation.

Into this group came a telegram from Postmaster General Hitchcock to Lieutenant Governor Woodruff. It was a proposal to carry a sack of mail to Mineola, L. I., hardly 10 miles away, not just as a lark or experiment, but as proof of Hitchcock's conviction that the flying machine could turn out a most efficient and speedy form of mail carrier.

Earle Ovington got the job. He became the first airmail pilot in the United States.

Today, Ovington, gray-haired, partially bald and nearly 52, still flies, but the ship he takes up is quite a contrast to the one he flew on that first airmail delivery.

"I brought that Bleriot over from France," Ovington recalls. "It had a 70-horsepower Gnome motor, a French 7-cylinder radial engine cut out of a solid steel block. Its curved wings were interchangeable with a set of flat wings with which I could make faster time than Bleriot himself behind a much more powerful motor.

"The open framework of the airplanes of that day made them quite difficult to manage. We had to hold on to our sticks at all times, for the least suggestion of a side-slip would almost be the end of us. We couldn't stop a side-slip unless we kicked the rudder over and dove right into the direction of the slip. It was something like tight rope walking on the invisible air currents."

DIFFICULT as managing the airplane of those days was, it became much more of a stunt with extra baggage of any kind along. For there was no room in Ovington's plane for anything besides himself. Hitchcock came down to Long Island during the meet, with the intention of accompanying Ovington on his airmail flight. But he had to content himself with flying another day with Captain Paul Beck in an army Curtiss biplane.

In fact, Ovington had difficulty even carrying the mail. He had to get in first, and the sack of mail had to rest on his lap—the only place he could put it.

There were 640 letters and 1280 postcards in that sack. Regular mail postage was enough to carry each piece, but a special cancellation stamp was used and a new cachet, or rubber stamp, also applied. Now, one of these pieces of mail, stamped "Aerial Mail Station No. 1"

and "Aerial Special Dispatch," and dated September 23, 1911, is the envy of "first flight" collectors. With Ovington's signature one is worth $60, and without it one of these envelopes will bring $30.

"It was difficult enough handling that plane without an encumbrance," Ovington says. "The Bleriot had no vertical stabilizers and no ailerons. This meant that we were just rudder flyers in those days. In place of aileron control, we had an arrangement of wires from the stick to the ends of the wings on each side, so that we had to 'warp' the wings to bank.

"On my machine, the apparatus in front of me was a cumbersome 'cloche' or bell-shaped device on the stick, to which wires to each wing were connected. I had to keep both my hands on this stick at all times, working it like a sensitive stabilizer to keep the plane level. With that sack of mail on my lap, that was no easy task."

But Ovington made that first trip without a mishap, and he continued to fly the mail daily during that meet. He had been sworn in by Governor Woodruff as the first airmail pilot and he was the only civilian for the job during the week.

SINCE that first flight Ovington has made flying his hobby. He has owned 12 airplanes in the last two decades, and his thirteenth today is a fast ship of his own construction.

An electrical engineer by profession, he gets more enjoyment out of flying the mail once every three weeks over an unofficial route from Santa Barbara, Calif., his home town, to Santa Cruz Island, about 30 miles off shore. He makes the flight in his land plane, although he carries a rubber boat, oars and a canteen of fresh water for safety.

Outside of that and his historic trip, Ovington has never flown the airmail!

He's a transport pilot, too, but he hasn't flown a passenger, either!

He has a boy and a girl, one nearly 20, the other 18, but he won't let them solo until after their college days!

When Earle Ovington first flew the mail, 20 years ago, the Post Office Department had to take that responsibility on its own shoulders. Ovington carried nearly 50,000 pieces of mail that week, all at the regular rate of postage, all at quite an expense to Uncle Sam.

Today, some 300 pilots are carrying airmail day and night over a total of nearly 24,000 miles of air routes, in more than a thousand round trips each month. Three of these routes cross the country from the Atlantic to the Pacific, and one of these cross-country flights is made in the record time of 36 hours.

THE rise of the airmail in this short time is a remarkable occurrence. For it has been only in the last five years that growth of any consequence could be observed.

For six years after Ovington's first flight, the Post Office Department had to use funds originally set aside for other purposes in its encouragement of airmail development. During that time it built up a route between Boston and New York, between Washington and New York, and other cities, all under its own operation.

Early in 1917, Congress appropriated $100,000 for airmail development. The World War, however, distracted all attention from this development and so it wasn't until after the Armistice that Uncle Sam opened his eyes.

Pioneer of the airmail routes. . . . Earle Ovington, who still makes flying his hobby.

IN those days, flyers had quite a problem to get their planes over the Alleghenies, the Rockies or the Cascades, without crashing blindly into a hillside. They had no beacon lights at night, or radio signals to guide them through the fog. Detailed weather reports were sadly lacking.

Yet so well was the work done, and with so remarkably little loss of life, that in 1922 the airmail service was awarded the Collier trophy for the most important contribution to the development of aviation, with its remarkable record of safety in the air lanes.

The next year, night flying came along. The stretch between Chicago and Cheyenne, where formerly the mail had to be transferred to trains, was equipped with airway beacons, powerful, revolving land lighthouses by which pilots even today are guided. For that development, and its success, the airmail service again won the Collier trophy.

It is only since February, 1926, that the job of flying the mails has been let out to commercial concerns. In February, 1926, 328 miles of airmail flying were done by contract. Five months later, this had grown to 3397 miles, and the Post Office Department had spent nearly $90,000 for the purpose.

Airmail, however, should not be regarded as a venture unique to the United States.

It is fast spreading all over the world, through South America, Australia, Europe, Asia, Africa. Even today, a pilot and his radio operator and navigator are trying to establish an All-American airmail route across the Arctic to Copenhagen.

Mail planes are flying daily between London and various important centers of Europe, even to Asia and Africa. And the mail is continually being speeded up.

OATH OF POST OFFICE EMPLOYEE
(TO BE FILED IN THE POST OFFICE)

A copy of the oath filled out and executed by Ovington in 1911 before he made the first airmail flight.

(Copyright, 1931, by EveryWeek Magazine—Printed in U. S. A.)

REPRINTED FROM EVERYWEEK MAGAZINE, ISSUE OF OCTOBER 11, 1931.

Article about Earle Ovington, the first official Air Mail Pilot of the United States Post Office, who in 1911, using his own Bleriot monoplane, made this record.

Succumbs

Earle Ovington, pioneer figure in aviation and a resident of Santa Barbara for many years, died last night in Los Angeles after an extended illness.

OVINGTON, AIR PIONEER, DIES

First Air Mail Pilot, S. B. Resident, Loses Fight Against Illness

Earle L. Ovington, Santa Barbara resident for past years, whose ten-mile flight in 1911 won him the distinction of being the first air mail pilot, died last night in a Los Angeles hospital as a result of heart complications resulting from a long illness and several operations.

Fifty-six years old, Ovington had never been an aviator by profession, but had seen the possibilities of flying in the first years of the century, shortly after his graduation from Massachusetts Institute of Technology in 1904. He enrolled in the Bleriot school of aeronautics at Pau, France, and returned to the United States in 1911 to persuade the government to allow him to make an experimental flight carrying mail.

Held Bag On Lap

Ovington took his ship to Garden City, N. Y., and on September 23, 1911, carried the mail bag given him by Postmaster-General Frank H. Hitchcock to Mineola, L. I., ten miles distant. Ovington held the bag on his lap, because there was no baggage compartment and worked the "stick" by circling his hands around it.

Letter to Bobbi from Adelaide Ovington, Earle's wife, just after Earle died. Earle and Adelaide met on a boat from Europe when Earle was bring his Bleriot home.

During the World war he served as lieutenant-commander in the United States Navy.

His interest was diverted to yachting upon his removal to Santa Barbara in 1920—not, however, until he had built the Casa Loma airfield near the northern city limits. At one time he was principal owner of the Casa Loma tract.

Active Locally

Ovington resided here at 3030 Samarkand Drive until several months ago, when he became ill. During his residence he served as a consulting electrical and aeronautical engineer, and took an active interest in the development of aviation in this city.

He was the inventor of the Ovington high frequency apparatus, the first of its kind in the world, and other electrical devices.

His wife, Adelaide Alexander Ovington, was with him when he died. Other survivors include a son and daughter, Kester Ovington and Miss Audrey Ovington, of Ojai.

Ovington was the son of Edward J. and Mary Wickes Ovington, and was born in Chicago December 20, 1879. He married Adelaide Alexander in 1911, following his graduation from the French flying school. He began his career as an assistant in the X-ray laboratory of Thomas A. Edison in 1898, later transferring to the experimental laboratory of the Edison Electric Illuminating Company.

He was affiliated with the New York Telephone Company from 1899 to 1900, and in 1905 founded the Ovington Manufacturing Company, serving as its president from 1905-1908. In the latter year he organized the Ovington Motor Company and served as president for two years.

In 1912 he became president of the Vitalait Laboratory, Inc., the Vitalait Laboratory of New England, and the Vitalait Laboratory of the Pacific Coast, remaining in this capacity until 1919. However, in 1918 he founded and was president of the Sandy Point (Me.) Shipbuilding Company, and, at the same time, served as president of the Curtiss Flying Station in Atlantic City, N.J.

He was winner of the Boston Globe Tri-State Air Race in 1911, and was awarded the $10,000 prize. The same year he won the John R. McLean trophy and the prize of $2,500.

First Day Cover Earle Ovington sent to Bobbi.

—Frank B. Howe Photo.

FAMOUS QUARTET—BUT THEY DON'T SING!—Left to right, Edna May Cooper, Lady Mildred Bruce, Bobby Trout and Lady Adelaide Spencer Cleaver, as Lady Bruce was greeted at United airport yesterday on arrival. Ladies Bruce and Cleaver are making 'round-the-world flights in opposite directions.

Highest Award

Bobbie Trout, local girl, who will be awarded a medallion of the Federation Aeronautique International, the h i g h e s t individual honor in aviation.

BOBBIE TROUT TO RECEIVE COVETED AVIATION AWARD

Highest Honors In Aviation To Be Given Local Girl In Washington

Bobbie Trout, flying ace from East Los Angeles, will soon receive the highest honor a flyer can receive—a medallion of the Federation Aeronautique Internationale, world honorary flying organization.

Miss Trout, bobbed hair graduate of Roosevelt high school and membere of the Trout family who run the Super Service station under their name at 4th and Soto strets, will be awarded the medallion at a banquet of the Aero club in Washington on January 30. This medal goes to the outstanding flyers and advancers of aviation during the year.

Miss Trout wins the coveted honor through her achievment of setting a new endurance flight for women in conjunction with Edna Mae Cooper, also of Los Angeles. The new mark was set last January over the Los Angeles Municipal airport and raised woman's endurance in the air to 123 hours and 50 minutes.

Hiram Bingham, president of the Federation Aeronautique will make the presentation.

Cross presented by King Carol

FA469 43 NL 6 EXTRA

TD SANFRANCISCO CALIF 2

THE MGR OF NATIONAL AIR RACES 1472
LOBA

PLEASE INFORM MISSES BOBBY TROUT AND EDNA MAY COOPER THAT THEY

HAVE BEEN AWARDED AVIATION GOLD CROSS BY KING OF ROUMANIA FOR THEIR

NINETEEN THIRTY ONE RECORD AND AM ANXIOUS GET THEIR ADDRESSES

TO SEND INSIGNIAS THANKS

DIMITRI DIMANCESCO ROUMANIA CONSUL 1980 WASHINGTON STREET.

Telegram and letter informing Bobbi that she will be awarded the gold cross and Decree by King Carol of Rumania.

LEGATIUNEA REGALA A ROMANIEI,

WASHINGTON, D. C.

San Francisco, July 11, 1933

Dear Miss Trout:

I ask you to kindly forgive this delayed answer. I was glad to receive your telegram and to know your address.

My friend , Mr. John Villiers Farrow of 1416 Haveanhurst Drive Hollywood, will hand to you the insignia and the Royal Decree signed by King Carol. May I ask you to be kind and acknowledge to me the receipt of both, cross and decree. Mr. Farrow will write or telephone to you soon.

I take this opportunity to congratulate you for this distinction awarded to you by my King. In our country they have not as yet forgotten your splendid performance, and the members of the Aeronautical Virtute Order are now proud to have you among their ranks. May I add that beside you, in America, only Colonel Lindbergh and Miss Amelia Earhard have received this cross.

Should you come this way, my wife and myself we will be happy to meet you personally.

Most respectfully yours

John Farrow and Bobbi

40 Planes Hunt Missing Aviator

Soaring low over rugged mountains and canyons on a 500-mile radius from Las Vegas, Nev., more than 40 planes yesterday pursued methodically the search for "Bud" Hussey, missing since Thursday morning in a North American Aviation training plane.

The hunt for the missing pilot turned again to the wild mountain country along the California-Nevada border, and beyond, after a plane answering the description of Hussey's had been reported over Kingston, near the boundary, just before 9 a. m. Thursday.

SEARCH POSTPONED

Previously it had been planned to center the search in the Hi-Vista section east of Lancaster, where a similar plane had been reported seen at 7:40 a. m. This search was postponed when it was determined the Kingston report more nearly checked with Hussey's probable course and time.

Basing at the Las Vegas airport, 15 planes from North American, 10 Army ships from March Field, 10 Navy trainers, four Lockheed Lodestars from the Lockheed factory, and several planes of the Sheriff's aero squadron began covering a 6000-square mile area in all directions from the Nevada city.

Each pilot was assigned a definite territory in the vast "grid," and North American officials hoped by this means to scan every mountain peak, hilltop and canyon.

REPORT CHECKED

Authorities also were checking carefully a report that a plane resembling Hussey's had been seen 10 miles east of Baker, near Barstow, at 8:15 a. m. Thursday, when it turned abruptly northward toward Silver Lake.

Apparent confusion in the many reports of the missing plane undoubtedly was due, according to E. L. Burla, assistant to the president of the North American company, to the fact that Hussey was flying one of eight planes that passed over the same general route the same morning.

Five planes got through direct from Los Angeles to Las Vegas. The other three, including Hussey's, started from Palmdale, but Hussey soon became separated from his comrades.

All eight ships were training planes being ferried to Canada as a routine flight in which Hussey had participated several times.

The other seven craft were checked in at Los Vegas by 9 a. m. Burla said, indicating the plane reported over Kingston was most likely Hussey's.

Wife for Whom He Gave Up Throne Only One at Bedside

LISBON, Portugal, April 4 (Saturday) (AP) — Rumania's Ex-King Carol II, who juggled his Balkan throne and gave it up for the red-haired beauty he later married at her supposed death-bed, died early today in exile. He was 59.

Death apparently was due to a heart attack.

His wife, the former Mme. Elena (Magda) Lupescu, survived him. She was alone with him at his deathbed in the swank Estoril colony of dethroned European monarchs.

Uncrowned Queen

Their romance before their marriage won her the title of uncrowned Queen of Rumania Twice she left Rumania to go into exile with him.

Carol, a handsome playboy of the world's resorts once gave up first claim to the Rumanian throne to his son Mihai (Michael) and then reclaimed it for a time before going into exile again.

Their last flight from Rumania was to escape the occupation of Hitler's Nazi legions and they were fired on as they left by train.

DIES IN EXILE — Former King Carol of Rumania, who died in Lisbon at 59.

As a virtual prisoner of the Franco government in Spain Carol made a spectacular escape during the war to Portugal.

Married Three Times

Rumania later ended the monarchy and is now ruled by a Communist government under Russian domination. Mihai himself is an exile.

Carol, son of Queen Marie and King Ferdinand, married three times. Divorces complicated the Carol-Lupescu romance but they were married in Rio De Janeiro in 1947 under Brazilian law that a person near death—"in extremis"—may be married under any circumstances.

The sad fate of Bud Hussey, one of the refueling endurance crew.

Obituary of King Carol.

Bobbie Trout to Get Medal for Air Feats

In recognition of her achievements in the air Miss Bobbie Trout, local woman pilot, is to be awarded one of the few medals granted each year by the Federation Aeronautique Internationale, she revealed last night.

The award probably will be made in Washington. Miss Trout will try to make the trip there to receive the honor.

Her outstanding air victory in 1931 was to set, with Edna May Cooper, a world's endurance record for women over Los Angeles Municipal Airport. Previously she had held the world's solo endurance record.

At present Miss Trout is directing construction of a single-seated Lockheed monoplane which she hopes to fly from Honolulu to Los Angeles.

Chapter Eleven

Friends and the Cycloplane

MARIE Kelly Sponholz, who sent up the chocolate birthday cake during Bobbi's second refueling endurance flight, called Bobbi in July 1931 for a special favor. She told Bobbi that her husband, Herb, was going to play golf on Sunday with a big dairy "butter and egg" man at the Pasadena golf course. She asked Bobbi to fly over the golf course and do a little stunting. Since they were old friends, Bobbi agreed and made the flight July 18, 1931. She had fun doing it. A hidden motorcycle cop reported it, however, to the Civil Aeronautics Administration and one of the C.A.A. officials called Bobbi to come down to the United Air Terminal office. He actually did not see what was so harmful, but in order to satisfy his boss, he asked Bobbi to let him keep her pilot's license for a couple of weeks. Since Bobbi had no particular flights to make, and this would satisfy the complaint, she surrendered it.

A couple of weeks later, Bobbi got her license back. She accepted employment as an instructor for Elizabeth Inwood and her husband at the Cycloplane Company, Ltd., based at the American Airport in Los Angeles. Bobbi's first student was Mary Wiggins, a movie stunt girl who later became an important member of the Women's Air Reserve. Mary flew for the Women Airforce Service Pilots (WASPS) when they were formed, ferrying bombers and fighter planes in the United States.

Bobbi and her friend, Marie Kelly Sponholz, first office manager of Lockheed in 1928. Picture circa 1979.

Bobbi told Mary that her first lesson would be on the basics of flying the Cycloplane. This unique airplane was designed to teach the lone student, in easy steps, by means of an adjustment to the throttle. First, only enough throttle to carry or pull the plane along the ground was provided. She showed Mary how to get the tail up in a flying position and then how to keep the nose straight while landing or taking off.

AVIATION

Edited by BOBBY TROUT

BOBBY TROUT

Nationally known aviatrix, holder of the Woman's World Re-fueling Endurance Record—time 122 hours, 50 minutes We are proud to announce Bobby Trout as editor of the new Aviation Department.

We're off—with the roar of our mighty engine pulling us forward at terrific speed we quickly realize ourselves flying through space, and as we look back we see the airport getting smaller and smaller. "Look at that sky of blue, splashed here and there with wisps of white; feel the warmth of the sun as it embraces us in its magnetic rays; what joys this new world unfolds to those of us who have chosen this fascinating adventure.

Our destination is everywhere, so prepare to be with us each month for an interesting and educational resume of our aerial explorations — we promise you thrills galore, and will reveal to you facts and achievements beyond your furtherest imagination. This department is for YOU so why not make use of it? We are open to helpful suggestions, so let us hear from you. How else can we be gratified?

Our good ship is now hovering over Rye, New York, so let us drop in on Ruth Nichols, aviatrix, speed queen, who is planning a solo flight across the Atlantic from Newfoundland to Paris. Ruth is a very modest girl and gives all the credit to the Crosley Radio Corp. which has so kindly sponsored the various flights as well as furnishing the Lockheed vega in which Ruth has been able to establish so many records. Of course we realize the Crosley Radio Corp. deserves a great deal of credit for their air mindedness in foreseeing the advantages of aerial advertising. We must not overlook, however, that Ruth must perform the work in establishing the air records that she now holds, which are: Women's Altitude record, Women's Trans-continental both east and west (incidentally she bettered the time made by Col. Lindbergh and his wife). She also established a new woman's speed record at the recent Detroit Aircraft show. So you can see that Ruth has had a very busy year.

As we may not return to Rye before June, at which time Ruth plans to take off for her hop to Paris, we wish to take this opportunity to wish her all success. And we can just see her now in gay Paree with her cute little New York accent telling 40,000,000 Frenchmen how she did it.

Speaking of gay Paree: We see that our good friend, Capt. Frank Hawks, is showing the Europeans that continent is merely an afternoon's hop.

It is now time to return to our home port, so we will be looking forward to many suggestions from our readers so as to make these flights more interesting and entertaining.

Bobbi advertising for Cycloplane Co., Ltd., May 1931.

(above) Tony Stadlman (l) one of the four partners of early Lockheed Company, Marie Kelly (c) hired as Lockheed office manager, and Captain Wilkins (r), famous arctic explorer in front of Lockheed. Circa 1927.

Mary Wiggins, Bobbi's first Cycloplane student, as a WASP in WWII.

Mary Wiggins first parachute jump, Clover Field, August 16, 1931.

After the student completed the ground maneuvers, he or she would gradually be allowed to use more throttle to become airborne a few feet at a time, until the student learned to fly the Cycloplane close to the ground. In little time Mary became proficient in handling the Cycloplane. The final lesson was to fly at higher altitudes. The Cycloplane was designed to give the student only enough throttle to complete the prescribed lesson, thus ensuring the student's and plane's safety.

Bobbi continued to work for Cycloplane in 1931. One day after completing instruction,

Bobbi struck up a conversation with Bud Campbell, who was the captain of the Goodyear "Volunteer" blimp. Bud said if Bobbi went flying with him he would let her pilot the blimp. She got his consent to fly over the family service station. Bobbi completed the maneuver and handed the controls back to him. He remembered her enthusiasm, for every now and then, he would fly over the station and yell down, "Hi Bobbi", giving the Trouts' patrons and neighbors a big thrill.

The summer of 1931, Bobbi heard her name called as she walked off the field at Grand Central Airport in Glendale. She turned and her face lit up when she recognized the familiar face of Tex Rankin, who had just landed. Tex was one of the most colorful acrobatic fliers of the time, and he asked Bobbi a few years earlier if she would consider being one of the girls in his tri-acrobatic flying team, with Tex's protege, Dorothy Hester. She had given it serious consideration, but time passed, and she heard no more from him until 1931.

Tex had just finished taking several pilots up for a few outside loops, and each of them had become nauseous. Bobbi and Tex discussed the flying trio he had proposed several years earlier. He now wanted Bobbi to go up with him for a trial run on an outside loop and a few other stunts.

Bobbi readily agreed, and they climbed into his little Great Lakes biplane. Grinning like a Cheshire Cat, Tex strapped Bobbi and then himself in. Unaware that Bobbi had never experienced seasickness or airsickness, Tex was surprised when she laughed in outright enjoyment while he completed his unusual gravity-defying maneuvers, an outside loop, and an inverted spin. She had done considerable acrobatics in the Jennies as part of her initial flying course, such as spins, loops, and wingovers, but nothing comparable to what she had just experienced.

Tex completed an inverted spin, brought the plane in to land, and turning to Bobbi told her that he was proud of her abilities and informed her that he would be in touch soon, when he was ready to train the act. However a trio was never formed. Several years later, Tex was killed in an airplane accident.

INTERNATIONAL ADVENTURERS HAVE BIG NIGHT

The last meeting of the year of the International Adventurers was a big success, and reflected great credit upon the organizer and president, Col. Edward P. Bailey.

It was held at the Mona Lisa Cafe in Los Angeles on Friday night last, and the speakers and guests included Lieut. Commander B. H. Wyatt, of the air squadron of the U. S. battle fleet; Capt. Alfred A. Grant, commanding officer of the 27th air squadron; Capt. John A. McCready, of international fame; Capt. J. A. Archibald, veteran balloonist and war correspondent; Capt. Frederick Libby, of the British Royal Air Force; Bobby Trout, Verne Speich, Captain Parker, Esten B. Kojer and many others.

It was truly a red-letter event in the history of the organization.

Some of Mary Wiggins early exploits inspired comic strips of the day, 1933.

FIESTA OFFERS FAMED FLYERS

Outstanding pilots in world aviation will participate in the huge international air meet to be held here September 12 and 13 as the climax of La Fiesta de Los Angeles, it was announced today by Col. Richard Barnitz, manager of the air carnival.

Among those participating will be Bobbie Trout and Edna Mae Cooper, Ruth Nichols, Florence Lowe Barnes, Capt. Frank Hawks, Amelia Earhart, Laura Ingalls, Art Goebel, Jimmy Doolittle, John MacCready, Al Williams and many others.

A special air event for motion picture notables who fly is being planned.

An amphibian race will be held. Planes will take off from Los Angeles Airport, pick up La Fiesta bathing beauties at sea and race back flying field.

Mary Wiggins, 1931.

Air Circus Slated At Lake Elsinore Sunday

There will be a stupendous Air Circus held over Lake Elsinore on Sunday, June 14th, 1931, in which over twenty planes will participate. Parachute jumping, balloon bursting, rolls, side slips, barrels and other hair-raising events will be included in the stunts these daring pilots will put on for exhibition.

In one of the races Bobbie Trout, internationally famous aviatrix will pilot a speedy Eagle Rock plane. This fearless young woman is looked upon as one of the outstanding and most daring pilots in the world today. She has twice broken the Women's World solo endurance record and on two occasions has broken the women's record for endurance refueling.

Vernon Speich, holder of a two year solo endurance record will be an added sensation of the air circus. Nineteen year old Sid Holland will perform some of his dare-devil stunts. Estel Coppock, one of America's youngest amateur parachute jumpers will give the spectators a thrill by his feats.

Many of the planes engaged in this circus are coming from Santa Ana and the Martin airport near there and it is said this will be one of the largest and most spectacular air circuses ever held in inland California.

The planes will fly to Lake Elsinore the afternoon preceeding the air circus. There a banquet and dance will be held at the Clevelin Country Club on Saturday evening, limited to the owners and pilots of planes, and their ladies who have arrived by air.

JUNIOR BIRDMEN OF AMERICA

LAWRENCE SHAW   NATIONAL DIRECTOR

DEVOTED TO THE INTEREST OF THE
YOUTH OF THE AMERICAS IN AVIATION

By Pat Hogan
Examiner Wing Commander

IMAGINE FLYING CONTINU-ALLY for almost a week. That was the experience of Miss Bobbie Trout when she established a re-fueling record flight in 1931 in company with Miss Edna Mae Cooper. Tonight over radio KFAC, Miss Trout will tell Junior Birdmen about this memorable flight as well as other record hops she has made.

Each Monday night at 8 o'clock the Examiner Wing of the Junior Birdmen of America presents a radio program wherein some famous figure of the flying world is interviewed. Don't forget to listen in on this Birdmen feature as well as read the daily and Sunday column devoted to the Junior Birdmen activities.

BOBBIE TROUT
She'll Tell Thrills

Bobbi in the newspaper, circa 1931.

Passenger's Log Book

VOLUNTEER

Goodyear-Zeppelin Corp.
Akron, Ohio

Passenger's Log Book.

The Volunteer

THE VOLUNTEER was christened on May 4, 1929, at Pittsburgh by Mrs. W. C. Young on occasion of the National Balloon Race starting in Pitt Stadium. The Volunteer with the Pilgrim and Puritan participated in the fleet's first formation flying on the trip to Pittsburgh.

Returning to Akron, the Volunteer was taken down and shipped to Los Angeles, where after a record job of assembly and inflation it made its initial appearance at the Shrine ceremonial.

The Volunteer is 128 feet long and 37 feet in diameter. It is equipped with two .70 h.p. Ryan-Siemens motors.

Dr. Karl Arnstein designed the Volunteer. He has made plans for some 70 Zeppelins including the two great airships ZRS-4 and ZRS-5 of the United States Navy.

In naming the ships of the Goodyear fleet, President P. W. Litchfield established the precedent of using the designations of international yacht cup winners. Blimps and yachts have something in common. They serve a similar purpose, one over land and the other on water.

Passenger's Log Book showing Bobbi's first ride in a dirigible.

FLIGHT LOG

From _____ Airport

Passenger's Name

Bobbie Trout

Other Passengers

Friday 13 - 1930

Remarks on Flight

Time in Air

Bud Campbell

Pilot's Signature

Bobbi Trout, circa 1929. Mrs. Bagnell gave Bobbi and Elinor Smith each a $100 gift after their first refueling endurance flight.

Thea Rasche.   Berlin W 15, 7.12.31.
                                Kurfürstendamm 203
                                Pension Stotzheim.
                                Tel: Bismarck 6154.

My dear Bobbie!

        Please don't be mad with me - I feel terrible bad, that
I did not write you sooner, to thank you for the sending of the
nice photos and your lovely letter. I was so glad to hear from you
and your plans. It is a bad time for aviation - no one has money
or will give money for aviation and unfortunately aviation is a
wonderful but very expensive sport! My great plan for a long
flight is also going to nothing - always the bad money! But -
keep smiling! Also with my book a had bad luck! Just before the
printing was an other book appearing about all us german women
pilots and many of my live and flying - I did not know anything
about this, only this newspaperman had interviewed me how many
others are doing this always. And this man has made a book about
this and my publication made me a big scene, that I had kept a se-
cret about this and that so the first orginality would be away
and so on - so that I took my manuscript and said: Hallo ! An
other newspaper has ask alraedy, but I was until too lazy to
dictate the whole thing again, but I will do it soon! I was traveling a great deal and flyers never have loved writing! Do you
use the photos soon or has the sending a little time? Becaus I
love to use them.
        What are you doing now, what are your plans, so many question
I have for you - you could not anther them all! What is with all
the girls I know and what are they all doing. Gee - would I love
to come over to America again to be together with you all - But
the money - the money ! How is aviation now by you - I hear so
different opinions and meanings, that I can't make a real picture
about it. They say all, that is going not so good with the sport-
flying and the difficulties also very great there. Are you pla-
ning a big race again for the next year! When you can make it
possible that I can fly in this race for a factory or so, I would
like to come. Or to do some other flying - only to be in America
again - really longing for it!
        Write me soon again, Dear, I am always so happy to hear from
you and really I am thinking very offen about you and all the nice
hours we had.
        Lots of luck - and best wishes for you

                                Lovingly yours

                                Thea Rasche.

                        *Merry christmas and
                        happy new year -*

Thea Rasche, German aviatrix, circa 1929.

Amelia Earhart (l), Thea Rasche (c), and Bobbi Trout, at United Airport, now Burbank Airport, circa 1936.

Bobbi in pants makes the news again!

Why All This Fuss About Men's Pants for Women?

Marlene Dietrich, Who Started Fad, Declares Americans Should Stick to Skirts

BY ALMA WHITAKER

Too late, Marlene, too late! Example, you see, is so much stronger than precept.

Marlene Dietrich, who has so effectively concentrated masculine attention on the provocative subject of trousers for women by adopting them to the complete exclusion of skirts for all off-screen occasions, raises her piquant eyebrows and remarks blandly:

"American women wear dresses so well. They should stick to skirts."

OLD STUFF TO HER

It may sound a bit incredible, but the lovely Marlene essays to be quite annoyed about the publicity attendant upon her preference for masculine garb for herself. As for that tuxedo outfit she donned at the premiere of "The Sign of the Cross:"

"Why, I wore that in my first picture for Paramount, 'Morocco,'

nearly three years ago—had quite an argument with the studio to let me. I'd been wearing men's clothes in Europe for long before that. No one ever got excited about it before. Why all this fuss now? I am suddenly besieged for interviews, and with requests for manufacturers to let them promote a Marlene Dietrich suit. It is all very tiresome.

"Why, I've practically always worn them—because I think I look well in them, because they are comfortable, because they are economical. But I'm no crusader. I wear what I like and expect other women to do the same. I think it would be a pity if all American women took to trousers; they look so well in dresses. But why pick on me? The girls have been wearing slacks in Hollywood since long before I arrived on the scene. What's the big difference between slacks and trousers, anyway?"

By which you will gather that Marlene is a trifle peeved about it all. Paramount's publicity brigade assures me that she really has been very cold and snippy with them, since they blithely seized her pants, as it were, for exploitation purposes. She deplores, she vows, ever having consented to be photographed in be things.

SKIRTS CONSPICUOUS NOW

"Why, if I started to wear skirts in public now," sighs Marlene, "it would make me horribly conspicuous. It is all very silly."

It is true the girls have been trousering for lo, these many seasons. One Hollywood store alone claims to have sold more than 5000 pairs of slacks in 1932. A department store man casually estimated that at least a million pairs of pants for women were sold in this territory last year, and that during the past three or four years the total for just this coast would reach a billion! As for this season, oh boy, how the stores are stocking up on 'em all over the country—not just feminized slacks, either, but honest-to-goodness trousers of masculine cut together with coats and shirts.

All the same, it remained for Marlene to establish them for formal attire, even if such pioneers as Bobbie Trout of aviation fame have

[...] ago, but one could not call that a truly formal occasion.

SHE REALLY STARTED IT

Marlene says she has worn men's suits for years, that a great many girls did in Germany, without anybody raising an eyebrow. But when she went shopping in Beverly Hills in a man's gray lounge suit, with fedora to match, all complete, and later appeared in that faultlessly cut tuxedo of strictly masculine genre at the Biltmore—well, something rather epoch-making was obviously in the air. She banished the last wavering barrier. She can tweet all she likes about American women sticking to skirts, she's been and gone and done it. Hope springeth anew in the human breast and every last one of us fondly expects to look as cutey in 'em as Marlene does. We'll be dressing our babies in 'em, too—you should see Marlene's small girl tricked out in her wee boy's outfit!

Bobbi and a couple of Disney friends.

NINETY - NINE CLUB MEETS
Southland Aviatrices Form Plans

Latest in Flying Togs
What is being worn in feminine aeronautical circles is demonstrated : this informal pose of five of the Southland's women pilots, left right, Adoree Neville, Gladys O'Donnell, Florence Lowe Barnes, Mi J. M. Keith-Miller, Bobbie Trout.

Ninety-nine out of 100 your women might want to become a plane pilots, and there's one flyin organization in which ninety-nh women flyers were original men bers.

So naturally the girl pilots call it the Ninety-nine Club. Its rost includes feminine names know throughout the world for their sl tricks and accomplishments.

In a meeting at the home of dred Morgan, in Beverly H bers of the club revealed th are plannig aerial vacations coming summer—substituting planes for automobiles.

At their parties the lady air ski pers are garbed in costumes ran ing from the latest in eveni dresses to what the well-dress aviatrix wears at the controls of plane. Florence Lowe Barnes, f mer holder of the world's air record for women, and Miss Bo Trout, co-holder of the women's fueling endurance record and now preparing for a Honolulu-to-Los Angeles flight, appeared in trousered ensembles.

The organization boasts more air speed, endurance and adventuring pilots than any other similar group.

A gathering of women fliers.

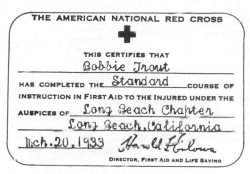

Bobbi's Red Cross card.

Bobbi remembers hearing all the wonderful publicity in May 20-21, 1932, when her friend Amelia Earhart successfully flew the Atlantic. At last one of her women friends was getting much acclaim, such as Lindbergh did in 1927.

Bobbi got her opportunity for another record-breaking flight in August. She received a telegram offering her the opportunity to fly from New York to Italy, and parachute jump over Florence, Italy, in commemoration of the famous nurse, Florence Nightingale. It happened that the Pennzoil Oil Company representative, who received a lot of business from the Trouts, was in the service station when Bobbi received the telegram. The representative thought the Pennzoil Oil Company might like to put up the necessary one thousand dollars for Bobbi's participation in the flight.

Within twenty-four hours Pennzoil sent a telegram to Bobbi confirming the offer of the one thousand dollars. An acquaintance of Bobbi's, who was a nurse, wanted to take this flight so badly that Bobbi big-heartedly gave her the offer. Before things were ironed out, Bill Ulbrich and Edna Newcomer set out from New York to Rome in a Bellanca Aircraft Corporation cabin monoplane called The American Nurse. The ill-fated flight was last seen somewhere near the Azores in the Atlantic. God was really watching over Bobbi.

In the early days, there were just too many accidents due to insufficient knowledge of aerodynamics and engineering. This was the era of early aviation and there was much to learn about accident prevention. In time, lives and better training equipment would prevent these losses as aviation progressed.

Telegrams from Dr. Pisculli inviting Bobbi to fly to Italy with the crew of the American Nurse.

PATRONS ARE REQUESTED TO FAVOR THE COMPANY BY CRITICISM AND SUGGESTION CONCERNING ITS SERVICE

CLASS OF SERVICE

This is a full-rate Telegram or Cablegram unless its deferred character is indicated by a suitable sign above or preceding the address.

NEWCOMB CARLTON, PRESIDENT

WESTERN UNION (55)

J. C. WILLEVER, VICE-PRESIDENT

SIGNS

DL = Day Letter
NM = Night Message
NL = Night Letter
LCO = Deferred Cable
NLT = Cable Night Letter
WLT = Week-End Letter

The filing time as shown in the date line on full-rate telegrams and day letters, and the time of receipt at destination as shown on all messages, is STANDARD TIME.

Received at Main Office, 608-610 South Spring St., Los Angeles, Calif. **ALWAYS OPEN**

032 JUL 27 AM 8 56

RXNB262 26 XU=NEWYORK NY 27 1153A

EVELYN TROUT=

418 SOUTH SOTO ST LOSA=

NO TIME FOR ADVERTISING NOBODY WILL ADVANCE MONEY ON FLIGHTS

ANYWAY STOP WIRE AT LEAST ONE THOUSAND DOLLARS AND COME TO

NEWYORK AT ONCE ANSWER IMMEDIATELY=

DR PISCULLI.

PATRONS ARE REQUESTED TO FAVOR THE COMPANY BY CRITICISM AND SUGGESTION CONCERNING ITS SERVICE

CLASS OF SERVICE

This is a full-rate Telegram or Cablegram unless its deferred character is indicated by a suitable sign above or preceding the address.

NEWCOMB CARLTON, PRESIDENT

WESTERN UNION (55)

J. C. WILLEVER, VICE-PRESIDENT

SIGNS

DL = Day Letter
NM = Night Message
NL = Night Letter
LCO = Deferred Cable
NLT = Cable Night Letter
WLT = Week-End Letter

The filing time as shown in the date line on full-rate telegrams and day letters, and the time of receipt at destination as shown on all messages, is STANDARD TIME.

Received at Main Office, 608-610 South Spring St., Los Angeles, Calif. **ALWAYS OPEN**

RXNB262 26 XU=NEWYORK NY 27

EVELYN TROUT=

418 SOUTH SOT ST LOSA=

IF YOU CAN WIRE IMMEDIATELY FIFTEEN HUNDRED DOLLARS

NATIONAL BANK STUYVESANT BRANCH TO HELP DEFRAY FLIGH

EXPENSES WILL ACCEPT YOUR COPILOT NEWYORK ROME FLIGHT TAKING

OFF WITHIN TEN DAYS WIRE ANSWER COLLECT=

DR PISCULLI   235 SECOND AVENUE.

WESTERN UNION GIFT ORDERS ARE APPROPRIATE GIFTS FOR ALL OCCASIONS.

Had Bobbi accepted Dr. Pisculli's invitation, she too would have disappeared like many ocean fliers in those days.

ROME FLYERS LONG OVERDUE; HOPE WANING

ROME, Sept. 15.—(U.P.)—Every airport and wireless station in Italy was alert today for word of the lost trans-Atlantic airplane American Nurse, many hours overdue in its attempted non-stop flight from New York to Rome.

On the Spanish, Portuguese and French coasts utmost vigilance was maintained, with coastal patrol boats cruising far beyond their ordinary ranges in the hope of finding the plane, in which a pilot, a student nurse and a New York physician left New York Tuesday morning.

HOPE FAST WANING

Air Minister Italo Balbo and the entire Italian air force waited throughout the day for word of the plane's whereabouts, but by nightfall it was apparent that hope was rapidly waning.

Italian airmen, who are notoriously superstitious, said that because Pilot William Ülbrich and his companions started on the 13th of the month, and because their flight was made in a total eclipse of the moon in Italy, they believe the plane was lost in the sea.

LINER REPORT LAST

No word of the flight's progress was received after the liner France, at sea 450 miles east of Land's End, England, radioed that "an aluminum-colored" plane passed, flying eastward, at 12:50 p. m., New York time, yesterday.

Aboard the American Nurse with Pilot Ulbrich were Miss Edna Newcomer, student nurse and co-pilot, and Dr. Leon M. Pisculi, native of Italy. Dr. Pisculi financed the flight for the purpose of obtaining the physical, mental and emotional reactions of trans-Atlantic flyers, and carried a veritable laboratory for his experiments.

Missing On U. S. Flight to Italy

—Acme Photo.

SOMEWHERE ON ATLANTIC — The plane American Nurse and its three passengers were lost yesterday, being long overdue on trans-Atlantic flight. Above photo, taken before flight, shows Stephen Miller, backer of flight; Edna Newcomer, nurse and co-pilot; William Ulbrich, pilot; Mrs. Stephen Miller, and Dr. Leon Pisculi, physician.

California Women of the Golden West

MRS. GEORGE DAVIDSON GILMORE, *President*
6366 MARYLAND DRIVE
LOS ANGELES

Feb.1,1932

> California Women of the Golden West
> MEMBERSHIP CARD
> 1932
> NOT TRANSFERABLE
> NAME *Miss Bobby Trout*
> ADDRESS *2400 East 4th St. L.A.*
> MRS. GEORGE DAVIDSON GILMORE, PRESIDENT
> TREASURER *Hattie E. Smith Hughes*
> PLEASE PRESENT THIS CARD AT ALL MEETINGS

Miss Bobbie Trout
2400 East 4th Street
Los Angeles,Calif.

Dear Miss Trout;

No doubt Mrs M.E.Ridenour ,our Aviation Chairman in this organization has informed you that we have appointed you as our' "AIR MASCOT" for 1932, at her suggestion.

As you were "Miss Aviation" for this club when we held out Los Angeles' Birthday Ball in 1930, we felt that you were already a warm friend of ours and so the idea went over very agreeablly with the whole executive board.

Mrs Ridenour informed us that you would accept and that pleased us greatly. Now we are asking you to come as an honor guest February 12th. to the Hotel Roosevelt,in Hollywood, when we hold our monthly social event, so that we may introduce you and ask you to say about from five to seven minutes of the "usual word" of greeting etc. Will you,my dear ? And if you can, will you wear an aviation costume? T

The affair will begin about noon. I am inclosing a bulletin so that you may read all about it. Of course from now on you are a member of the club with all privileges--a complimentary member .Your card is also inclosed.

Will you please ley me know if you will be with us on the 12th. and we also hope that you will be able to attend other meetings of the club also.

Sincerely yours,
Betty Gilmore (Mrs.Geo.D.Gilmore)

BGJC

Bobby Trout Plan: Honolulu-L. A. Flight

LOS ANGELES, Oct. 24.—(AP)— The first west-to-east flight between Hawaii and the mainland is planned for early next year by Bobbie Trout, woman flier, it was announced here today by her financial backer, Gordon S. Davidson, manufacturer.

Carl Squire, general manager of the Lockheed Aircraft corporation in Burbank, said Davidson had entered an order for a high-powered, speedy, one place Lockheed-Alstair plane.

Davidson said Miss Trout would take off at Honolulu for Los Angeles.

MISS TROUT TO ATTEMPT PACIFIC HOP

Girl Flyer to Take Off on Honolulu-Los Angeles Jump Early Next Year

Some time after the first of the year a low-wing Lockheed Altair monoplane is scheduled to leave Honolulu for a nonstop flight to Los Angeles with Bobby Trout, Los Angeles aviatrix, at the controls. That was the plan outlined yesterday by Gordon F. Davidson, Los Angeles manufacturer, who said he is prepared to finance the flight and has already ordered the plane.

Davidson said Miss Trout, who, with May Cooper early this year established a new endurance flight

Bobbie Trout

AVIATRIX PLANS PACIFIC FLIGHT

(Continued from First Page)

flight record for women, will be provided with a new plane equipped with radio for both sending and receiving, and with every appliance known to insure safety.

An innovation in ocean flight ventures will be attempted, Davidson said, if present negotiation with Lloyds in London can be completed. The insurance on the plane has been tentatively set at $16,000.

"I am giving Miss Trout this opportunity to make the Honolulu-Los Angeles flight," he explained, "because I have always admired her good sportsmanship and I believe she is entitled to the chance."

Carl Squires, general manager of the Lockheed Aircraft Company, yesterday said the plane has been ordered for delivery in February of next year and that it will probably have a motor capable of delivering 500 horsepower and driving the plane at a speed of 180 miles an hour.

Miss Trout enrolled as a flying student three years ago and after four months of training made her first solo flight. She was subsequently given her pilot's license and the first two passengers to go aloft with her were her parents. She now holds a transport pilot's license which permits her to pilot any type of plane.

A PACIFIC FLIGHT ASPIRANT CHECKS UP ON HER PLANE: MISS BOBBY TROUT
Examining Details of the Fast Machine, Now Building at Burbank, Cal., in Which She Plans to Fly From Honolulu to Los Angeles.

This Cachet was carried from Hawaii to America by Miss BOBBIE TROUT in the first successful solo ocean flight made by a woman and bears her original signature.

HONOLULU TO LOS ANGELES

BOBBIE TROUT

A First Day Cover Bobbi was to have carried on her flight.

Bobbie Trout To Attempt Pacific Flight Next Year

Speedy Plane Being Built For Hop; First Planned By Woman Pilot

Bobbie Trout, East Los Angeles noted woman flier, will attempt a non-stop flight from Honolulu to Los Angeles early next year, it was announced this week. Upon completion it will be the first successful flight by a woman over the Pacific Ocean.

Miss Trout, co-holder of the woman's endurance flight record with Edna Cooper, will use a high powered, speedy one-seater Lockheed-Attair plane which was recently ordered from the Lockheed Aircraft corporation in Burbank. Delivery of the plane will be made shortly before the flight attempt.

The plane, to cost about $30,000, will be shipped to Honolulu upon delivery.

Gordon S. Davidson, soap manufacturer, is backing the flight.

The Bobbie Trout Transpacific Solo Flight

(PROPOSED NAME OF PLANE - MISS COMMERCE)

ADVERTISING CONTRACT

NEWSPAPER SERVICE, INC., and

_____, Director

We, the undersigned, hereby subscribe _____

for special advertising space on the plane of Miss Bobbie Trout, said plane to be used in her proposed Transp_____ United States, during the month of August, 1932, the date of flight to be between the 1st and 7th of the month, _____ the take-off at that time.

It is mutually agreed between the two contracting parties that the advertisement furnished by this firm (_____)

shall occupy space on plane in position hereby designated_____, and that

the size of said advertisement shall be_____feet,_____inches.

It is agreed by the contracting party that this contract shall be in full effect from_____, 1932, until

_____, 1932. In the event that Miss Bobbie Trout should crack up, or any other unavoidable accident should happen during the take-off, or during the flight, or during the preparations for the flight, that circumstance, or circumstances shall not relieve the subscriber hereto from fulfilling his contract, and under no consideration or circumstances can same be cancelled without the permission of both the contracting parties.

It is understood and agreed that the only condition upon which this contract can be terminated by subscriber is in the event the plane to be used in said flight should, for any reason, not be completed and no space, therefore, furnished on which the advertisement can be placed. In such event the said sum advanced for said advertising shall be returned to the subscriber.

It is fully understood and agreed, however, that under no circumstances is Bobbie Trout to be held liable for failure to make said flight, or for failure of the backers of said flight to complete said plane, and the subscriber hereto expressly waives any right of action against said Bobbie Trout personally on account of any loss or damage sustained under or by reason of this agreement.

It is agreed that the undersigned shall furnish copy for the said advertisement, or in the event that same is not submitted within ample time we authorize the Directors of the flight to use any available copy.

It is further agreed that this advertisement shall remain upon the plane used by Miss Trout until the same is dismantled; upon the actual dismantling of the plane upon completion of flight, this copy shall be returned to the contracting advertiser, (as part of the plane) to be used in any manner that the advertiser shall see fit.

MAKE ALL CHECKS PAYABLE TO

BOBBIE TROUT TRANSPACIFIC FLIGHT.

_____
(Firm Name)

_____
(Address)

_____
(Authorized By)

❰ **THIS CONTRACT IS NOT SUBJECT TO CANCELLATION** ❱

Salesman_____   Date_____, 1932.

(Please retain duplicate copy)

Bobbi inspects her Lockheed Altair under construction, 1931.

PUBLICITY HEADQUARTERS
THE BOBBIE TROUT TRANS-PACIFIC SOLO FLIGHT
HONOLULU TO LOS ANGELES

Los Angeles, Cal.,
May 23, 1932.

Attention:
Gentlemen: Re: Bobbie Trout Trans-Pacific Solo Flight.

In placing your advertising you wish to do so through a medium that will attract not only attention but one that will produce results, do you not? Herein contained you will find information that will be of vital interest to you concerning a medium that will prove both effective and unique, and of much more value than any other type or form of advertising offered the business world today.

Without a doubt you have heard that Miss Bobbie Trout, woman champion aviatrix, and holder of many aviation records and who was recently awarded the highest honors by the Federal Aeronautical Internationale, will make a solo flight from Honolulu to Los Angeles during the forthcoming Olympic Games. We have chosen this time (between August 1st and 7th) so as to take advantage of the hundreds of thousands of people who will be in Los Angeles to witness the Olympiad. It is also planned to have Miss Trout dedicate a new million dollar airport here in connection with a three day air circus that will be held at the time of her completion of the trans-Pacific flight, and we expect two or three hundred thousand people to attend during the three days' festivities.

We are placing advertisements on the plane which is to be made of plywood, the advertising to be painted on the plane (as part of the plane) and to remain on same until it is actually dismantled.

During the latter part of June or the first part of July, Miss Trout will make a test flight with her plane "The Miss Commerce" to New York City and return. In so-doing, our advertisers will receive national publicity from their advertisements. After the return flight from New York, Miss Trout's plane will be shipped to Honolulu, to stand by for the U. S. Weather Bureau's signal to take off for the States.

Miss Trout's plane will carry a radio telephone transmitter and receiver. The National Broadcasting Corporation is now considering a nation wide hook-up of Miss Trout's conversation during the flight. This is very important, especially to the firms carrying representations on the plane. It is now our plan to have Miss Trout CASUALLY mention the products of the firms who participate in the advertising program that we have planned.

World wide publicity has already been given this flight. Hearst Newspaper Syndicate, which controls as you are aware, eighty-three newspapers in the U. S. A., has approached us for exclusive rights to a feature story before and after the flight. Just consider the front page publicity this will obtain -- space that can not be bought. It is also planned to have Miss Trout make interstate and international good will flights before and after the Honolulu flight.

*Two page publicity on
Bobbi's plans for her
Trans-Pacific solo flight.*

We need not tell you that Miss Trout is famous. She is capable, and is officially recognized in the aviation world. Her record is a worthy one.

We believe that this is a natural and extraordinary opportunity for your firm to advertise its products. No other opportunity today equals this when one takes into consideration the importance of a woman flying a major ocean alone. The channels for publicity are many and varied, such as radio, newspapers and newsreels. Consider the effect it would have upon the buying public if Miss Trout should broadcast that she selected your product for use during her flight because it is best. This statement would have tremendous appeal; after all, a life is at stake. Consider the number of times this plane will be photographed, and the number of times that your advertisement if placed on this plane, will appear on the front page of the nation's newspapers and magazines. Just deliberate upon the possibilities this medium of advertising presents to you by virtue of its diversified channels for publicity throughout the nation -- the world.

Regarding her ship, she will use a Lockheed Altair, equipped with every known device for safety; gas tankage 475 gallons; a Wasp motor, generating 520 H. P., with a cruising speed of 150 M.P.H., top speed 225 M.P.H.

The price of an advertisement on the plane varies from $100.00 to $2500.00. Attached herewith you will find card setting forth the different sizes and the amount of each space. Please be advised that should you take part in this program, upon completion of the flight the original covering of the plane (ply-wood) will be removed and the ads will be very carefully cut out and turned over to the advertisers respectively to be used by them in any way that they see fit, along with a letter from Miss Trout explaining just what part of the plane the advertisement covered. Then the plane will be recovered with regular canvas and silk, the advertisements will be replaced on this second covering to remain on the plane until it is finally dismantled for all time; thus you will receive publicity wherever the plane may go after the Honolulu flight.

Contracts will be mailed to you immediately upon request. Two-thirds of the cost of the advertising is payable at the time contract is signed, the balance being payable upon completion of the flight. Additional information will gladly be furnished upon request.

We trust that you will give this matter your most careful consideration, and that we may hear from you regarding it within the next few days.

Yours truly,

Address:

A. J. Young,
Director of Publicity,
Bobbie Trout Trans-Pacific Flight,
544½ No. Kingsley Dr.,
Los Angeles, California.

A. J. Young,
Director
Bobbie Tr

This Certifies Bobbie Trout
is an Associate member.
Complimentary   Date 1936 To 1944

Women's International Association
of Aeronautics
LOS ANGELES
CALIFORNIA
U.S.A.

Secretary

Lady Hay Drummond-Hay
President

MISSION INN
RIVERSIDE, CALIFORNIA
U.S.A.

WINGS AROUND THE WORLD FOR PEACE, PROSPERITY, AND WORLD FRIENDSHIP

Lockheed's Herb Boen, aviation historian, takes Bobbi back to where her Hawaiian flight plans began in the Lockheed factory, 50 years later.

CREDIT: BOB FERGUSON, LOCKHEED-CALIFORNIA COMPANY

BOBBIE TROUT PLANS HAWAII TO L. A. FLIGHT

$30,000 Lockheed Plane Being Built for Nonstop Hop Next Year; Soap Maker Backer

Bobbie Trout, noted aviatrix, will attempt a non-stop flight from Honolulu to Los Angeles some time early next year—either in January or February.

Announcement to that effect was made yesterday by Gordon S. Davidson, soap manufacturer, who is backing the flight.

A high powered, speedy, one-place Lockheed-Attair was ordered Friday from the Lockheed Aircraft Corporation at Burbank, Carl Squire, general manager, said yesterday. Delivery of the plane will be made shortly before the flight attempt.

The plane, to cost about $30,000, will be shipped to Honolulu, Davidson said, and Miss Trout will take off for Los Angeles from there.

GIRL FLYER WEIGHS HER 'PAY LOAD'

Cargo Carefully Figured as Aviatrix Prepares for Honolulu Journey

The weight of a single envelope ordinarily does not come in for a great deal of consideration, but when 10,000 envelopes get together that is another matter — particularly when the 10,000 are to be carried in an airplane where every ounce counts.

Miss Bobbie Trout, local aviatrix and coholder of the world's refueling air endurance record for women, learned this in ordering envelopes that will be aboard her Lockheed Altair monoplane which she plans to fly from Honolulu to Los Angeles within a few weeks.

Not only the weight of the paper had to be taken into consideration, but also the weight of the blue ink that was to be used in coloring the beautiful cachet stamped on each envelope.

The 10,000 carriers had to weigh less than seventy pounds. It took Miss Trout nearly a month to obtain a suitable light weight combination of paper and ink, but last night she received the first of the order.

The envelopes are to be autographed by her, shipped to Honolulu and carried back over the 2500-mile ocean skyway. Miss Trout declared she has received hundreds of letters ordering the aerial cachets and she is confident she will sell all of the 10,000 before leaving here.

Her intention is to help pay for her airplane and to establish a home for sick children on the desert.

She will fly alone.

BOBBIE TROUT
FAMOUS AMERICAN AVIATRIX
TO FLY FROM
Honolulu to Los Angeles
ALONE

Miss Bobbie Trout, holder of many air records for women pilots, is going to attempt a solo flight across the Pacific Ocean from Honolulu to Los Angeles, shortly after the first of March, 1932.

To gratify the wishes of philatelists and others, Miss Trout is going to carry some specially printed and cacheted air covers which are offered to philatelists and others as follows:

COVER No. 1——The SPECIAL CACHET COVER will be carried by Miss Trout, will be autographed by her, and will be post-marked HONOLULU the day of her departure for Los Angeles. Upon her arrival at LOS ANGELES it will again be stamped and postmarked, and then forwarded to the addressed by Air Mail.

COVER No. 2——For every SPECIAL CACHET COVER ordered, Miss Trout will have a Special Cachet applied on a self-addressed and stamped envelope. In addition, Miss Trout will autograph this cover, which will be mailed from Honolulu the day of her departure. This cover will be carried by boat to the mainland and then forwarded to the addressed by Air Mail.

COVER No. 3——In addition, a Special Cachet will be applied to a second self-addressed and stamped envelope which will be autographed by Miss Trout upon her arrival in LOS ANGELES. This cover will then be forwarded by Air Mail to the addressed. Note: Covers No. 2 & 3 must be sent with your order and stamped.

The rate of the above three covers—one Commemorating Miss Trout's departure from HONOLULU, one carried by Miss Trout in her flight from HONOLULU to LOS ANGELES, and one Commemorating her arrival in LOS ANGELES—is five dollars ($5.00). Each of these covers will be personally autographed by Miss Trout.

ALL ORDERS FOR COVERS MUST BE IN BEFORE MARCH 1st, 1932. Cashiers' checks or Postal Money Orders must be made to the order of THE BOBBIE TROUT FUND and sent to

EARL MILLS

750 NORTH HAYWORTH AVE.   HOLLYWOOD, CALIFORNIA

Hazards of the flight prevent assuming responsibility for return of covers. If flight not started, all remittances will be refunded

Note: Anyone interested in a West Coast Advance Air News Service, write to Mr. Mills.

Bobbi (r) and Amelia Earhart (l) in 1936.

BECAUSE OF DEPRESSION AND LACK OF FINANCING, BOBBI'S PACIFIC FLIGHT PLANS FELL THROUGH. Amelia Earhart successfully completed this flight in 1935.

First Day Cover commemorating Amelia's Pacific flight.

Christmas card from Bill Cottrell in 1936. He was a friend of Bobbi's and a Disney employee when Walt Disney had but one camera!

(left to right) Forest O'Brine, Dale Jackson (who in 1929 set men's refueling endurance records), Bobbi, and their Disney friends.

CREDIT: BILL COTTRELL

CREDIT: BILL COTTRELL

CREDIT: BILL COTTRELL

Bobbi and her Mickey Mouse friends advertising for Disney.

Bobbi flies with Mickey Mouse!

AMELIA EARHART

Locust Avenue
Rye, New York

November 25, 1931

Dear Bobbie:

From time to time there have been sporadic
attempts to form among women pilots an
honorary society. So far each one has been
unsuccessful for one or more reasons. Lack
of time on the part of those who can lead has
certainly been a contributing cause. Then,
too, some pilots have felt that the "99's" covered
the general field and the later organization,
the "Betsy Ross Corps", the specific one. Others
expressed the opinion that there were too few
flyers to be spread around throughout any more groups.

It seems to me, despite these criticisms, that
a different sort of society could advantageously
be sponsored now. Therefore, I am submitting this
ready made plan for the yes or no of those to whom
it is sent, i.e., the first derby group.

If most of it is passed, I shall be glad to attend
to details of printing stationery and forms,
obtaining the small file necessary for members'
records, making arrangements for securing emblems,
in short put everything in readiness for the
secretary. I shall be glad to contribute the
expenses incurred in these preliminaries as tangible
evidence of my belief in the purpose to be served.

Sincerely yours,

Amelia Earhart

Amelia Earhart

*Letter from Amelia Earhart, submitting a plan to various women pilots to form ANOTHER
women pilots organization in 1931. Nothing became of this idea.*

After Amelia's Trans-Atlantic solo flight in 1932, a group of aviation friends congratulate her. (left to right): Pancho Barnes, Mrs. Elizabeth McQueen, Amelia, Clema Granger, Elizabeth Kelly Inwood, Gladys O'Donnell, unknown, Mildred Morgan, and Valentine Sprague.

"FLYING CONDITIONS ARE PERFECT IN LOS ANGELES COUNTY"... SAY THE FLIERS

AERIAL POLICE, LOS ANGELES COUNTY – *Officers Caris, Goebel, Waterman, Turner, Barnitz, Campbell, Noville, DeSilva, Thomas, Richter*

FLIERS determine the aircraft market. Where the fliers are, where they like to stay, where they like to fly... there is the market for the products of airplane factories.

Today Southern California leads by a substantial margin, every comparable community in America in the number of pilots, licensed aircraft, gliders, airports and mechanics.

Here the manufacturer, in addition to the market and perfect flying conditions, finds air-minded communities eager to cooperate with low cost and well situated plant sites. And when labor conditions are considered, manufacturing costs in Los Angeles may be easily proved the lowest in the United States.

*Complete detailed surveys and information supplied on request
to Industrial Department, Los Angeles Chamber of Commerce.*

LOS ANGELES COUNTY
FLYING ALL YEAR

Art Goebel
of California to Hawaii fame. "No place in the world where conditions for aviation advancement are better."

Col. Chas. A. Lindbergh
Col. Lindbergh has many times praised the flying conditions of Southern California and its great aviation development.

Lt. Henry H. Ogden
Round-the-World Flyer, Pres. Ogden Aero Corp. "No other section can compare with Los Angeles County in its number and diversification of aviation advantages."

Ruth Nichols
Women's East to West and West to East record holder. "There is almost always a fine airport within gliding distance, a source of intense satisfaction."

Edna May Cooper
Co-Holder of world's endurance record for women–122 hrs. & 50 min. "Southern California climate is inducive to year 'round flying and record-breaking flights."

Bobbie Trout
Co-Holder of world's endurance record for women–122 hrs. & 50 min. "The flyer learns here as nowhere else the meaning of 'The joy of flying'."

Earle Ovington
First U.S. Air Mail Pilot (1911). "Los Angeles County is a pilot's heaven with better flying weather than any spot in the world."

Ruth Elder
Transatlantic Flyer, gives Los Angeles County the credit of having ideal flying conditions and of being the aviation center of America.

Amelia Earhart
Transatlantic Flyer. "Southern California airports and flying conditions are the best I have found anywhere in the country."

Roger Q. Williams
Transatlantic Flyer New York to Rome. "I consider Southern California the ideal spot of the world for aviation in all its phases."

Wallace Beery
M. G. M. star, transport pilot. "Southern California is the ideal playground for the aviator, this location is the center of flying activities."

Lt. Com. Geo. O. Noville
Aide to Byrd North Pole and Transatlantic Flights. "Los Angeles County furnishes ideal flying territory, weather conditions permit all-year flying."

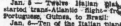

Jan. 5 — Twelve Italian planes started trans-Atlantic flight from Portuguese Guinea, to Brazil.
Jan. 6—Ten of the Italian planes reached Natal, Brazil; two forced down at sea; five men killed.
Jan. 9—Edna May Cooper and Bobbie Trout set new endurance record for women for airplane staying aloft 122 hours and 50 minutes.
Jan. 11—Mrs. Beryl Hart and Lieut. W. S. MacLaren lost in hop from Bermuda to the Azores.
Jan. 31—Big German flying boat DO-X flew from Lisbon to Canary Islands on trans-Atlantic flight.
May 27—Prof. August Piccard of Brussels and an assistant made balloon flight to the stratosphere, being in a sealed aluminum ball, reaching record altitude of 52,500 feet.
June 4—German flying boat DO-X flew from Cape Verde Islands to Fernando Noronha, Brazil, in twelve hours fifteen minutes.
Otto Hillig and Holger Hoiriis left Harbor Grace on a flight to Copenhagen.
June 25—Hillig and Hoiriis landed at Crefeld, Germany.
July 1—Post and Gatty landed at Roosevelt Field, Long Island, having completed flight around the world in eight days, fifteen hours, fifty-one and one-half minutes.
July 16—Endres and Magyar landed fourteen miles from Budapest after flight from Harbor Grace, N. S.
July 28—Hugh Herndon and Clyde Pangborn took off from New York on flight to Moscow; Russell Boardman and John Polando started from New York on flight to Turkey.
Col. and Mrs. C. A. Lindbergh left Washington on air tour of Japan.
July 29. Herndon and Pangborn landed in Wales, went on to London and started again for Moscow.
July 30—Boardman and Polando landed in Istanbul, setting new nonstop distance record.
Aug. 27—DO-X, big German flying boat, arrived at New York.
Sept. 1—Graf Zeppelin reached Brazil.
Sept. 7—Lowell Bayles won Thompson trophy at Cleveland with average speed of 236 miles an hour.
Sept. 8—Don Moyle and C. A. Allen started from Samushiro, Japan, on nonstop flight to Seattle.
Sept. 13—Lieuts. J. F. Boothman and G. H. Stainforth won Schneider Cup permanently for Great Britain, the latter setting new speed record of 379.05 miles per hour.
Sept. 16—Moyle and Allen found alive and safe on island off Kamchatka.
Oct. 4—Pangborn and Herndon started nonstop flight from Japan to United States.
Oct. 5—Pangborn and Herndon landed at Wenatchee, Wash., completing first continuous flight from Japan to United States and winning $25,000 prize.
Nov. 25—Bert Hinkler started flight from Natal, Brazil, to Africa.
Nov. 26—Hinkler landed in British Gambia, West Africa, completing first eastward flight across the South Atlantic.
December 18. Lieut. William A. Cooke in Hawaii set new records for gliders for endurance and possibly altitude, staying aloft twenty-one hours and thirty-six minutes.

Advertising for flying in the Los Angeles County, circa 1931.

Letter from Bobbi about her refueling endurance attempt with John E. Sheasby from Sept. 28–30, 1932. Bobbi and John departed from Grand Central Air Terminal in a 225-hp Wright J-5 Universal Fokker dubbed the "Spirit of 76." The flight was sponsored by the Union Oil Company and lasted 40 hours. The refueling crew consisted of Garland Lincoln and Gus Axelson, flying a Douglas M-2 and a Stinson. The flight was terminated due to a vibrating prop and electrical failure.

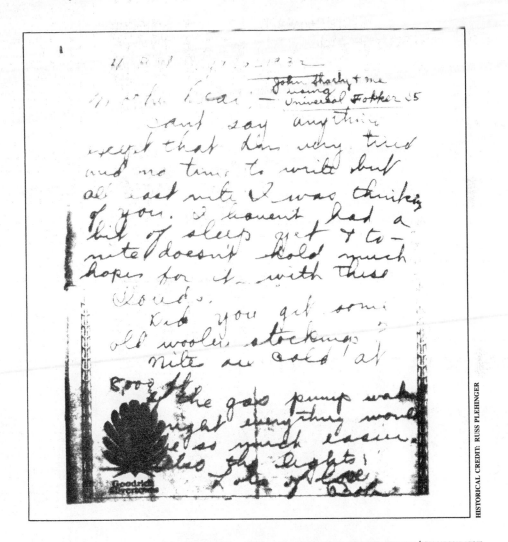

HISTORICAL CREDIT: RUSS PLEHINGER

September 28–30, 1932.   ATTEMPTED FLIGHT RECORD/UNSUCCESSFUL
Landplane endurance record.
Refueled.
Grand Central Air Terminal, Glendale, California.
Evelyn "Bobbi" Trout, Fred Murillo.
Fokker Universal "Spirit of 76"/NR-3317.
220hp Wright J-5 Whirlwind.
Sponsored by Union Oil Company. Takeoff at 2:48PM. Forced down by damaged
    prop. Flight lasted 40h. Refueling crew—Garland Lincoln, Gus Axelson.
    Refueling planes—Douglas M-2 NR-1490, Stinson NR-7738.

PATRONS ARE REQUESTED TO FAVOR THE COMPANY BY CRITICISM AND SUGGESTION CONCERNING ITS SERVICE   1201-S

WESTERN UNION

CLASS OF SERVICE

This is a full-rate Telegram or Cablegram unless its deferred character is indicated by a suitable sign above or preceding the address.

NEWCOMB CARLTON, PRESIDENT   J. C. WILLEVER, FIRST VICE-PRESIDENT

SIGNS

| DL = Day Letter |
| NM = Night Message |
| NL = Night Letter |
| LCO = Deferred Cable |
| CLT = Cable Letter |
| W'T = Week-End Letter |

The filing time as shown in the date line on full-rate telegrams and day letters, and the time of receipt at destination as shown on all messages, is STANDARD TIME.

Received at 6360 Hollywood Blvd., Hollywood, Calif.   Phone GLadstone 4191

SA71 36 .2 EXTRA VIA DLY DL=RYE NY 13 110P

MISS BOBBIE TROUT=

TRY 6606 SUNSET HOLLYWOOD CALIF

WAS THRILLED AND OVERWHELMED AT HONOR OF YOUR INVITATION
BUT CANNOT GET WEST AT THIS TIME AM WISHING YOU EVERY
LUCK AND SUCCESS IN THE WORLD BOBBIE DEAR WITH MY BESTEST
LOVE TO YOU=

RUTH NICHOLS.

Telegram from
Bobbi's friend, Ruth
Nichols.

Bobbi and all her
Mickey Mouse
friends!

Chapter Twelve

Women's Air Reserve Goes To Gilmore

DURING the year that she worked for Cycloplane, Bobbi heard rumors of a flying club, strictly for women, forming in New York. She was enthusiastic about the idea, thinking this type of organization was just what women in aviation needed. When the Betsy Ross Corporation was formed, she and the other Los Angeles women fliers immediately joined. However, it somehow didn't catch on well enough, and the membership fizzled out.

A month or so later the New Yorkers tried again. This time it was better organized and was called the Women's Aeronautical Air Force. Uniforms were ordered, and everything went well for a few months, but again interest lagged. At last the western women decided to form a new organization. Pancho Barnes was the principal organizer. A viable plan emerged from their meetings, and the Women's Air Reserve, W.A.R., was born. It was registered in Washington, D.C., with the Department of Commerce, and Bureau of Air Commerce.

The purpose of the W.A.R. was to aid in disasters, where it was impossible to reach people in need of medical attention, except by plane. The group wore military uniforms and trained in first aid, navigation and military maneuvers. They consisted mainly of doctors, nurses, fliers, and parachutists who could go directly to the scene of the disaster by air, or at least have the know-how to drop medication and first aid equipment to the survivors on the ground. They also trained to help in case war broke out; they wanted to be prepared.

The W.A.R. had a bona-fide doctor enrolled. Dr. Emma McNair Kittridge, known as Kit, was the first woman doctor appointed by the Bureau of Air Commerce for the express purpose of checking on the health of any pilot obtaining a license, or renewal of a license, and okaying them for flying. The W.A.R. met on Monday nights of each week and studied first aid under Kit. On the first Sunday of each month, they drilled on the Army Parade Grounds at Long Beach, which had been generously offered to them by Army Air Corps officers. They also practiced their marching at Alhambra Airport and Mines Field. Their drilling proficiency improved. The months passed, and the sounds of marching feet and the strident voice of Captain Mary Wiggins, a perfectionist, yelling to keep in cadence echoed across the field. Bobbi thought they looked like a bunch of tin soldiers doing their marching; it was a waste of time.

WAR regulation book and Preamble. Bobbi's membership cards.

Typical membership application for Women's Air Reserve (WAR).

PREAMBLE

The name of this organization shall be the WOMEN'S AIR RESERVE.

❧

The primary object of this organization shall be to train women pilots in practical mechanics, as pertaining to any skilled workmanship, academic work, and in flying, so that they may be qualified and available for military or civic service in these UNITED STATES OF AMERICA in any national or civil emergency.

❧

It shall be the aim of the WOMEN'S AIR RESERVE to build and maintain an organization in so far as may be practicable along the tenor of the AIR CORPS, UNITED STATES ARMY.

❧

Jan 1934

Allen, Jean 2nd Lt. 1742 N. Edgemont, LosAngeles Mo 17307

Barnes, Florence Lowe Col. 1350 Gabfield, San Marino Syc 1011
Benson, Margaret Private 1317 N. Crescent Hts Cr 12650
Bond (Fikes) Edith 1st Lt. R3 Box 276 Santa Cruz, Calif
Braun, Friedel Cadet 303 So. Central, Glendale Du 9351
Bronish, Estelle Sherman Private 1458 Euclid Santa Mon SM28683

Chapman, Gertrude Marie Cadet United Airport, Burbank Va 6151
Charles, Mary Capt. 2716 Reservoir St. Los Angeles, Calif
Culver, Gladys Vivienne Private 3114 West 75th L. A. Ca 3161
Curley, Eileen Lt. St. Arthur Apts., Santa Monica SM 27173

Deems, Sylvia M. Private 227 St. Joseph, Long Beach LB815-88
Drake (Chaffee) Nancy Capt. 1669 La Cresta Drive Pasadena
Sta 3704Colo 2521
Dudrey, Frances I Cadet 1958 N. Normandie L. A. Mo 16062

Fyle, Gretchen 2nd Lt 1125 Tower Road Beverly Hills Ox 0617
Fyle, Marybeth, 2nd Lt "   "   "   "   "(reported wed)

Gilliland, Peggy 2nd Lt 520 East Elk Glendale Douglas 6973
Glidden, Elizabeth Private 305 West Laurel Sierra Madre SM 3224
Gorby (Beard) Melba Capt 756½ S Marengo Pasadena Terr 1740

Inwood, Elizabeth Kelly 2nd Lt 201 So. Granada Alhambra 649 J

Lawhorn, Della 323 E. 6th St. Downey Tel Downey 43230
Lyon, Bebe Daniels Cadet 972 Ocean F

Mantz, Myrtle Lt. United Airport, Bru
McCandless, Helen M. 1420 So. Bonnie
Mc Gaffey, Georgialee 2nd Lt. Clovert
Merrell, Frances Private 42 Glendora,
Mertens, Ruth 2nd Lt 222 North Ave 5
Miller, Julia Anna 112 So. Westmorel
Morgan, Mildred Capt 5818 McAndrew Dr
Murphy Margaret Private 4210 Lincoln

Neill, Viola 1st Lt. 1801 W San Ferna
O'Connell, Josphine 1414 So. Hope L

Peacock, nchsa % Fellows & Stewart, W
Selck, Bee Private 2131 So. Hoover P
Sherman, Peggy Master Sgr Moana Hotel
Sloan, Vinetta-Mary Lou Apts Long Bea
Spirito, Yolanda Capt 896 N Raymond
Sprague, Valentine Capt. Monarch Hote
Trout, Bobbie Capt. 418 So. Soto L.
Van, Ruth, 1376 N. Ridgewood Place, L
Walker, Vera Dawn Capt. 677 So. Westl
Wallce, Marguerite 679 So. Ardmore,
Wiggins, Mary Cadet 1376 No. Ridgewo
Williams, Mary 230 Brighton Burbank
Willis, Patty 1st Lt. 2721 Bellvue Av
Wilson, Dorothea 2nd Lt. 100 N. Broad
Wice, Josephine PERSONNEL SQUADRON #1

Anona Hansen, in 1931, as a member of the newly formed Marvel Crosson Glider Club.

CREDIT: ANONA HANSEN BROWN

WAR's original membership list, January, 1934.

Letter from Capt. Bobbi Trout, new Squadron Commander, requesting attendance of a WAR meeting on Nov. 19, 1933.

Women's Air Reserve
HEADQUARTERS—U S ARMY AIR BASE
LONG BEACH, CALIFORNIA

BULLETIN

Nov. 11, 1933

TO THE PERSONNEL:
SUBJECT: Regular Meeting

1.(a) A Regular Meeting of the Women's Air Reserve will be held at their headquarters at the Officers Club, U. S. Army Air Base, Long Beach, California. *Nov. 19th - 10 AM*

(b) One Hundred Per Cent Attendance is requested as the Reserve has missed a Regular Meeting and there is much business and many plans to be put into action.

2.   It is the hope of the new Squadron Commander that the girls will be ready to put forth their best effort, bearing in mind the real spirit of the Women's Air Reserve, which is a patriotic organization for which the country has an especial need at this time as it has need of every organized and truly loyal unit.

Bobbi Trout

CAPTAIN BOBBIE TROUT
SQUADRON COMMANDER
1st Squadron, 9th Corps Area

CREDIT: ANONA HANSEN BROWN

WESTERN AIR COLLEGE
Airport Management, Inc.
ALHAMBRA AIRPORT
620·E·VALLEY BLVD.
ALHAMBRA, CALIFORNIA
ATLANTIC 26891

September 20, 1938

Miss Bobby Trout
2400 E. Fourth
Los Angeles, California

Dear Bobby:

Enclosed find flight course that we more
or less follow. In drawing up this course,
I have taken it for granted that the
student is "plenty dumb." So naturally
the average student would not require
quite so much check time.

Don't worry, I'll not forget you in the
first trip I have in the Stinson, where
I only have two passengers.

Yours very truly,

WESTERN AIR COLLEGE

W. H. Coffin
Chief Pilot

WHC:vaw

*A WAR gathering at Alhambra Airport
waiting for a chance to fly. (left to right)
Monte Orman, Carolyn Terrill, Bobbi, Mary
Pike, and Gale "Smitty" Smith.*

*Charlie Babb, from whom Bobbi
purchased her J-5 Stearman
for $3500.*

Waldo Young taught Bobbi to ride his motorcycle about 1923. Waldo was a long-time service station customer and very good friend.

Margaret Sugars Kane, Hank Coffin, and Bobbi at Hank's Western Air College.

Bobbi and Myrtle "Mitzi" Mantz in 1934 on their Indian Pony motorcycles, riding around Paul Mantz's United Airport Terminal.

After one of the Sunday morning W.A.R. marches, Dr. Peggy McClean, Mary Wiggins, and Bobbi decided to rent a Kinner Fleet to make a flying trip up the San Joaquin Valley. The day was beautiful, the sky was blue, and the women knew they just wanted to go flying, but did not have a destination in mind. They took turns piloting, and Bobbi started out for Bakersfield. They refueled, and it was now Mary's turn to pilot. Mary, seated in the back, was a very good pilot by now. The other girls were in the front.

About noon, Mary made an uneventful takeoff to the north and they were on their way to Visalia. After the one-hour flight, Mary made a perfect landing and used the rudder to keep the plane on a straight line. While Mary's feet were on the rudder, her right foot slipped

down a few inches. Her tall boots had regular boot heels about an inch high, and her right heel caught between the front end of the floorboard and the rudder pedal. She frantically tried to remove her heel. Before it could stop, the plane veered sharply and ground-looped. Mary was only going forty miles per hour, but she did not have enough time to free her heel. The plane spun to the right and stopped, with a damaged lower right wing.

People came out of the Visalia Airport offices and hangars and helped get the plane off the runway. It was towed back to the hangars, and the girls sat all afternoon waiting for help. They called the plane's owner, Hank Coffin, at Alhambra Airport and waited for someone to arrive and help. They were anxious to get home.

California Women Flyers Form Air Reserve Unit

Members of the California Women's Air reserve, which has been organized at Los Angeles as a defense unit in event of national emergency. Most of them are flyers of long experience. Included in the group are Nancy Drake, Viola Neill, Yolanda Spirite, Lavelle Sweeley, Patty Willia. Florence Barnes, Alice J. Kelly, Beatrice Selck, Mildred Morgan, Vinetta Slaon, Eileen Curley, Lean Thomas, and Valentine Prague.

Some of the Women's Air Reserve, 1934.

About midnight, help arrived, and the situation was evaluated. The wing was not terribly damaged, but it still had to be repaired before anyone could fly the plane. The women arrived home by automobile in the early morning hours. They were most heartsick because the day had started out so beautifully. The next day the girls were back at work, but tired.

One weekend Bobbi was with her friend, Bea Selck, and they were riding in the countryside on Bobbi's Indian Pony Motorcycle. The orange trees were blossoming, filling the air with their alluring aroma. Close to El Monte, Bobbi and Bea rode through a subdivided walnut grove. On the outskirts of El Monte they spotted a "FOR SALE" sign in front of a partially built home. It was Bobbi's idea of her first home away from her mother, and just the thing to get away from city life.

Bobbi bought the house in no time. Her new moneymaking scheme was raising jumbo frogs. Since Bobbi had a small ravine crossing the back of her property, and it was the ideal place to put a concrete pond to raise jumbo frogs, she traded her Nash coupe for a dozen jumbo frog breeders. After hard work putting in a concrete pond, finding the necessary plants and green growth, Bobbi anticipated that money would come rolling in. Frogs produced thousands of eggs a year, and by the fall of 1933, Bobbi could see the pond full of tadpoles, swimming to their hearts' content. Each day Bobbi and her friends checked on the tadpole growth.

In the summer of 1933, fires in the hills around Los Angeles were terrible. Most of the watershed growth was burned in this fire, especially around the La Crescenta and Tujunga areas. On New Year's Eve, 1934, it rained hard. The entire Los Angeles area was flooded. Bobbi watched the water come up in her back yard, and her ravine overflow. When the water came to the edge of her home, she decided it was time to leave her house and frogs.

Two days later, when the water began to recede, Bobbi returned to her house. She found the concrete pool washed out, and her aspiring business venture washed away. Discouraged with the catastrophe and longing to get back into flying, Bobbi sold the house to Denny, moved back home with her mother, and used the money from the sale of her home to purchase a J-5 Stearman from the Glendale dealer, Charlie Babb, who was located at Grand Central Airport in a big hangar. Two years later, Bobbi returned to that area on a rainy day drive, and heard nothing but frogs croaking. She wondered how she could round up her valuable lost frogs.

Aviatrices Form Emergency Corps

Bobbie Trout

Part of the corps

Mrs. Frorence Barnes

LOS ANGELES America's women flyers decided to take a leaf from the books of Soviet Russia's aviatrices and demonstrate that they, too, are able to compete with men in handling ships of the skies.

This decision is due mainly to the fact that they still are smarting from the humiliation of being excluded from the recent National Air races in Cleveland, because "women and other amateur flyers" reportedly tended to rob the aviation of its thrills and "slow down the speed tournaments."

Two of the queens of the air, Mrs. Florence "Pancho" Lowe Barnes, chubby California pilot, and slim Bobby Trout, who have handled planes with veteran skill during recent years, are leading a group of famous feminine flyers in demonstrations to show how indispensable and useful they can be.

Unlike their Russian sky sisters who are thickly scattered among the powerful bombing squadrons and handle the stick of scores of huge passenger planes, America's women flyers always have had to take second choice "pickings," they contend.

"We can't handle machine guns or war planes," they declare, "but there are other jobs we'll be able to take over."

Ever-smiling "Pancho" Barnes, whose paternal grandfather was a famous balloonist during the Civil war, virtually has lived and breathed aeronautics since she was a child. And when air meets became the rage, "Pancho" and her friends became familiar figures at the tournaments.

Slick-haired Bobbie Trout, who likes to wear mannish looking garb most of the time, climbed into the air from behind a west coast store counter.

Now she and Mrs. Barnes are going to lead the women flyers to show how they can battle for mankind during peace years and wartime. From the air, they'll help fight floods, forest fires, riots, or whatever else comes up in the way of catastrophe, tragedy and disaster.

They've developed a technique for emergency relief work, too. For stricken areas unapproachable except by plane, they'll drop food and medical supplies by means of parachutes.

America's women flyers are on the warpath. Not yet recovered from the humiliation of being barred from participating in the National Air Races, held recently in Cleveland, the aviatrices are determined to make themselves worthwhile and "show up" the men. Under the leadership of Mrs. Florence (Pancho) Barnes and Bobbie Trout, of California, they are organizing an emergency flying corps for use in case of forest fires, floods, earthquakes and other disasters.

Aerial Ambulance Service
L.A. Eastside Airport
300 Whittier Blvd.
Montebello
Calif.

John Nagel
Manager

W.A.R. had full use of John Nagel's ambulance ship for emergencies.

1936 gathering of some W.A.R. members.
From left: Bobbi, Smitty, Peggy, unidentified, Pike, Edie, Ruth, D. Kit, Joe, and Gere below.

Women Will Fly to March Field

Women airplane pilots of Southern California yesterday completed arrangements for the invasion Sunday of March Field, the Army's flying base near Riverside.

Approximately 25 members of the 99ers and the Women's Air Reserve will fly to March Field during Sunday, it was announced.

Those reported "rarin' to go" include Bobby Trout, Mary Wiggins, Mary Pike, Hilda Jarmouth, Ethel Sheehy, Wilma Fritchy, Dorothy George, Dorothy Ruther, Evelyn Kilgore and Lucille Orman.

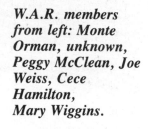

W.A.R. members from left: Monte Orman, unknown, Peggy McClean, Joe Weiss, Cece Hamilton, Mary Wiggins.

W.A.R. members at airport for Sunday morning exercises: (left to right) Peggy McClean, Joe Weiss, unknown, Cece Hamilton, Mary Wiggins and Monte Orman.

VOL. 3 NO. 9   Published by GILMORE OIL COMPANY   SEPTEMBER, 1934

WOMEN START NATION AIR TOUR

RED LION FLIGHT OF WOMEN'S AIR RESERVE WINS GILMORE AID FOR ADVANCE OF AVIATION AMONG WOMEN. PHOTO SHOWS THE 3-SHIP FLIGHT ON LINE, WITH PILOTS AND CO-PILOTS AT THEIR SHIPS. Left to right—COL. FLORENCE LOWE BARNES AND LIEUT. VIOLA NEILL, CAPT. BOBBIE TROUT AND CAPT. NANCY DRAKE CHAFFEE, CAPT. MARY CHARLES AND LIEUT. PATTY WILLIS.

AVIATRICES IN CROSS-COUNTRY HOP

CREDIT: GILMORE OIL COMPANY

*Bobbi and the gang
ready to begin
transcontinental trip.*

WOMEN'S GROUP IN FORMATION FLIGHT TO EASTERN AIR RACES

The first transcontinental formation flight by members of the Women's Air Reserve, was launched at 7:20 this morning from Union Air Terminal, when six officers of the organization in this area took off for the National Air races and Atlantic seaboard points in three planes, under command of Col. Florence Lowe Barnes, with Capt. Mary Charles executive officer.

Having ships of one make and all painted alike in cream and red colors, the detachment presented a smart appearance in formation as the women pilots and co-pilots took the air lane in the two-seaters equipped with dual controls.

Pilots of the ships are Colonel Barnes, with Lieutenant Viola Neill as co-pilot; Capt. Mary Charles, with Lieut. Patty Willis as co-pilot, and Capt. Bobbie Trout, with Capt. Nancy Drake-Chaffee as co-pilot. Besides participating at the Cleveland air races, the women are to visit Chicago, New York, Philadelphia and, most important, Langley

field for official consultation with department of commerce aeronautic advisors and inspectors. Dr. Emma McNair Kittredge, flight surgeon of W. A. R. here, is expected to join them somewhere in the east, it was reported.

Safe and sane flying is the order given by Colonel Barnes and no spectacular speed efforts are to be made. Eastbound to the races, easy hops were scheduled to include Kingman, possibly Winslow, Albuquerque, Amarillo, Wichita, Kansas City, Indianapolis and Cleveland.

The tour was made possible for the women, Mrs. Barnes explained, by the generosity of the Gilmore Oil Co. in furtherance of aviation among women, and the uniformity of paint jobs for the ships also was credited to this company. In recognition of this aid, the fliers adopted the red lion as insignia for the flight, and military men among the airport attaches promptly dubbed the three ships the "Red Lion Flight" in the manner of groups.

The W.A.R. began to flourish when more women joined. In order to increase membership, they needed publicity, and the group asked the Gilmore Oil Company if they would finance a trip to New York City for six women fliers and three airplanes. All three ships would be Stearman biplanes with the Gilmore colors painted on the ships, together with the company emblem. It would make an outstanding gimmick for Gilmore and garner the W.A.R. a lot of press coverage.

Gilmore accepted, and gave the W.A.R. leader, General Pancho Barnes, five hundred dollars to pay for the gasoline, oil, and supplies. Gilmore Oil Company also painted their three Stearman planes "Gilmore Yellow" with red trim and painted its insignia, the red Gilmore lion.

Nancy Chaffee flew with Pancho in her J-5 Stearman, Patty Willis flew with Mary Charles in her J-6-7, and Viola Neill (Washburn) flew with Bobbi in her newly purchased J-5.

On August 31, 1934, dressed in their W.A.R. uniforms and with hopes high, they took off for New York, making side trips to Cleveland, Washington, D.C., and Philadelphia along the way. Mary Charles and Patty Willis made it only as far as Meteor Crater, near Winslow, Arizona, before having to set down, being out of gas. The landing gear was damaged so badly on landing that it was impossible for them to continue. Mary and Patty returned to Los Angeles broken-hearted. This accident cost the trio a flying job with Gilmore Oil Company.

Pancho, Bobbi, Nancy, and Vi taking a break shortly before taking off for the Cleveland Air Races and New York.

Nancy, Vi, Pancho, and Bobbi ready for eastern take-off.

CREDIT: VIOLA NEILL

(right) Viola Neill on a hiking trip.

Bobbi and her Stearman after the eastern trip.

The two remaining ships flew on to Cleveland, landing at the National Air Races where they spent a week being entertained and renewing old friendships. Their next stop was Washington, D.C., where Pancho, Nancy, Viola, and Bobbi made a scary, but uneventful landing on a dark and unlighted field. Phoebe J. Fairgraves Omlie met them at the airport and had arranged for a motorcycle escort for the group through the city to her home. Phoebe won a major triumph for women pilots three years previously when she placed first in the 1931 National Sweepstakes Race from California to Cleveland. It had been the first major air race in which women were allowed to compete with men.

Earlier, in 1932, Phoebe flew around the country promoting the election of Franklin D. Roosevelt during his presidential campaign. Through this contact, she was appointed Special Assistant for Air Intelligence on the National Advisory Committee for Aeronautics at Wright Field. In this capacity, she set out to air-mark every city and town in the United States with signs painted in a conspicuous place—usually a rooftop—to give pilots their bearings. She and her co-worker, Amelia Earhart, enlisted the aid of several famous eastern women fliers of the 1930s, including Louise Thaden, Blanche Noyes, Helen Richey, Helen McCloskey, and Nancy Harkness.

Enjoying conversation at Peggy Rex's home, September 5, 1934.

THREE GIRL PILOTS FROM WEST COAST HERE

United Air Terminal on August 31, 1934, flying via Kingman, Arizona and on to Winslow, Arizona. Arrived in Cleveland on September 4, 1934. Spent one week at the Cleveland Air Races and continued to Washington D.C. and Philadelphia, arriving September 18, 1934. Final destination: New York City.

Phoebe was a wonderful hostess. With Pancho's jovial personality, the two kept them laughing for hours with their anecdotes. While Pancho took care of personal business, Phoebe took Bobbi, Viola, and Nancy on a tour of the famous landmarks in the nation's capital: the White House, Mount Vernon, Tomb of the Unknown Soldier, and Annapolis, where they saw the Naval Academy. Bobbi especially enjoyed

the U.S. Mint tour. She watched all those beautiful bills rolling off the press and was amazed to see the printers rubbing the plates with ink by hand. Turning to Phoebe, she said, "Wouldn't it be wonderful if they gave out samples?" Phoebe acknowledged the comment with a pained smile, for it was not the first time that comment had been made.

Five Women Of Air Reserve Arrive Here

Five women . . . all high fliers . . . arrived in Philadelphia yesterday from California.

They are Dr. Emma Kittridge, the first woman to be appointed medical examiner by the aeronautic division of the U. S. Department of Commerce, and four women pilots, members of the Women's Air Reserve of Los Angeles.

This organization is the first flying medical unit composed of women in the United States. Sixteen women fliers, six of them nurses, are members of the Reserve.

They aim to give medical care in times of disaster or distress—fire, flood or famine—using the advantages of air service.

The planes by which the four pilots flew here from California are at Patco Airport, outside of Philadelphia. They started from Los Angeles with three, but one was forced down in Arizona.

Record Flight by Women.

"This is the first cross-country formation flight of women pilots."

explained Dr. Kittridge, when interviewed at the Woman's Medical College Hospital, of which she is a graduate. "The flight was broken by various stops along the way. We stayed for a time in Cleveland to see the air races, and also spent some time in Washington.

"Our organization is patriotic. We realize that when medical care is needed by a large number of sufferers, communication and transportation are two important obstacles which must be overcome. We aim to bring to medical care the advantages of radio and aviation, and to show that women are capable of rendering the same efficient service in these lines as men.

Parachute Jumpers.

"One phase of service which our organization renders is to contact land when the conditions are such that it is impossible to land the plane. We have a division of parachute jumpers who can land by jumping. They are equipped with first aid kit and radio apparatus, can make a survey of the situation, and send back a radio report to headquarters so that further assistance may be planned and given."

The party of women fliers looked attractive and businesslike in their regimentals of horizon blue, with black belts, ties, berets and puttees.

One of their number, Captain Bobbie Trout, Los Angeles, broke the first endurance record for women in the air. Colonel Florence Lowe Barnes, San Marino; Captain Nancy Drake, Pasadena, and Lieutenant Viola Neill, R. N., Burbank, California, are also members of the flying squadron. Miss Neill is in charge of the medical work. Colonel Barnes and Captain Drake are both married. Dr. Kittridge isn't . . . yet.

Eligible for Membership.

"Any woman pilot," explained Dr. Kittridge, "is eligible for membership in the Reserve. Of course, she has to prove that she is the fearless, daring type of person who is willing to take risks, and do really hard work."

Asked what women she regarded as important in the flying field, Dr. Kittridge named Amelia Earhart for her spectacular flight of the Atlantic, and Phoebe Fairgrave Omlie, Special Assistant for Air Intelligence, at Washington, D. C. "From the point of view of technical knowledge Miss Omlie has done more to advance the place of women in aviation than any other woman in this country," Dr. Kittridge said.

Meanwhile, Pancho tried to arrange the release of her European friend, Duncan Renaldo. Renaldo, the mascot of the Women's Air Reserve, was an actor who overstayed his visa in the United States and was detained, by United States authorities, in New York. Renaldo was finally released, and later became famous for his role as the Cisco Kid.

A week passed, and Pancho had no luck in Washington, but she was determined to pursue her cause when they reached New York City. From Washington, they headed for Philadelphia to meet Kit. They visited her alma mater, the Woman's Medical College, where a press conference was set up to welcome them.

The next morning, after a drive through Prospect Park, they were forced to wait at the airport until the fog lifted. When it had at last burned off, they began the last lap of their journey.

Soon, they could see the towering skyscrapers of New York City ahead of them.

Shortly afterwards, Bobbi and Pancho were flying wing tip to wing tip around the Statue of Liberty. They then headed for Floyd Bennett Airport, named for the man who was Admiral Richard Byrd's pilot on his first flight over the North Pole. They were greeted at the airport by members of the press and had to explain the absence of the third airplane. After detailing Mary Charles's mishap, they were escorted to the plush St. Moritz Hotel to rest and prepare for a gala press and cocktail party that evening.

Dressed in their military W.A.R. uniforms, the four women arrived at the party. Shocked murmurs circulated among the crowd and members of the press. Someone finally explained that it was against the law in New York City for a female to wear masculine attire in public. Their full blue dress uniforms consisted of jackets and pants. "In the eyes of the law," one reporter haughtily informed them, "you are impersonating a male."

THE PHILADELPHIA INQUIRER,

NOTED WOMEN FLIERS VISIT CITY

CREDIT: PHILADELPHIA INQUIRER

The above group was photographed yesterday at the Woman's Medical College, Henry ave. and Abbottsford rd., when Dr. Emma Kitteridge (at the right in front), flight surgeon of the Women's Air Reserve of California, visited the college, from which she graduated in 1929. Beside Dr. Kitteridge is Dr. Martha Tracy, dean. In the rear are four widely-known women fliers who accompanied Dr. Kitteridge. They are, left to right: Colonel Florence Lowe Barnes, Captain Nancy Chaffee. Captain "Bobby" Trout and Lieutenant Violet Neill, R. N.

Bobbi could not understand. She had been wearing pants almost all her life, and it was no crime in California. It was so impractical to wear a dress while piloting a plane. Alma Whittier, a columnist for the Los Angeles Times, had recently written a long article describing Bobbi and Marlene Dietrich as style setters for the "slacks" generation.

Among the guests was Gert Yancey, wife of Lon Yancey, a famous pilot and navigator. Lon was on a flying mission at the time, so Gert had brought her friend Edie Curtis in his place. Later, Bobbi would become good friends with Edie after Edie moved to Los Angeles. Edie worked in the publicity department of the national Girl Scouts, and her office was within walking distance of the St. Moritz.

W.A.R. in Cleveland (left to right): Peggy Rex, unidentified, General Barnes, Nancy Chaffee, Bobbi Trout, Viola Neill, Dr. Emma Kittridge Quinn and friend. This was taken while they attended the Cleveland Air Races.

Lon Yancey was a famous pilot and navigator.

Women Fliers Hop for West After Spanning Nation

The four women spent almost a month in New York City. Bobbi, Viola, and Nancy sometimes accompanied Pancho to visit various officials, lending support in her cause, but more often explored the city. The girls saw all the sights from Staten Island to Greenwich Village, rode the merry-go-round in Central Park, walked down Fifth Avenue, visited Times Square, and went to plays and movies. One evening they even went to see Gypsy Rose Lee do her striptease act in Greenwich Village. Afterwards they were invited to her apartment, where she read poetry to them. She was a charming hostess.

Fall weather had already started to turn the leaves in Central Park to red and gold. Pancho was at last persuaded to abort her mission of freeing Duncan Renaldo in New York City. They wanted to stay, but they knew that their cash reserves were perilously low.

With a few dollars left, and after paying their bill at the St. Moritz, they headed back to Washington. Pancho insisted on making a final plea for Renaldo's release there. Once again they were the guests of Phoebe while Pancho pursued her crusade. At last Pancho was able to get justice moving, and the others persuaded her that Renaldo was going to be released, they were tired and running out of money, and it was time to go home.

BOBBY TROUT   "PANCHO BARNES"
Pictures from International News Photo Service.

Bobbi and Pancho in the news.

Yesterday, four women draped about a suite of a mid-town hotel discussed New York shops, styles and queer funny places where they might go for luncheon and cocktails.

Today, their shiny, vivid nails presenting a brilliant contrast to the horizon blue of their uniforms, these four women flyers, members of the Women's Air Reserve of the United States, took off at Floyd Bennett Field en route for Chicago, the World's Fair, and more queer, funny places, where they can have luncheon and cocktails.

They are Commander Florence Lowe "Pancho" Barnes, Captain Bobby Trout, Captain Nancy Drake and Lieutenant Viola Neil, the first women flyers to complete a transcontinental formation hop from California to New York.

HOLDS SPEED RECORD.

"Pancho' Barnes, founder and head of the Women's Air Reserve, holder of the women's world speed record in 1930, and mother of a 12-year-old son, is an aviatrix by birthright. Her grandfather, General Thadeus Lowe, organized the first military air unit in this country during the Civil War, having five balloons and 50 men under his command and was credited with saving the Union Army on two occasions. When she was a small child, her grandfather took "Pancho" to the first air meet of the world, held in 1910 at San Domingo air field in California.

Bobby Trout, the girl flyer of 25, who looks like a boy of 16, needs no introduction. The first woman endurance flyer of the country, she holds four world's records; two for solo endurance flying and two first refueling records.

Nancy Drake, whose husband is a well-known California sportsman, is captain of Squadron No. 1, of California. Someone led Nancy to a flying field seven years ago and said they'd teach her how to fly. She said "swell." And the pretty red-haired girl has been up in the air, figuratively and literally ever since.

FOURTH OF GROUP.

The fourth member of the group is Viola Neil, who is seeing the East for the first time and getting a tremendous kick out of it. Lieutenant Neil is a registered nurse and chief of the Medical Detachment of the W. A. R.

Bobbi packed her few remaining articles in the bag and snapped the lock shut. She slipped her arms into her jacket and shivered in anticipation of the biting cold outside. She put on several layers of clothing to combat the freezing weather, but knew that the flight back to the West Coast would undoubtedly be a cold one.

They borrowed money from Phoebe and headed for California, sleeping in airport hangars, and having nothing to eat but a few sandwiches. It was quite a comedown from the flight out. Bobbi, Viola, Pancho, and Nancy arrived back at United Airport two months later, October 28, 1934, in the late afternoon. Bobbi had seven cents in her pocket. Friends transported the four tired and broke fliers to their homes.

Reserve Displays Methods

If flood prevents planes from landing, Capt. Bobby Trout shows how she will push food and medical supplies out of the medical corps plane as it dives toward a stricken family.

Chapter Thirteen

Women's Air Reserve Antics

SHORTLY after the Women's Air Reserve returned from New York, Kit asked Bobbi if she would like to fly to Parker Dam so she could visit her fiance, Dr. William Quinn. The next day Bobbi, Kit, and Viola Neill took off in Bobbi's Stearman J-5.

On the way, Bobbi landed at March Field to gas up for the trip. She was perturbed to discover that they were out of regular gas, which her J-5 required. The commanding officer, however, sent two cadets to Riverside for the right gas, and the trio were on their way, two hours behind schedule.

Dr. Quinn expected the trio to arrive by noon and, not being a flier, became frantic, thinking the worst. He told his friends he should not have trusted a woman pilot to deliver his precious Kit to him. After their safe arrival, and learning the reason for the delay, he apologized profusely for even thinking such terrible things about women pilots. After his marriage to Kit, the W.A.R. adopted him as another mascot.

Life in the W.A.R. was never dull. Some Sundays, after drilling at the Long Beach Army Airport, the W.A.R. had a quick sandwich and went to San Pedro Harbor, where W.A.R. officer Peggy McClean kept a sailboat. In their uniforms and hard-heel boots, they scrambled onto the boat. Everyone had a chance to steer during the trip. Peggy was the only good sailor among them, but what the others lacked in skill, they made up in enthusiasm.

Vi, Kit, and Bobbi readying for take-off from Parker Dam visit, Circa 1934.

A group of the W.A.R. enjoying a Sunday afternoon on Peggy's sailboat at San Pedro Harbor.

The weather was gusty one Sunday, but not bad enough to cancel their plans. They started out under sail heading toward the ocean, only to come upon a sand bar. Much to their embarrassment, many other boaters began to watch their antics. The W.A.R. members acquired an audience. Their boat moved steadily toward the sea gull-occupied sand bar—there was no way to avoid it. Peggy gave orders for Bobbi to grab the boat hook and fend them off the sand bar.

Bobbi made a dash for the boat hook, aimed it at the sand bar, and leaned on it in hopes that it would meet with resistance. The porous sand caused the hook to become embedded, sent the sea gulls squawking away, and made the shore crowd of people laugh. The sailors felt very foolish, especially since they were dressed in their uniforms. With the oars and much work, the sailors got back to shore safely.

Other weekends, they drove to Santa Barbara, where they practiced archery. One occasion, after practice, they went to a Mexican restaurant for dinner. It was dark inside, and they were seated before their eyes became adjusted to the candlelight. The W.A.R. members accidentally chose an established high-class society restaurant. People around them were dressed in beautiful dresses and summer suits. Bobbi tried to slink down into her seat, but their uniform shirts and slacks could not be hidden.

Bobbi being greeted by one of the March Field officers.

Bobbi, Kit and Bill Quinn (her fiancé) just after landing at Parker Dam for a short visit.

Kit, Vi, and Bobbi arriving at Parker Dam.

(left to right) Margaret Perry, Pancho Barnes, Bobbi, Art Gobel, and Vera Dawn Walker enjoying an evening at Pancho's.

W.A.R. members in Santa Barbara around 1937. From left to right: Edie Curtis, Bobbi, Smitty Smith, Ruth Vargas, Peggy McClean and Patty Willis.

Once again Bobbi and the others had inadvertently furthered their image of pants-wearing females.

There were also jovial and fun times on weekends. Once the W.A.R. members did some target practice with pistols in a remote area. Edie Curtis, who was from New York, claimed she had been shanghaied into the W.A.R. group for comedy relief alone. She knew nothing about nursing, parachuting, doctoring or flying, but wanted to be part of the group.

Looking back, there were foolish things Bobbi did as a young woman that she wouldn't do today. One time Bobbi and Edie walked to a ravine where a target full of dents hung from a tree. The iron target was old and had become rusted from being outdoors for a long time. Most of the painted circles had become obliterated and the shooter's score could only be seen if someone climbed the tree and watched over her shoulder to see where the shot landed.

The bullets often ricocheted. This happened when Edie was taking her turn at calling the score. She received a direct hit on her back end from the ricocheting bullet. It turned into a colorful bruise. Later Edie found out two other girls received a similar bullet in the same place. All had a big laugh over what could have been an embarrassing situation.

Women's Air Reserve Displays Emergency Methods for Disasters

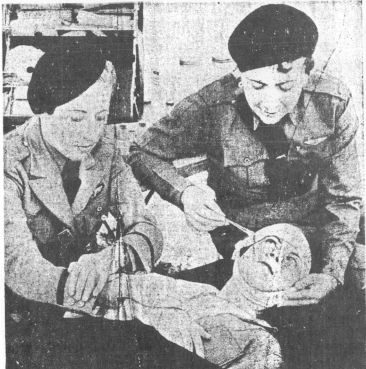 

Skilled women nurses and doctors will take care of the injured. Lieut. Viola Neill, registered nurse, and Lieut. Emma Kittridge, M.D., demonstrate. Grace Cooper plays the part of patient. At the Oxnard airport opening the medical corps will give first aid to any injured.

Ready to rush aid in disasters, Mrs. Paul Mantz of the Women's Air Reserve shows how she will take a call. The Reserve will attend Oxnard's airport opening Thursday.

W.A.R.'s picnicking, target practicing and having fun!

Mary Charles was instrumental in arranging for the appointment of five W.A.R. members as honorary aero policewomen by Los Angeles Chief of Police James E. Davis. Chief Davis presented police badges to them and allowed the new members to use the Police Academy for target practice. Bobbi did considerable practice there with a .38 revolver, which she purchased from an officer. She had it worked over with a hair-trigger pull and a new hand grip. At a policewomen's competition shoot, Bobbi won second place. During the day of shooting, she also let an expert marksman shoot cigarettes out of her mouth and shoot holes through a two-inch square piece of cardboard held in her hand.

The W.A.R. members' medical education was often conducted by experts. On one occasion, they invited a snake expert to tell them about rattlesnake bites and effective methods to administer first aid. The "snake man" stood by the desk and he invited them to sit anywhere they wished in the classroom. They sat scattered around the room.

He made his speech, and they studiously made notes. When he finished, he introduced his *piece de resistance*. He had with him a pillowcase containing a live rattlesnake, and he invited the group to sit close up front and get a better view. He had assured them that there was no chance of the snake escaping or biting anyone. To his amazement the women all moved to the front row leaning forward, wanting a closer look.

Bobbi's Chief of Police card originally issued in 1931.

Bobbi at target practice at the Los Angeles Police Academy, 1931.

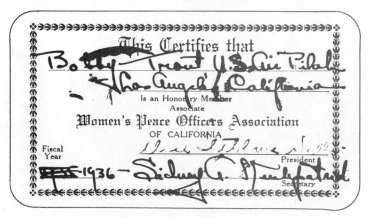

Bobbi's Honorary Member card of the Women's Peace Officers Association.

Air Policewomen Get Honor Today

Members of the Women's International Aeronautic Association will gather today at Riverside Mission Inn to honor the newly organized Aero Policewomen.

The new organization, headed by Mrs. Ulysses Grant McQueen

Members of the International Aeronautic Association honoring the newly organized Aero Policewomen at Mission Inn, Riverside, California.

Bobbi had no problem staying awake during this meeting. She was often kidded about her tendency to fall asleep while in inoperative motion, especially right after dinner. One evening, during a first aid lecture by Kit, Bobbi fell asleep while standing up. Kit was explaining the arterial system of the human body and she pointed to a human skeleton that was used for a training aid. The skeleton had red rubber tubes running through the body to represent the arteries.

In the middle of Kit's lecture, she turned to find Bobbi fast asleep while standing in the group viewing the skeleton. Kit tapped Bobbi on the shoulder, waking her. Later, she told Bobbi to come in for some tests. Kit found that the sugars in Bobbi's body burned immediately after she ate. The body does not normally burn sugars so fast. Bobbi was not a vegetarian, so Kit told Bobbi the solution was to eat more proteins like meat, eggs, and dairy products because they burn slower in the body.

Bobbi began eating a lot of proteins, and to her surprise, she stayed awake until early evening. She was used to falling asleep right after dinner, no matter what company was at her home, or what she was doing. A change in diet paid off in later months. It made her feel better, and in the evening, she could stay awake until nine or ten p.m., no longer being embarrassed by falling asleep wherever she was.

Bobbi especially enjoyed Sundays at the Women's Air Reserve meetings. The W.A.R. regularly reserved three Fleet planes for the members to fly. They arrived at Mines Field shortly after dawn, and were each assigned to their special mission. Each plane carried a pilot and a navigator. The mission for the day was to fly to a certain airport, circle the field, and return within a given time. The destination of each plane was never known before that morning. While the pilots checked out the plane, the navigators figured out the direction, airspeed, groundspeed, and course to be traveled. Their fingers were often blue from the early morning cold while each navigator plotted her pilot's course to a separate location. The pilot could watch the terrain below and enjoy the flight, but the navigator was too busy writing and checking the landmarks, the airspeed, the time when they passed checkpoints, and the altitudes. All this information went into the navigator's log. They had to be accurate because the pilots were instructed to fly as directed—right or wrong, or until they were convinced that the navigator was completely turned around. Her duties really began before they took off and did not end until they returned and the final entry was made at the end of "Remarks."

All of this was good practice for members of the organization, because it helped them to be better equipped for emergencies or any other aviation activity that might present itself in the troubled times prior to World War II. The W.A.R. was a group of very good friends, all dedicated and with one goal in mind.

Aviatrix Shot to Death in Home

Tragedy Takes Life of Former Pretto Bell

(Picture on Page 3.)

Victim in a double tragedy after a day-long quarrel with her husband, Mrs. Pretto Bell Clithero, 28-year-old former girl pilot of Santa Monica, yesterday was found shot to death in her Laramie (Wyo.) home.

Near-by was her husband, Ray Clithero, 40, retired orange grower, formerly of Santa Barbara, who died a short time later.

A maid reported that Clithero shot his young wife and himself after the couple had quarreled throughout the day. Undisturbed in his crib was their six-months-old son.

MADE AIR TOUR

Laramie authorities reported that the Clitheros had resided there since last summer, after a five month honeymoon by airplane through Latin America.

Mrs. Clithero, the former Pretto Bell, daughter of Mrs. Dan R. Bell of 1134 Glendon avenue, Westwood, was a graduate of the Los Angeles campus of the University of California, and a flying enthusiast. Holder of a private pilot's license, she organized a flying club for women in Santa Monica.

Just Plane Sense

By MARION FERGUSON
1454 Lemoyne street.

Let me introduce you to one of California's foremost pilots. To do so, however, we must go to the flier's place of business, the Holly-Wood Craft Co.

We step into the shop.

"Where's Bob?" This after presenting you to Gale Smith, my friend's partner.

"Busy back there with a cabinet order." She nods toward the rear of the shop.

As we walk through the door, into the other room, a young, slim figure in sweater and slacks is bending over a whining table saw.

"Hello, Bob!"

You look surprised as the boyish-looking girl straightens and grins.

Oh, didn't I tell you? This is Bobbie Trout, transport pilot par excellence... Four times the holder of the women's endurance record, her last being in 1931, when she and Edna Mae Cooper stayed aloft nearly 123 hours under very bad flying conditions. Besides that, she has been prominent in cross-country air derbies, shows, and races, and was at one time the only woman test pilot. Bobbie is also a radio operator, captain in the women's air reserve, a trained singer, and...What's she doing here, you ask?...Speak for yourself, Bob, I'm out of breath!

Bobbie leans against the workbench and explains how she and "Smitty," a student flier, opened the shop last year.

"We make anything of wood, from toys to bars...."

She is interrupted by Gale's excited announcement that the cabinet order has just been doubled by telephone.

We make a hurried exit as Bobbie returns to the noisy machinery with renewed vigor.

Bobbie always has liked the roar of motors.

(left) Death of one W.A.R. member and a dear friend of Bobbi's in the 1930's.

A group of W.A.R. members at gunnery practice.

Chapter Fourteen

Inventions and Business

THROUGHOUT the mid-1930s Bobbi's flying was intermittent because of the Depression, and she primarily flew with the W.A.R. Many women were vying for new records, though. Bobbi's friend, Louise Thaden, took the refueling endurance record from her in 1932. Louise and a Texas woman, Frances H. Marsalis, established a new refueling endurance record between August 14–22, 1932, of .ight days, four hours, five minutes.

Frances Marsalis later made another endurance record. She and Helen Richey were up nine days, twenty-two hours, forty-two minutes between December 20–30, 1933. During the flight, their refueling plane ripped a hole in the fabric of their aircraft, and Helen Richey crawled out onto the wings, far from the fuselage, and repaired it. These were risky things few would attempt today.

Helen Richey was the first woman pilot to be hired by an airline, which was the Central Airlines. On December 31, 1934, she made her first flight from Washington D.C. to Detroit, in a Ford Tri-Motor. She was happy in her position until October 1935 when she felt her name encouraged the airline to use her as a lecturer and not as a pilot. Bobbi thought a lot of Helen and was saddened when Helen became despondent over the lack of a steady job and the Depression, and then committed suicide.

When Jacqueline Cochran, head of the ATA's American contingent was recalled to the United States late in 1942 to organize the Women's Airforce Service Pilots (WASP), Helen was placed in charge of the group. She remained in command until April, 1943 when she returned to the United States to be with her seriously-ill mother.

Hearing that Helen was back in the United States, Miss Cochran invited her to join the WASPs. Helen accepted, and after a period of training in Texas she spent 16 months ferrying bombers and fighters from aircraft factories to air bases throughout the nation. When the WASP organization was disbanded in December, 1944 she returned to McKeesport.

Unable to readjust to life in a small town Helen moved to New York City in 1945 and attempted to get a job in aviation as a pilot, instructor or consultant. However, thousands of military pilots who had flown in all parts of the world were returning from service to seek jobs in aviation, and Helen found the doors closed wherever she turned.

Unable to find a job in aviation, and unable to afford private flying, Helen became discouraged. Her small savings dwindled and she moved to a tiny one-room apartment in lower Manhattan where friends watched her grow bitter and despondent with the passing weeks.

She spent more and more time thumbing through her old scrapbooks and thinking about the many wonderful people she had known, like Frances Marsalis and Amelia Earhart, who were gone. During a December visit to McKeesport in 1946 she sadly remarked to her sister Lucille that her flying days were over and life was a bore to her. She appeared listless and withdrawn.

On January 7, 1947 her lifeless body was found sprawled across the bed in her apartment, an empty pill bottle clutched in her hand.

The first lady of the airlines had made her last flight.

CREDIT: GLENN KERFOOT

Article about Helen Richey, first woman pilot instructor for U.S. Army Air Force in 1940. Helen died January 7, 1947.

Bobbi also grieved when her W.A.R. friend, Mary Wiggins, whom she taught to fly, also committed suicide right after she was discharged from the WASPS. Mary had severe back pain from her movie stunt work. She lost her WASP severance pay to a Hollywood con artist. This, plus Mary's severe pain, caused her to be so depressed she put a bullet through her head.

Bobbi keenly felt the loss and was saddened, when the Lindberghs' son had been kidnapped in March 1932.

Another of Bobbi's friends, Amelia, was the first pilot to make a solo trip from Hawaii to California on January 11–12, 1935. Bobbi wanted to make this flight in 1932, and almost did. Lockheed was building an Altair for the flight, and there was a lot of publicity in the west. Bobbi's financial backing, due to the Depression, fell through and Bobbi could not organize the flight before Amelia made it. Amelia's tragic loss on July 2, 1937, stunned Bobbi. That tragedy had once again touched a member of the charmed circle of those who had reached the pinnacle of fame in the aviation world and this was unthinkable.

Anyone who knew that Bobbi was a friend of Amelia's always asked her, "What do you think happened to Amelia?" Bobbi's answer was, "The same thing that happened to many other ocean flyers. They were lost at sea."

Margaret Sugars Kane was a great assistant to Bobbi in her Aero Reclaiming (rivet sorting) business.

LAST SCENE—Mary Wiggins, who doubled for film actresses in spectacular stunts, shown in plane cockpit during recent service as Wasp. Yesterday she ended life.

Veteran Woman Stunt Artist Ends Own Life

In life, Mary Wiggins worshiped excitement.

As a double for such screen stars as Barbara Stanwyck, Dorothy Lamour, Norma Shearer and Claudette Colbert she loved to climb the facades of tall buildings, to leap from a running horse to a speeding automobile, to fly a plane while blindfolded.

Perhaps that is why she chose a sudden death.

Alone in Last Scene

Mary Wiggins apparently had twirled a .25-caliber automatic a time or two and fired into her head.

She had played her last scene alone.

There was no gallery such as had gasped in the days when she made high dives while her clothes were aflame and plunged into a pool of flame. There was no spectacle of a balloon ascension, of driving a motorcycle through a burning building, of being locked in a mail sack and thrown into a swimming pool.

All these things the 35-year-old lover of thrills had done since she was 16 as a double for Madge Bellamy, Mildred Harris, Clara Bow, Bebe Daniels, Lupe Velez, Ruth Chatterton, Eleanor Boardman, Sally Eilers —for a list of actresses and famous pictures too long for her mother to begin recounting.

Despondent and Alone

She had not picked wing walking or parachuting this time. She died despondent, alone.

"I don't know why," sobbed her mother. "She was starting a business with a paint refinishing man a month ago and that fell through but she had plenty of money. I guess she was just disappointed in everything."

Only a few days ago Mary Wiggins had appeared at Monogram Studio in her last picture, one with a tombstone-like title, "Face of Marble."

She came to Hollywood in 1927 after winning State high-diving championships for two years while a high school girl in Florida. Her first roles were as a bathing girl in Mack Sennett productions.

Career of Hazards

Directors quickly learned that the petite (five-foot-two) brunette knew no fear. She learned to fly in 1930 and was off on a career of hazards.

Three years ago she joined the Wasps as a ferry pilot, then as a group commander, finally as an instructor at an Army airfield at Hondo, Tex. She returned to pictures a year ago when the Wasps disbanded.

Yesterday one shot had done what thousands of risks had failed to do. She was dead.

The death of Mary Wiggins in the fall, 1945.

THE SPOTLIGHT THE PAPER YOU CAN TRUST

CHARLES LINDBERGH
... An inventor, too.

AVIATOR, ENGINEER, AUTHOR, POPULIST AND INVENTOR. According to "Parade" magazine, Charles Lindbergh, famous as the first flyer to solo across the Atlantic non-stop, also is credited with inventing the first successful artificial heart. He announced the invention in 1935, after working on it secretly for four years with Nobel Prize laureate Dr. Alexis Carrel. Lindbergh's "heart" became a museum piece after Carrel retired in 1939. But 25 years later, scientists at the U.S. Naval Research Institute realized that it worked better than their own equipment. At their request, Lindbergh redesigned his pump for their use.

Lindbergh was an inventor too.

CREDIT: HARVEY CHRISTEN

Amelia and her Lockheed Vega, 1928.

Bobbi uses her new Leica camera, circa 1938.

Frank Wiggins photography class "on location" in 1938.

Throughout 1937 and the first part of 1938 the country was still in the grip of Depression and flying jobs were scarce. Bobbi flew with the Women's Air Reserve and took a few jobs, when available. She was always busy at the family service station when she did not have other things to do. In August of 1938, Bobbi decided to try another line of work. Because she knew that she was fairly good with a camera, but not quite enough to be a professional, Bobbi enrolled in a photography class being offered at Frank Wiggins' Trade School in Los Angeles.

Bobbi told one of her friends, registered nurse Margaret Sugars Kane, about her intention and Margaret also enrolled. A few months later, Bobbi and Margaret received their commercial photographer's license. Through the school, Bobbi was fortunate enough to get a job teaching photography to a wealthy man from the east named Jeff Blount.

Jeff Blount, Bobbi's photography student, in 1938.

VANISHED FLIER —
Amelia Earhart vanished
on Pacific flight in 1937.
(A) photo

Earhart Rites Recall Mystery of 1937 Flight

MIAMI, June 1 (AP) — Memorial services were conducted at an out-of-the-way airfield today for Amelia Earhart, the tousle-haired adventuress who left here 20 years ago for an around-the-world flight which ended in a tragic mystery.

At dawn on June 1, 1937, the 38-year-old Miss Earhart gunned her twin-engine monoplane down the runway and flew off on the first leg of the historic flight.

One month and two days later Miss Earhart and her navigator, Fred J. Noonan, took off from Lae, New Guinea, in the homestretch and most dangerous hop of their planned 29,000-mile flight. They were headed for Howland Island, about 1200 miles away.

Headed for Island

A Coast Guard cutter picked up intermittent radio messages throughout the day from Miss Earhart but she was never known to be seen again.

The last messages picked up by the cutter indicated her plane — the Electra — was circling, looking for the island, but may have been way off course.

Declared Legally Dead

Two years later, in Los Angeles, Miss Earhart was legally proclaimed dead. But what actually happened to her has long been one of aviation's greatest mysteries.

In 1944, there came reports from the war-torn Pacific that a native had seen the woman flier taken aboard a Japanese fishing vessel, but the Japanese government later denied any knowledge of what happened to her.

A huge search in the Pacific, involving 300 ships and more than 100 planes, failed to turn up any sign.

Today aviation pioneers and a few close friends of Miss Earhart gathered for memorial services at the little airfield which bears her name.

One of many services for Amelia.

Bobbi admires this wonderful and courageous woman, Sept. 6, 1936.

Markham Plane Ends Sea Flight in Nova Scotia Crash

Woman Pilot Escapes With Cuts; Head Winds Use Up 'Gas' Meant to Carry Her to New York

Trip Through Fog Held 'Miraculous'

Flyer's 2,700-Mile Journey Is First East-West Crossing by a Woman; Crowd Waits in Vain

Mrs. Beryl Clutterbuck Markham, English flyer, who took off at 6:50 p. m. Friday (1:50 p. m. New York time), from Abington Airport, Berkshire, for Floyd Bennett Field, Brooklyn, was forced down at 1:05 p. m. Atlantic standard time (1:05 New York time) yesterday at Baleine Cove, near Louisburg, N. S. Her face was slightly cut and her plane damaged, but she had made a solo flight of about 2,700 miles and was the first woman to cross the Atlantic alone by air from east to west.

Spans Ocean; Then Crashes

Herald Tribune photo—Acme
Mrs. Beryl Markham

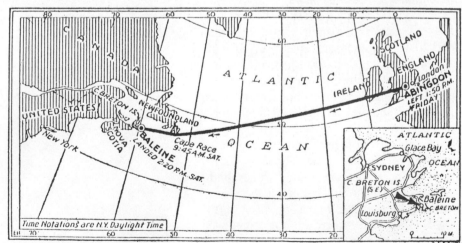

Here is the course of Mrs. Markham's flight across the Atlantic Ocean

Blount had recently moved to California on the advice of his doctor, who informed him he should take up knitting or photography to help him calm down—if he wished to avoid a stroke. He had become a nervous wreck from too much active living and the stress of running his large machine shop in Detroit. Blount purchased a Van Nuys estate from the early screen actress, Pauline Fredericks. There was a house on the five-acre plot that Pauline lived in, but Blount gave it to his divorced wife and built himself another home on the same five acres. He added buildings for a storeroom and darkroom in which to learn about developing and printing, but he really was not interested in doing anything more than the trips to get pictures. He did not learn much about photography, but his nerves did quiet down as his health improved.

Blount one day told Bobbi he had just met Harry Forsythe, who remembered Bobbi. She studied engines under Forsythe at the Curtiss Wright Company at Grand Central Airport. The trio got together and discussed Forsythe's riveting class. The class started in his chicken coops in the back yard—when he first began to offer classes—and he was making plenty of money. He said the aircraft plants were junking thousands of pounds of good rivets each day because the men got more rivets from the tool crib than they needed for their riveting job. They threw the extras into fifty gallon drums or onto the floor. That was all Bobbi needed to hear to put her inventive mind to work. She could not stand waste.

Woman pilot-inventor, Bobbi Trout

Forsythe explained that they weren't exactly wasteful: the labor to put them back in the right bins was too expensive. During World War II, the U.S. was building airplanes for England and the terrible waste bugged Bobbi. She kicked around a few ideas the next few days about sorting and grading the rivets. She then went to see Pop Lingerfelt whom she met through his daughter, Edith, a student, at U.S.C.. He was very interested in the rivet-sorting project, and together they worked out the final ideas. Pop and Bobbi started a business in a little building behind his machine shop in Vernon. Bobbi got the financing from her mother, in exchange for ten percent of the profits. Pop and Bobbi split the remaining profits. Bobbi was in charge of the business and Pop kept all the machines running. They named the business "Aero Reclaiming Company." Blount recovered his health by this time and was anxious to get back to Detroit. Bobbi was now free to devote all her energy to the rivet separating business. Bobbi hired Margaret to do final inspection of all the rivets before they were packaged.

Bobbi's defense employee identification card.

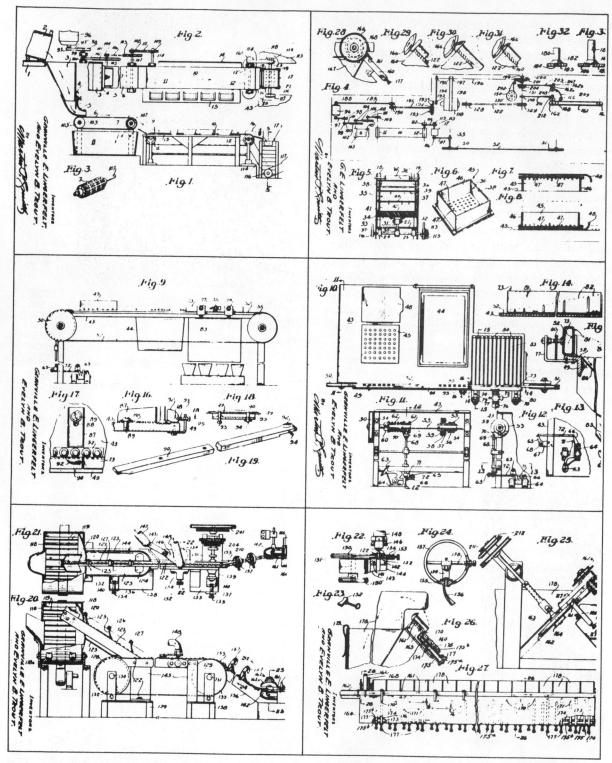

A few of many pages of the Trout & Lingerfelt's Rivet Sorting Patent. Walt Disney's photographers filmed the complete operations of the business and the film was shared with all aircraft manufacturers for support in speeding up the U.S. WWII war effort.

The first customer was the Douglas Aircraft factory at Santa Monica Airport. Time proved Bobbi's idea a winner. Bobbi and Pop patented their inventions and kept improving the process, speeding up production. Bobbi employed a staff of forty-nine women and Harry Marshall, the only man, who used to sell gasoline to the Trouts' family service station. Bobbi felt good that she was doing her bit for her country, but regretted all the wasted training in the Women's Air Reserve preparing for flying with the armed forces in case of war. She longed to be up flying instead of confined to an office and keeping the business running.

Bobbi was dedicated to her work. When Douglas Aircraft called, needing an immediate shipment of particular rivets, she would often stop all other operations to fill the order. She knew it was important that the airplane production schedule not be held up.

Florence "Pat" Lewis, Ph.D., 1943.

Letter regarding Bobbi's deburring service.

Bobbi's partner in the Civil Air Patrol (CAP), Pat Lewis.

WAR DEPARTMENT
AIR CORPS
MATERIEL DIVISION
OFFICE OF THE AIR CORPS REPRESENTATIVE
Vernon Sub-Area Office

ASM:ob
January 30, 1943

2835 Santa Fe Avenue
Los Angeles, California

Subject: Parts Salvage.

To: Miss Bobby Trout
        216 Irving Avenue
        Glendale, California

1. In accordance with your telephone request to this office the early part of this month, together with visit and discussion held with our Production Engineering Section on January 27th, it is the opinion of this office that you have a meritorious scheme that deserves consideration.

2. It is the understanding of this office that your proposition is to canvass prime and sub-contractors of the aviation industry with regard to cataloging and, if possible, stocking in a central location salvagable standard items of equipment such as bolts, nuts, fittings, etc.

3. Your idea of accumulating these for eventual re-distribution to the industry has been discussed with this office and this is to advise you that no objection to the plan is apparent.

ALBERT S. MENASCO
Major, Air Corps
AAF Resident Representative

For a while she continued to run the plant, but it somehow had lost the challenge that it once had for her. She wanted to do something more concrete for the war effort, even though friends and family tried to convince her that running the plant was doing a lot to keep the planes rolling off the assembly line. Two years after Pearl Harbor, all of the rivet problems were conquered. The rivet reclamation processes were perfected and the business was profitable. She perfected their most difficult and final sorting problem using a flotation system for separating the different harnesses of rivets. Bobbi eventually decided to sell out to Pop. She sold out before she realized how much money the new process was bringing in.

Shortly after selling out to Pop, in April, 1943, the Civil Air Patrol, C.A.P., of which Bobbi was a member, had a "fly-in" at Quartzsite, Arizona. They practiced their flying there because pilots were not permitted to fly within one hundred fifty miles of the coast during wartime. The group was commanded by actor Robert Cummings when he was not busy with his acting profession.

To do some flying, Bobbi and Pat Lewis, an ex-music teacher who taught at the Jordan Conservatory of Music in Indianapolis for years before coming to California, drove to Quartzsite. On the way to meet the C.A.P. group, Bobbi and Pat took a detour through Glamas to check on Bobbi's and her mother's manganese mine interest. Glamas, located right at the edge of the American Sahara Desert, consisted of a grocery store and beer pub. They stayed all night at the mine site in the trailer they were pulling behind their car. The next morning they started out on a dusty, dirt road to Blythe. After a couple of hours, they drove through some soft sand in which the trailer became stuck. No matter what they did, it would not move.

Bobbi was unhitching the trailer to go by car for help, when two Mexicans who could speak no English came out of the bushes on the roadside. They helped push the trailer out of the sand and in return Bobbi and Pat gave them a ride to Blythe. That night Bobbi was delirious from the sunstroke she received as a result of her work in the hot afternoon. The next morning she felt miserable, but by afternoon she had recovered enough to rent an airplane at the Blythe Airport and take Pat for her first flight.

Bobbi's CAP officers, included Bob Cummings, her Commanding Officer.

Bobbi in 1947.

1944 *1950* *1967*

Letter that contained the idea that started the W.A.S.P.'s.

ADDRESS REPLY TO
CHIEF OF THE AIR CORPS
WAR DEPARTMENT
WASHINGTON, D. C.

WAR DEPARTMENT
OFFICE OF THE CHIEF OF THE AIR CORPS
WASHINGTON

July 29, 1941

To all women holders of licenses

A survey is being made to determine the feasibility of forming under Government auspices, an auxiliary organization of women pilots for the ferrying of certain categories of airplanes. No conclusions have been reached as to the future of such an organization, and it has not been determined whether it should be formed on a military or civilian basis, temporary or permanent.

You will aid in a prompt compilation of such a survey by filling in and returning immediately the questionnaire in the addressed envelope, enclosed for that purpose.

Even if you are unable or unwilling to participate actively in such an organization, if formed, nevertheless you are requested to fill in and return the questionnaire so that the survey may be complete as to both available and unavailable women pilots. It may be assumed, for purposes of the questionnaire, that, if the services of women pilots are utilized, they will obviously receive compensation.

Please note that a space has been left in the questionnaire for the insertion of such additional data as you believe necessary for the completion of the records as to your availability now or in the future.

Your very prompt attention is urged.

Air Corps Ferrying Command

Colonel Robert Olds
Air Corps Ferrying Command
War Dept. Munitions Building
Wash., D.C.

After landing they met six girls who were very upset. The girls had paid in advance for their flying courses. Bobbi and Pat, who came with cash, rented a plane which left the girls waiting. Bobbi felt heartsick because the girls had already paid their money and had high hopes of joining the WASPS. Had Bobbi only known she never would have rented the plane.

Bobbi and Pat arrived at Quartzsite and Bobbi registered her license number 2613. A commotion began behind her. She looked back and saw a group looking at her license number in disbelief. It had been quite a while since she had obtained her license, and in the interim the digits in license numbers had gone up considerably. By 1943, they had begun to look like Social Security numbers. In 1975, the F.A.A. began using Social Security numbers for private pilot's licenses.

Pat Lewis was not a flier, but Bobbi and Margaret wanted her to be a part of the C.A.P. The commander, Bob Cummings, insisted that everyone have a responsibility. Since her father was a telegraph operator for the railroad and taught her International Code, Pat taught the code to the C.A.P.

UNITED STATES OF AMERICA
DEPARTMENT OF COMMERCE . . . CIVIL AERONAUTICS ADMINISTRATION

MEDICAL CERTIFICATE, STUDENT AND PRIVATE PILOT

THIS CERTIFIES that I personally examined

Evelyn Bobbie Trout
(FIRST) (MIDDLE) (SURNAME)

Address 1648 Victory Boulevard

Glendale California

1/7/06 126 65½ Brwn Brwn Fem
(DATE OF BIRTH) (WEIGHT) (HEIGHT) (HAIR) (EYES) (SEX)

and find him free from any disease that would be likely to cause sudden incapacity and, except as noted hereon, that he possesses no structural defect or limitation. I have forwarded the report of my findings to the Civil Aeronautics Administration.

Date May 24, 1949

Place Los Angeles, California

Signed _____ M.D.

Degree M.D. State Board License No. ____

STRUCTURAL PHYSICAL DEFECTS
List defects. If none, so state

Impaired vision R. 20/40 L 20/40
Impaired hearing None
Deformity None
Limited motion None
Muscular weakness None
Amputation None
Remarks: Holder shall wear correcting lenses while exercising privileges of his airmens certificate.

Bobbie Trout
(SIGNATURE OF APPLICANT)

Any alteration of this certificate is punishable by a fine of not exceeding $1,000, or imprisonment not exceeding 3 years, or both

Bobbi's pilot license renewal in 1949.

(center) these are the little burrs Bobbi had to de-burr.

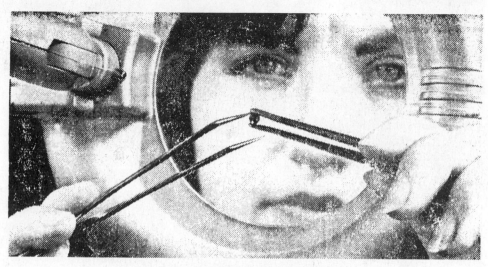

OF PRIME CONCERN

Getting careful attention of inspector at Omark Industries' plant is a tiny ammunition primer—the element that sets off the charge in a cartridge—turned out by the millions at Lewiston, Idaho. Tweezers and high-powered magnifying glass are the tools of the trade.

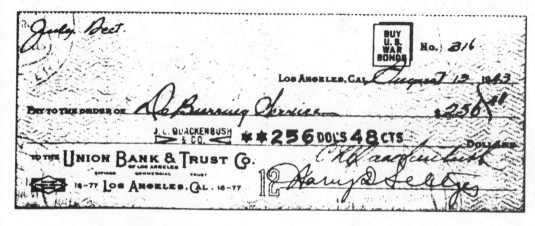

Bobbi's first check from a customer in her new deburring service.

Bobbi and her Arabian horse named Murad.

The C.A.P. had regular meetings and the subject at one of these was on cumulus cloud formations. As usual, Bobbi, Margaret Kane and Pat were a little late arriving. This one evening the place was packed and there were only three seats left. Bobbi took a seat in front and before long her head was at a strange angle. Bobbi was fast asleep.

At the end of the lecture Margaret and Pat noted Bobbi finally begin to move. Apparently, the stirring of the people at lecture's end awakened her. The lecturer made his final comments to the audience, saying, "Well, Bobbi's awake. I have never had anybody go to such trouble to tell me I was such a bore." Of course, Bobbi was embarrassed and knew her body was again burning sugars as fast as she ate them.

Bobbi was ready to again find some way to contribute to the war effort. One day, she met an old friend who had soloed the same day Bobbi did at Burdett's flying school. He mentioned the need of a de-burring service for the aircraft plants, because they were using files to de-burr their parts. Bobbi again began to think.

She rented a cement mixer and tumbled various small, machined parts together to determine whether or not her idea would work. Metal machined parts have rough edges which need to be smoothed or de-burred. Bobbi needed parts from a machine shop to de-burr so she went to the Quackenbush Machine Shop in Glendale. Mr. Quackenbush was amazed to see her. He told her that he remembered seeing her at the banquet at the end of the 1929 first Women's Transcontinental Air Derby and at the Cleveland air show. A few days later, Bobbi was working on Quackenbush parts in her back yard. He became one of her best customers.

Bobbi and Pat together founded the De-burring Service. They found a building on Flower Street in Glendale, about two blocks from Grand Central Air Terminal. With Pat's Irish wit and fun personality, she became their first sales representative. Pat's first sales call was to Menasco Manufacturing Company in Burbank. It resulted in a huge truck and trailer loaded with parts to be de-burred.

Bobbi managed the business and worked out new methods and ways to accomplish what the

U. S. DEPARTMENT OF COMMERCE CIVIL AERONAUTICS ADMINISTRATION		
AIRMAN IDENTIFICATION CARD		
This is to certify that the person whose picture, fingerprint, signature, and descriptive data appear hereon has registered with the Civil Aeronautics Administration and otherwise complied with the procedure prerequisite to the issuance of this card.		FINGERPRINT

AIRMAN'S NAME AND ADDRESS
EVELYN BOBBIE TROUT
1648A VICTORY BOULEVARD
GLENDALE 1, CALIFORNIA

DESCRIPTION OF AIRMAN

HEIGHT	WEIGHT	COLOR OF HAIR	COLOR OF EYES
65½"	129	BROWN	BROWN

DATE OF BIRTH	PLACE OF BIRTH
1-7-06	GREENUP, ILLINOIS

CITIZENSHIP
UNITED STATES OF AMERICA

DATE OF ISSUE	ISSUED BY: *H.W. Kattelmann*
12-13-51	H. W. KATTELMANN AVIATION SAFETY AGENT

tumblers were not able to handle. Business was booming and they soon had to hire more people to finish the orders on schedule. Denny was hired as a salesman. Bobbi always said Denny could sell anything. Within a short time she was proven right; their profits continued to escalate. The business got all the tough de-burring problems to solve, which was not always the easiest thing to handle. But then, that made the work interesting and challenging, something Bobbi was always seeking.

Shortly after World War II ended, Denny walked into the de-burring building and within ten minutes bought the business from Bobbi and Pat. Denny continued to build it into a successful business, still in operation today.

Chapter Fifteen

More Business Ventures

WANTING a new challenge, Bobbi and Pat built a building at Western and Victory Boulevards in Glendale where they purchased some lots. They manufactured an item that Pat invented: a plastic container they called the "EG-CEL." They named their business, Trout and Lewis.

The "EG-CEL" held a dozen eggs and was made of slightly tinted transparent plastic. The trouble Bobbi and Pat had with the plastics was a nightmare. A little carbon would collect on the nozzle during manufacture and cause black streaks to shoot into the light pink, blue, or green plastic. This was corrected within a month.

Bobbi ran into Dana Boller, after not having seen him for the eighteen years since she was learning to fly at Burdett's. He learned that Bobbi had never flown an Engineering Research Corporations' Ercoupe, a low-wing, two-place monoplane. He told her that the Ercoupes at the corner of the airport were his, and he was the distributor for them. The following day Dana came by and insisted she close the business early and go flying with him. He finally ushered her out of the shop and before long they were at the Grand Central Airport, climbing into an airplane.

After Bobbi and Dana were seated, Dana said, "It's all yours." In no time they were airborne. She was amazed to find the plane handled so easily. It had no rudder pedals. The rudder automatically moved in coordination with the ailerons. There was also a radio, which

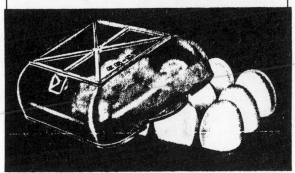
One of Bobbi's inventions.

impressed her. Everything came in mixed up, like a citizens band radio. When she came in to land, she wanted to sideslip, but could not because it is impossible to cross control the Ercoupe.

In 1946 Bobbi piloted Dana Boller's Ercoupe for one hour, at Grand Central Airport.

PIONEER AIRMEN °

OFFICIAL PUBLICATION OF

OX5 CLUB OF CALIFORNIA

?NIA WING HEADQUARTERS - P.O. Box 281, BURBANK, CAL

JULY- AUGUST 1962

DANA BOLLER

It was sad to pick up the morning paper and learn that Dana has made his last flight the day before, when the helicopter in which he was a passenger tangled with an overhead wire and crashed in New Mexico. Dana was a devoted OX5er and during the 1958 Pre-convention period worked hard to assure the success of the event. He did much in later years to develop the use of helicopter. His many friends in the OX5 Club will miss him.

1946 I piloted his air coupe with him for 1 hr Grand central air Port

Dana Boller
Ernest E. Tattersfield
Thomas Charles Bannon
George W. Cook

This is to Certify that

Bonnie Trout

has ridden in the

FIRST COMMERCIAL HELICOPTER

in the State of California

ARMSTRONG-FLINT HELICOPTER CO.

FIELD ADDRESS
Whiteman Airpark
PACOIMA, CALIFORNIA

MAILING ADDRESS
P. O. Box 343
PACOIMA, CALIFORNIA

Bobbi paid $5 for her first ride in a helicopter at Pan Pacific Grounds in 1947.

Normally, Bobbi liked to be plenty high when approaching the field. She would side slip down, then ease the stick back for a three-point landing. With all these new things to occupy her, plus fighting the involuntary instinct to use her feet, time rushed by and flying the airplane became fun.

For over an hour she was captivated with the ease of piloting this unique plane. She landed, and they climbed from the plane. Bobbi thanked Dana. He told her about his whirlybird and how he would like to take Bobbi up for a ride. Bobbi would have enjoyed the ride, given an opportunity. She thanked Dana again and departed, unaware that this would be the last time she would be pilot-in-command of an airplane.

During World War II, private flying was restricted, especially within 150 miles of the coast. As Bobbi turned her attention and energies to her businesses, she lost contact with her close flying friends.

After the war, flying had changed for many of the early pilots. It became so big and regimented that it lost its appeal to an adventurer who like the freedom of being able to fly "by the seat of her pants," wherever and whenever she wanted to go. This, and Bobbi's many businesses, left little time for flying.

About twelve years later, Dana Boller was fatally injured when he crashed his helicopter. The tragedy shocked Bobbi again.

A few months after the "EG-CEL" went on the market, other less expensive models came out using recycled plastic. A lot of people bought these for paints and other applications. They sold for only twenty-five cents apiece. Pat's and Bobbi's were much better, made out of quality materials, and one could see through the container at a glance to see how many eggs were there. Their "EG-CEL" sold in quality stores at the retail prices of one dollar seventy-five cents per container, which could hold a dozen eggs. With this much competition, Bobbi and Pat decided to sell the dies and start something else.

About this time a man had developed a remote control rear-view mirror for automobiles. He was interested in hiring employees who had been manufacturing Trout and Lewis "EG-CELs." He needed help developing and streamlining his rear view mirror. Trout and Lewis was the company name and Bobbi and Pat worked out an agreement where they would streamline the mirror and pay him a royalty for the use of his patent. They began with a first order for five thousand mirrors.

PILOTS OWN GLENDALE PLANT
Aviatrix Bobby Trout Bobs Up in Mirror Biz

By ANNE STERN

Some weeks ago, a Mirror columnist raised the question, "Whatever became of Bobbie Trout?"

The famed gal pilot of the early thirties dropped out of the aviation spotlight over a decade ago. But she is still making her mark—in business, in small-goods manufacturing and selling.

With as much zest as she ever put into her handling of an airplane "stick," she and a feminine partner operate a concern called Trout-Lewis Manufacturers, with headquarters at 1646 Victory Blvd., Glendale.

Chief item on Trout-Lewis' production schedule, which has included gadgets and household items of many kinds, is the Saf-T-View remote control mirror for cars.

It is a sideview mirror which can be adjusted from inside the car by turning a handle. No fumbling around outside and getting one's sleeve drenched on a rainy day.

The mirrors are obtainable for both sides of the car. "And you can actually see something in the one on the right side," Miss Trout explained proudly.

She and her partner, Miss Pat Lewis, hold the rights on all their inventions; contract their manufacture out to various firms, and are in sole charge of their distribution and selling.

Built Own Plant

If Bobbie took a roundabout way into business world, so did Pat. She was a piano and music teacher in Indianapolis before the war. Then the two met while working for war industries.

They set up their own "think" shop, where they helped manufacturers unravel vexing production problems and devise manufacturing short-cuts.

Since then, they helped in the actual building of their Glendale plant. Miss Trout turned mason and helped erect the walls.

In back of the 50-foot building, in which Trout-Lewis lease out four rental units, is a living studio for the two partners. Adjacent to that is a stable, where they keep horses.

Miss Trout, once so enthusiastic about the wild blue yonder, has taken to terra firma with the same gusto. Whenever her busy schedule permits, she goes riding —thinking, meanwhile, about new gadgets and inventions.

Bobbi, and her partner Pat Lewis, working at their Trout-Lewis Manufacturers Safety-View mirror business.

Bobbi put reflective silver stars on her blue jeep, which she sold to her father, in 1957. Driving behind the jeep at night was like following the Milky Way!

Obituary in October 1960 of Ruth Nichols, one of her friends in the first Women's Transcontinental Air Derby.

Bobbi's step-mother, Helen, driving the blue jeep.

Suicide Note Left by Noted Aviatrix

NEW YORK—UPI—An autopsy was to be conducted today to determine the cause of death of Ruth Rowland Nichols, 59, one of the world's most famous women fliers.

Miss Nichols was found dead on the bathroom floor of her apartment at 400 E. 49th St. yesterday by the building superintendent. Police said she left notes indicating suicide.

The aviatrix took to the skies in 1921 when she was a student at Wellesley College. Soon she became known in headlines as "The society flier" and shared with Amelia Earhart the adulation of the public.

In 1931 she held the three major international women's records—the speed mark of 210.6 miles an hour over a closed course; the distance record of 1,977 miles on a flight from Oakland, Calif. to Louisville, Ky., and an altitude record of 28,743 feet.

In 1930 she clipped an hour off Charles A. Lindbergh's transcontinental flight record, making the Los Angeles to New York trip in 13 hours and 21 minutes.

In 1932 she became the first woman airline pilot when she joined the New York and New England Airways. She had a number of close brushes with death, notably her escape from a flaming plane at Columbus, Ohio, in 1921, and from an exploding passenger plane at Troy, N.Y., in 1935.

Her latest record was set in 1958 when she was the first woman to fly an Air Force jet

—AP Wirephoto.
RUTH NICHOLS
. . . found dead.

faster than 1,000 miles an hour at an altitude of 51,000 feet at the Suffolk County Air Force Base, N.Y.

Miss Nichols was the daughter of a distinguished New Yorker, Erickson Norman Nichols. He was a noted sportsman, onetime member of Teddy Roosevelt's Rough Riders, and a member of the New York Stock Exchange.

Bobbi's step-mother died November 29, 1963.

MEMORIAL SERVICE FOR

Helen Marjorie Trout

Born
February 19, 1901
Washington

Passed Away
November 29, 1963
Los Angeles, California

Services at
Grace Chapel
Inglewood Park Cemetery
Inglewood, California
Monday, Dec. 2, 1963 - 3 p.m.

Bobbi's father died on October 3, 1962.

GEORGE EVERETT TROUT

George Everett Trout, 76, of 73-925 Rocky Road, Twentynine Palms, passed away in an Indio hospital, October 3. He had been ailing for 14 years.

Mr. Trout was a retired electrician. He had resided in Twentynine Palms for five years, and in the state of California since 1917. He was born in Illinois, April 29, 1886.

He is survived by his widow, Helen; a daughter, Bobbi Trout, Cathedral City; and a son, Ben Trout, Los Angeles.

He is a member of the Los Angeles Masonic Lodge. A Masonic service will be held at Inglewood Park Chapel, Inglewood, Friday, October 5, 1 p.m.; interment to follow.

After the War, cars were scarce and in order to buy one, dealers would make their profits by loading the car with all the accessories available. The buyers had to take all these accessories in order to buy the car, as that was the only way they could buy the car.

Trout and Lewis was getting low on mirrors when they had a big order from the east. They started to work on the order when a Kiplinger investment newsletter arrived stating there would be a shortage of cars for about two years. With this in mind, they stocked up on a lot of steel tubing and ordered another five thousand mirrors. Soon after, a large eastern company cancelled their order when cars started to appear by the thousands from storage in warehouses. People hated to drill holes in their cars, so nobody wanted to buy a mirror. Trout and Lewis sold its remaining mirrors for ten cents on the dollar, losing about twenty-five thousand dollars—quite a sum of money in those days.

After losing so much money on the mirrors, Bobbi's partner, Pat, took a job helping one of their tenants, Menton & Johnson, who specialized in air conditioning and sold home appliances. Pat only worked for a day or two when a buyer came in and bought about forty refrigerators. Pat was a terrific salesperson.

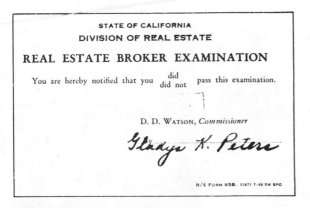

Bobbi became a broker without having been a real estate salesman in 1949.

About 1949, Bobbi went into a business venture with a real estate broker. She studied for her own broker's license, passed, and the two brokers started a real estate office in one of Bobbi's empty building rentals on her Glendale

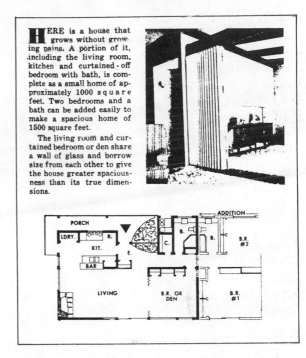

HERE is a house that grows without growing pains. A portion of it, including the living room, kitchen and curtained-off bedroom with bath, is complete as a small home of approximately 1000 square feet. Two bedrooms and a bath can be added easily to make a spacious home of 1500 square feet.

The living room and curtained bedroom or den share a wall of glass and borrow size from each other to give the house greater spaciousness than its true dimensions.

Spec house that Bobbi designed and built in Studio City about 1955.

property. Real estate was in a big slump at that time.

Bobbi always wanted to know more about offset printing and in 1949, she took a night class to learn how to run a 1250 Multilith offset printing press. She found a good buy on a used press and started a printing business in the same empty rental that she used as a real estate office. A year later she sold the printing business and rented the office "shop" to the buyer/printer. He stayed for several years.

In 1955, after building some homes, Bobbi learned about mutual funds. Pat wanted to move to Long Beach and start her own business, a pre-school for children. Bobbi bought Pat out. Bobbi traded her Glendale property for twenty-three acres of land in the Thunderbird area of Palm Springs in 1955. She ended up, after many costly experiences, selling lots for the buyer who purchased fourteen acres of her property. In her four-plex she had built on the twenty-three acres, she opened her real estate, life and disability insurance, and mutual funds office.

Bobbi in her real estate office sitting across from her partner, George Orlich (below).

(center right) Bobbi retrieving dates from one of her date-palm trees in front of her real estate office in Jan. 1966.

1961 view of Bobbi's real estate office in Rancho Mirage, California.

Phoebe Omlie "Flight Plan" Closed

BY FRANCES W. BURK

Associate Editor

Death has stepped in and silently closed the flight plan on Phoebe Omlie. It was probably the only "silent" thing Phoebe Omlie was ever connected with for the pioneer aviatrix was always vocal in the many aviation projects she pursued. Phoebe died in mid-July in Indianapolis, Ind. She was 72.

The history of Phoebe Omlie and her late husband, Vernon, is a history of pioneer aviation in Memphis, TN., although the stories of barnstormers struggling to settle in American communities bear a strange similarity.

As the first husband and wife barnstorming team in the country, Phoebe and Vernon started off romantically on a barnstorming honeymoon from St. Paul, Minn., down thru the Mississippi Valley. But just as they flew into Memphis, stormy weather (not marital, but of the climatic type) closed in. It lasted long enough to see their last bit of money trickle away.

They hocked their clothes to the hotel owner where they found a roof over their head and once the weather cleared, gave passenger rides and flight instruction, paying their way out of hock all the while. They based at old Memphis Driving Park at first, the airstrip being located right in the middle of a race track. "We never flew while Pop Geers was training his horses," Phoebe once recalled. "By 1925, there were so many cross-country fliers landing in the circle and scaring the horses that we had to stop flying there."

The old Memphis Aero Club was formed that year and built a new airstrip at nearby Woodstock and the Omlies moved there. Phoebe had to content herself with teaching primary because her legs weren't long enough to reach the rudder pedals of the Flying Jennies, Standards or Canucks.

They formed Mid-South Airways and were the first FBO on Memphis Municipal Airport when it opened in 1929. The Depression brought on bankruptcy, but by then the Omlies had long ago paid the hospitalities extended them on that first visit. Whenever Ol' Man River went on a rampage and flooded the farmlands, Vernon and Phoebe flew over the victims, dropping food and medicine. They rescued flood victims clinging to treetops and to houses floating down the river. And more importantly, they made Memphis air-conscious.

Vernon was killed in an airliner crash in 1936, but Phoebe carried on. An active member of the Ninety-Nines (she had won the very first Powder Puff Derby a-way back in 1929), Phoebe instructed Air Force students during World War II, then went to Washington to work for the old Civil Aeronautics Administration (now FAA) and her record of promoting an aviation education program around the country is a story in itself.

Working at a department store candy counter, she earned $8 a week. With grim determination, she saved up $15 and shot it all on her first airplane ride. Her second flight was with Vernon—a flight that was to set her course and her flight plan for life.

Mrs. Dorothy Crosno, president of Memphis Aero Corp., and a long-time friend of Phoebe's, has suggested some type of permanent memorial to Phoebe's contribution to aviation in Memphis.

Indianapolis, Indiana.
Sept1 24, 1971.

Dear Bobbi:

Thanks a lot for your card. I was especially interested to learn of your concern about our schools - "This busing is not American".

Busing is not the only issue. It is just a beginning in the complete "take-over" of the local schools by the federal government. As far back as 1966, the "ultra-liberals" in the Department of Health, Education and Welfare (HEW) have been promoting, openly, large park-schools, changes in curricula - so they can "brain-wash" children from the "Head-Start" program through the colleges. This curricula-angle was, again, introduced in the court testimony regarding the public schools in Indianapolis by one of the bureaucrats from Washington.

When I was asked, back in 1960, by some of the committee people who helped we aviation zealots in our fight for airport bond-issues to get aviation "off-the-ground", to help them fight to alleviate their exhorbitant taxes for schools, I didn't hesitate a minute to join them. It's been a long, hard, rough and rugged road. It hasn't been easy.

At first, I tried to interest aviation folks in helping - a reciprosity act, if nothing else - but met with complete failure. The "99's", like in the fight against limiting womens pilots licenses, at which time you were so cooperative back in 1934, I was turned down in no uncertain terms - The OX-5 Club, also - and many individual pilots throughout the country. Needless to say, I gave up. They are so non-appreciative, so selfish and self-centered, that I will not waste any more of my time with them.

We are going to win this battle. In Indianapolis, I have been asked to help prepare legislation to submit to the Legislature that convenes in January. If we fail there we will go to the people by the "Convention" route that is provided in the United States Constitution.
FOR
It might be interesting to watch.

Everyone concerned for these past ten years has contributed their time for-free. There has been no money and no national political leadership that has had "guts" enough to help.

Now, because of the pressure from the "grass-roots" they are beginning to offer "make-shift" legislation in regard to busing - only.

"Nuff" of that.

The mail just came in. There was a letter from "Jimmy" Doolittle. I had written to he and Joe about verification of some anecdotes of yesteryear. I, also, asked them about Pancho. Jimmy tells me that he saw her about a month ago at Lancaster where she was guest of honor at a fund-raising dinner to acquire money for the Antelope Valley Museum. He said I could reach her through her son "Billy" at P. O. Box 1939, Lancaster, California - 93534.

There is so much that must be done by we older aviation folks so that the true aviation-story can get down in print before the present-day "head-line" hunters and their myths are accepted as history of the true struggles - and fun too - of the early development of aviation.

I will be tied-up here for, at least, six months. Give me some ideas.

Bestus Always,

Phoebe Omlie,

Bobbi and one of her four-plex tenants, Charles Van Tress (l), developer of the large meaty chickens we eat today, in front of his luxury jet. With Bobbi (c) and Charles is Mary Hamilton

Mrs. Trout, 88, Mother Of Famed Aviatrix, Dies

Lola Denman Trout, 88, mother of famed aviatrix Bobbi Trout of Cathedral Ctiy, died Saturday and two days later was followed in death by a woman who had given up her own business to care for Mrs. Trout.

Frances Becerra, 60, was owner and operator of Frances Beauty Snop, 210 W. Olympic Boulevard, Los Angeles, for 10 years before closing it in 1965 to come to the desert and take care of her adopted "Mamacita," Mrs. Trout.

Graveside services for Mrs. Trout were held at Forest Lawn Hollywood Hills Wednesday at 3 p.m. with Rev. Sidney Lawson of the First United Methodist Church of Oceanside officiating.

She died at her residence, 70-231 Thunder Road, Cathedral City. Born in Greenup, Ill., Feb. 4. 1885, Mrs. Trout had been a resident of the desert 10 years and of the state 53 years.

In addition to her daughter, she is survived by a son, Denman O. Trout of Glendale.

Miss Becerra died Monday at the same address. Born in Mexico Sept. 17, 1912, Miss Becerra had been a resident of the desert seven years and of the state 43 years.

She was the sister of Maria Becerra of Fontana, Rosa Becerra and Conception Becerra of Talpa Ayende, Jalisco, Mexico, and an aunt of Josephine Sanchez.

Funeral services and interment for Miss Becerra will be held at Municipal Cemetery in Talpa Ayenda, Jalisco, Mexico.

Obituary of Bobbi's mother, May 1973.

Bobbi at Palm Springs, in front of her gold Riviera, circa 1968.

Bobbi asked George Orlich, who worked out of the same mutual fund office, to come and join her in her business activities. They shared her office and worked together well for eight years. Bobbi received a good offer for the four-plex from a long time friend, Lee Gerson, and sold it to her. Bobbi and George moved to a new building they had built and worked out of this office until the building was sold in 1976.

In 1976, Bobbi bought a condominium in Rancho La Costa, California, thirty miles north of San Diego, where summers were not so hot, and decided to retire. In the past thirty years, Bobbi started seven businesses and has many inventions to her credit. She was happy with the way it all worked out; however, when winter arrived, Bobbi longed for the Palm Springs weather.

Bobbi and her 99 friends in 1966 (from left): Eleanor Wagner, Vera Dawn Walker, Clema Granger, and Bobbi.

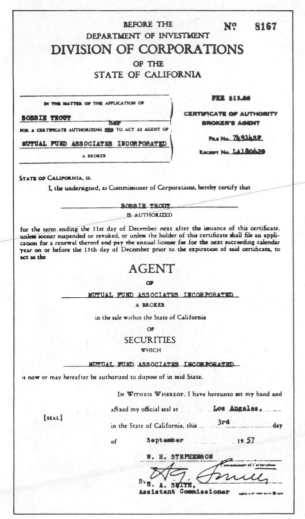

Bobbi's Life & Disability Insurance Agent's License.

Bobbi's Securities License.

*Photographer Bobbi takes a picture of
Margaret Kane (r) and a friend, on their
way to do some gold-dredging in the high
Sierras, 1938.*

*Obituary of Golden Eagle designer, Mark
Campbell, June 1963.*

Early Stunt Pilot Dies

A Burbank man who personified an era of aviation died Friday.

Mark A. Campbell, 65, of 632 N. Florence St., was the originator of wing walking and formerly the oldest living stunt pilot in the United States. His death further reduces to history the infant and daredevil age of flight.

Graveside funeral services will be held Tuesday at 2 p.m. at the Portal of the Folded Wings at Valhalla Cemetery. Pierce Bros. Mortuary is in charge of arrangements.

Mr. Campbell had returned home last week from a lecture-fact finding tour of the United States after becoming ill. He died while undergoing an operation in a Hollywood hospital.

The former aviator had hoped to publish a series of books on the history of flight.

Campbell was a member and state president for two years of the Silver Wings Fraternity, a national organization of pilots who had soloed more than 25 years ago. He was a member of the OX-5 club, a group of pilots who had flown planes with old-time OX-5 engines.

In addition, he had been a member of the Burbank Elks Lodge and a captain in the California Wing of the Civil Air Patrol.

He had retired from Lockheed California Company in December, 1962, but then took on the task of collecting information and photographs for aviation history books, the likes of which reportedly have never been published.

Campbell is survived by his widow, Betty; son, Mark Jr., of Pacoima; stepson, W. L. McKelvey, of Seattle, Wash.; two daughters, Mrs. Joy Hagin of Kansas and Mrs. Marjorie Winburn of Burbank; brothers, Mathew of Hemet, and Daniel of Alhambra; sister, Mrs. Mary E. Moore of Atwater, and nine grandchildren.

Campbell's calculating mind enabled him to survive the 1920's when many of his fellow stunt pilots and barnstormers met violent death.

MARK CAMPBELL

Chapter Sixteen

Recognitions and Achievements

BOBBI Trout's early retirement years were spent taking trips in her motor home, treasure hunting and gold dredging in the high Sierra, working with the Inventor's Workshop International, and doing some photography when she had the chance. She still had many ideas for new inventions, but new ideas were just too hard to market. She was not active in women's flying organizations for many years, but remained very interested in what other women fliers were accomplishing. Being a charter member of the Ninety Nines, she was especially interested in that group.

In her early retirement years, she had a Honda motorcycle she carried on the front of her motor home which she used now and then. She sold it in 1976 when she turned seventy years old and "retired." Even at age eighty she wanted another one and was scheming how to keep her friends from thinking she wasn't "just plain crazy."

In the early 1970's, Bobbi received a call from Professor David D. Hatfield. He invited her to come to Northrop University where he had assembled a photographic book he wanted to present to her. She took her good friend and aviation pioneer, Clema Granger, to Inglewood to visit Professor Hatfield. Professor Hatfield was actively creating the American Hall of Aviation History at Northrup University in In-

glewood, California. He told Bobbi how bashful he was in those early days when he was taking pictures of her on her flights. He was now proud to give her an album that he had taken special time to prepare.

Professor Hatfield contacted Bobbi six years later to invite her and other aviation personalities to his first videotaped production program called PIONEER'S REUNION on Saturday, June 11, 1977. He invited aviation personalities, including Tony Stadlman, Moye Stephens, Dave Grant, Cliff Henderson, Morton Bach, John Nagel, Tony LeVier, Gladys Ingle, and Martin Jensen.

Bobbi and friends, Skip Mazzio and Donna Veca, talking over **Just Plane Crazy** *in her condo.*

Bobbi relaxes in her Rancho La Costa condominium. (left) Certificate of Invention for the She-Wee (below).

INVENTORS WORKSHOP INTERNATIONAL
ANNUAL AWARDS DINNER
FEBRUARY 9, 1980

CERTIFICATE OF ACHIEVEMENT

awarded to
BOBBI TROUT
the inventor of
SHE-WEE

WHEREAS Inventor has conceived, given form and brought into being something that did not exist before, and
WHEREAS Inventor has displayed great Ingenuity, Resourcefulness, Dedication, Enterprise and, most importantly,
PERSISTENCE
NOW THEREFORE be it known that this Inventor is being honored by his peers and fellows for exhibiting that most
noble of all human traits,
CREATIVITY
And he has proved himself worthy of being recognized as an
INDIVIDUAL INVENTOR
The elite of the elite in the society of man.

INVENTORS WORKSHOP INTERNATIONAL

Melvin E. Fuller, Chairman
LeRoy Andrews, Vice Chairman
M. E. Weisberg, Secretary
Norman Fredriksen, Treasurer

"Hang-It" invention for drip-drying clothes on the shower head pipe.

Bobbi in her wet-suit, gold-dredging in the North Fork of the American River, 1965.

Bobbi and Professor David Hatfield.

*Professor David D.
Hatfield, aviation historian,
using his newly purchased
videotape equipment to
prepare a documentary of
flight in 1979.*

HISTORIC FLIGHT — Bobbi Trout, aviatrix, Realtor and investment broker, set
a women's endurance flight record in
1931 when she and co-pilot, Edna May
Cooper, remained aloft for 122 hours
and 50 minutes over Los Angeles, refueling from another airplane during that
time. David D. Hatfield, aviation historian, presents Bobbi with a scrapbook,
and collection of pictures of the historic flight which have never been published, at Clover Field, Santa Monica,
during 50th anniversary festival ceremonies.

Letter of invitation to aviation pioneer, Bobbi, from Professor David D. Hatfield.

American Hall of Aviation History

May 24, 1977

Dear Bobbi:

We are preparing to produce a two-hour video tape of the five rooms of photographic displays of leading events in aviation history and some of the personalities who were involved in making that history.

In so doing, we have invited a number of people who participated in these events to be present to make a one or two minute comment about their part in the story of aviation's progress. A series of photographs in which you are shown, or in which you played a prominent part, will be on display in a group. We would be pleased if you can be present to make a few comments on the subjects and events shown.

The filming will be done all day Saturday, June 11, 1977, from 9 a.m., to 3 p.m. If your time is limited, your part may be filmed at any time since the film will be edited later. If at all possible, we suggest that you visit the Hall any time before June 11, and see your display in order to know what is proposed.

We expect about 35 or more who were connected with the development of aviation to take part, and it will be an occasion for a meeting of old friends; so please feel free to bring guests. Refreshments will be served, a lunch hour observed and there will be a no-host bar set up in the American Hall of Aviation History.

Please let us know as soon as possible if you will be here. You may call us for further information at 213-670-6339. A list of those expected at the filming is attached, as well as a map directing you to the Hall, located at 5520 W. Arbor Vitae, corner of Aviation Blvd., next to a Gulf Station. We are directly across from Northrop University, which has an Inglewood address. Ours is a Los Angeles address, hence the difference in numbers.

Meanwhile, Maintain Airspeed, and we'll see you then!

Sincerely,

D. D. Hatfield, Director

Vitae, Inglewood, California 90306 • Phone (213) 776-3410

Pioneers Reunion Day, Saturday, June 11, 1977. Professor Hatfield (l) videotaped aviation notables including Tony LeVier (c) and John Nagel (r).

EAA...
the SPORT AVIATION ASSOCIATION
THIS IS TO CERTIFY THAT

Bobbi Trout

NO. 120770 IS A

Experimental Aircraft Association

LIFETIME MEMBER
AND IS ENTITLED TO ALL BENEFITS AND PRIVILEGES

PRESIDENT

Later that month, the Experimental Aircraft Association, EAA, in Oshkosh, Wisconsin, invited Bobbi to be one of twenty-five "antique fliers" to attend a huge meet in which they gave a whole day's celebration to the older fliers. Bobbi and Blanche Noyes were the only two women of her era to attend. The air meet was the largest ever assembled. Ten thousand planes were at Oshkosh, and it was the first time Bobbi had seen pilots camping under the wings of their airplanes.

Bobbi and the other antiquers gave talks to about two thousand people. The antiquers kept their listeners enthralled with tales about the early years of aviation. Bobbi spoke about women's acceptance in aviation in the early years. The younger generation listened eagerly, realizing how much change had taken place in seventy-three years, since the Wright Brothers first flew.

Dear Bobbi,

The Atchison Bicentennial Committee has received a contribution from H. Glenn Buffington, 818 West Crockett St., Seattle, WA. 98119, naming you as the honoree in the Memory Lane section of the International Forest of Friendship.

The Ninety Nines have done a tremendous amount of work in helping our committe have a most successful and worthwhile Bicentennial project. it is one that will increase in beauty for many years. We hope you will be able to visit the Forest and see for yourself what has been done to memoralize the Ninety Nines.

Sincerely,

Atchison Bicentennial Committee

John E. Smith
Treasurer

A letter from John E. Smith of the Atchison Bicentennial Committee telling Bobbi that her friend Glen Buffington (below right) sponsored her for Forest of Friendship, Memory Lane.

Bobbi Trout, '29 Derby entry, and Glenn Buffington during her Seattle visit in August, 1974.

GLENN BUFFINGTON ... *native of North Dakota, reared and schooled in Iowa and Missouri. Has been with The Boeing Company (Seattle) for the past 35 years as a flight technician and executive aide in the Production Flight Test organization. For two years prior to joining Boeing, was a flight radio operator with Northwest Airlines on their ATC routes in Canada and Alaska. Worked with Dr. John D. Brock, who made daily flights for ten years, for three years after high school graduation. During the depression years, attended three trade schools — Dickinson Business, Rearwin Flying School and Midland Tech, combining the training in avocation and vocation. Lived in Kansas City at the time of the '29 Derby and watched the girls wing eastward to East St. Louis.*

EAA gathering in Oshkosh, 1977, with Blanche Noyes, and Bobbi's hosts, Bill and Gail Turner (with young son), courtesy of EAA.

KNXT

CBS Television Stations
A Division of Columbia Broadcasting System, Inc.
6121 Sunset Boulevard
Los Angeles, California 90028
(213) 469-1212

Dear Bobbi:

I am writing this up at Santa Paula. Yesterday, Bill Hackbarth and I flew his wonderful old Stinson SM8A monoplane. Great bird with a 300 Lycoming on it.

This morning at dawn I was up in my little Buhl Pup. Flying up here is like going through the "Time Machine." Do hope you can drop by sometime and visit us at the airport. You would be most welcome, and we would be honored.

Bill Hackbarth sends his best regards.

Thanks for those kind words about the broadcasts.

Kindest and best,

CLETE ROBERTS

Last letter Bobbi received from famous TV announcer, Clete Roberts.

Obituary of Mary Von Mach in 1980, friend and contestant in the first Women's Trascontinental Air Derby.

Pioneer pilot Mary von Mach

By CATHY TROST
Free Press Staff Writer

She was a teenager in Detroit during World War I, destined to follow her father's footsteps into the comfortable world of interior design. But her soul was stirred by the fighter pilots half a world away.

"I was fascinated by planes and saddened to see them used for war," Mary Elizabeth von Mach explained after she had embarked on a remarkable career as a pioneer woman aviator. "I wanted to see them used for more useful purposes. I decided this would be my life's object."

Michigan's first licensed woman pilot, the first woman to own and operate her own plane here, the first woman to become a transport pilot, Miss von Mach collected a string of "firsts" with wry good humor and quiet pride.

SHE DIED Monday, at the age of 84, in Harper Hospital.

An open-faced woman with broad cheekbones and short cropped hair most often shoved beneath a leather flight helmet, Miss von Mach passed her pilot's exam in 1927.

A year later, at the age of 29, she was awarded her commercial airline pilot's license and immediately purchased her own plane. It was an open biplane and she named it Mary Ann after her mother.

She set her sights on a transport pilot's license. "Spectacular exhibition flights that have brought considerable note to several women pilots do not interest me," she said. "I believe women will find a place in the business of flying."

IN 1929, when solo flights by women were virtually unheard of because there were only 18 licensed women pilots in America, Miss von Mach flew more than 1,000 miles alone, from Dallas to Detroit, in her Mary Ann. Several

months later, she competed in the first Powder Puff Derby, the arduous Santa Monica-to-Cleveland race that celebrated its 50th anniversary last year.

The fanfare did not seem to affect her.

And it took her 44 years to admit that she was the mystery woman pilot headlined in a Dallas newspaper in 1929. The paper reported the story of a woman who appeared every morning for two weeks at Love Field, boarded a Travelair plane, and took a solo spin.

HER FAMILY was supportive, but she recalled with laughter her first gliding experiment on Grosse Ile.

"My mother was watching," she said. "I was on the left wing, it broke, my shoes fell off, and my mother fainted."

Miss von Mach was the first woman to graduate from Parks Air College near St. Louis.

"She had a little trouble getting them to let her go to school there," Antoinette Le Bay, her niece, recalled Monday. "They took her on probation. But at the end, the rest of the pilots got together and gave her a big trophy because of the help she gave them."

Miss von Mach renounced her dream of opening her own flying school to work in the Willow Run bomber plant during World War II. She inspected the Pratt Whitney engines that powered the B24s and was recognized for her efforts by the War Congress of American Industries.

AN ACQUAINTANCE of famed aviator Amelia Earhart, she was a charter member of the Ninety-Niners Club, a woman pilots organization, and an active member of the OX5 Club of America, named after the Curtis OX5 engine which powered early planes.

"She was very humble," her niece said. "She always said that you can do what you

Mary Elizabeth von Mach in 1928. She was the state's first licensed woman pilot.

start out to do."

Miss von Mach is survived by two sisters and one brother.

Prayers will be said at 8 p.m. Wednesday at the Verheyden Funeral Home, 16300 Mack, Grosse Pointe Park. Services will be at 11 a.m. Thursday at the Cathedral of the Most Blessed Sacrament, Woodward and Boston Blvd. Burial will be in Mt. Olivet Cemetery.

FLAMBOYANT AVIATOR RUTH ELDER DIES AT 74

SAN FRANCISCO (AP)—Ruth Elder, a flamboyant aviator whose 1927 attempt to fly the Atlantic ended in mid-ocean, is dead at 74.

She died quietly in her sleep Sunday at the apartment she shared with her husband of 21 years, Ralph P. King, a man she married twice.

In the half-century that followed the flight that began at Roosevelt Field in New York on Oct. 11, 1927, Miss Elder made movies, met a President, hobnobbed with royalty, married six times, made a lot of money—and spent it all.

Ruth Elder in 1929
Times photo

"She was a beautiful person, a real woman," said King, 79.

King said his wife had been suffering from emphysema for several years and from complications from a broken hip.

Five months after Charles A. Lindbergh made the first solo flight across the Atlantic, Miss Elder and co-pilot-navigator George Haldeman took off from New York in a single-engine Stinson dubbed "The American Girl."

The newspapers that morning remarked on the fancy figure the 23-year-old pilot cut in her flightsuit over checked golf knickers, checked stockings and two-tone shoes.

As the world waited, the frail aircraft droned on toward Paris. The two had flown 2,625 miles in 36 hours when an oil line broke near the Azores.

The aircraft had been without oil pressure for several minutes when a ship appeared on the sea beneath them. Miss Elder dropped a message on its deck, asking assistance. The captain turned the ship toward the nearest land to point the way, then had a message painted on deck.

It said land was 350 miles away at Cape Finistere off the coast of Spain. But this was too far for the crippled plane. Miss Elder ditched and she and her companion were rescued by the ship, which docked at Lisbon.

For Miss Elder the flight brought instant stardom. She was welcomed by European royalty. She went on tour and made silent movies with Richard Dix and Hoot Gibson. She had lunch with President Calvin Coolidge. Her bank account stood at $250,000.

"The money slipped through my fingers and soon there was nothing," she said in an interview years later.

En route, she acquired six husbands, including New York socialite Walter Camp Jr. She divorced them all—including the six-times-married King, her husband when she died.

"We were married about three years when she divorced me," King said. "One day she rang me. She says, 'Daddy, are you married again?' I says no, and she says, 'Can I come home?' I says yeah, and there it was. We got married again. A real love story."

King, a retired Hollywood cameraman, said his wife's remains would be cremated, in accordance with her wishes. Following his death the ashes of both man and wife will be scattered over the sea from an airplane, he said.

FAMOUS—Ruth Elder, "Miss America of Aviation," in 1932.

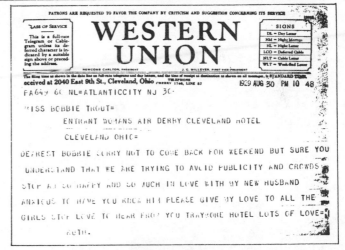

Telegram from Ruth Elder in 1930.

Obituary of Ruth Elder, 99 friend and contestant in the first Women's Transcontinental Air Derby.

In 1978, Bobbi took a special trip to Phoenix where her friend, Vera Dawn Walker, had a mobile home. Vera was a small woman, and after her flying days, she did a lot of prospecting for gold. She even owned a few gold claims. For years before that, Bobbi and Vera wrote back and forth trying to decide when they would get together to look over her properties and look for new claims. Bobbi made an audio taped interview of Vera, talking about her career in aviation. Bobbi gave a copy of it to the Ninety Nines when the group became interested in preserving their fifty-year old history. Vera died a short time later of cancer.

Dear Bobbi:-
I have recieved your cards — and I do thank you very much —
In your 1966 events for April you say: "Visits to skin Doctor Bobbi must stay out of seen." I think you might mean that you had skin cancer. I had it very badly for several years & I finally got an ointment that cured mine! Let me know, if I can help you!
I have been up in The Antelope Valley since 1933 — Remember I had already moved

Pancho was a strong-willed true character with a brain that never stopped. She was a leader, great flier, big-hearted person and wonderful friend.

here when we made our flight (W.A.R.) to N Y and Washington — Remember?
I met my last husband in 1946 — married him in 1952 — After fighting him for 5 year finally was devorced in July 27th — 1966 — Even at that time I was very sick but I didn't know it — My ex — has continued to make life very bad for me — To go into this detail is too lengthy — However after much drama I wound up in The California Hospital very nearly dead! They found out that I had a thyroid deficiency — Now I take little pink pills and

Group of Betsy Ross Members who soon became W.A.R.'s.

I'm getting well — It is a little slow — but I must have taken about 5 or 6 years getting that way — So it will take a little time to get back where I belong —

My husband has appealed the divorce case and says he'll keep everything tied up for 7 more years —

When I was in the Hospital — Kit Quin found out about it and told Curley — She phoned me and wrote — She is married now + lives a Costa Mesa —

Famed Woman Flier Dies

Florence Lowe (Pancho) Barnes, the first woman stunt pilot in the film industry, was found dead in her Boron home Saturday. She was 73.

Authorities said she had been dead for a few days. An autopsy is planned today.

Mrs. Barnes worked as a stunt pilot in the 1929 Howard Hughes film: "Hell's Angels."

An aviatrix who held many speed records in the late 1920s and 1930s Mrs. Barnes participated in the first woman's cross-country airplane race in 1929. She competed against such familiar figures as Amelia Earhart and Jacqueline Cochrane in that race.

Before her death she spent her time between horse racing and raising dogs.

Married and divorced four times, her survivors include a son, William E. Barnes, of Lancaster.

FLORENCE BARNES
Noted aviatrix, 73, dies.

In 1933, Mrs. Barnes moved to Antelope Valley where she bought an alfalfa ranch on what is now Edwards Air Force Base. Shortly before World War II, when the Army Air Corps was building the base, she turned the ranch into a resort called Happy Bottom Riding Club.

The federal government tried to have the land condemned in 1952 after accusing her of operating a house of prostitution. Acting as her own attorney, she sued for defamation and won $414,000.

I will drive down and see you some time — I have a lot of work to do — So have to get a few things cleared up here first —

Do you remember Granny Nourse? — He helped us recover + paint our airplanes for our trans-continental trip — He wrote me in September

With all my best wishes to you As Always

Pancho —

Aviation pioneer found dead in Calif. home

BORON, Ca. — Florence (Pancho) Barnes, the pilot who broke Amelia Earhart's air speed record in 1930 was found dead in her home recently at the age of 69.

The cause of death was not immediately determined and Sheriff's officials said an autopsy was scheduled.

Legend has it she earned her nickname "Pancho" while serving as a crew member of a boat running guns to Mexican revolutionaries. She is also thought to have been the first woman to fly in the Mexican interior.

Four times married and divorced, Mrs. Barnes did not devote her entire life to aviation. After her days as an aviation pioneer ended she owned and operated a guest ranch in the desert near Edwards Air Force Base.

She was very often embroiled in legal disputes, but perhaps her most famous lawsuit concerned her business, called "The Happy Bottom Guest Ranch."

The suit was the result of Mrs. Barnes' efforts to prevent the Air Force from tearing down the ranch to make way for a new runway. During the court proceedings she was accused of running a house of ill repute, to which she responded the Air Force had threatened to bomb her ranch. In the end, she lost the suit.

She is survived by one son, William Barnes, who operates a flying school at Fox Field in Lancaster, Ca.

Pancho Barnes death in 1975.

Bobbi and Vera Dawn Walker, who both flew in the 1929 first Women's Transcontinental Air Derby, died in 1978.

On May 16, 1979, "Hughes AirWest Air Race Classic" conducted a "Women in Aviation" forum, hosted at Northrop University's American Hall of Aviation History, and Bobbi represented the pioneer women of the air again. Also speaking were Mary Wallace "Wally" Funk II, a well-known flier, the first woman air safety accident investigator; Julie Clark, a young woman who talked about her job as a captain for Hughes AirWest; and Dr. Margaret Seddon, who, after becoming a doctor, was so enthusiastic about space that she became a United States astronaut candidate. Dr. Seddon became the third woman astronaut to ride the space shuttle. The four of them represented the history of women in flying.

Since Bobbi was one of the twenty entrants in the first Women's Transcontinental Air Derby in 1929, and one of the five who was still living at that time, she was given the honor of flagging the Hughes AirWest Classic off on June 16, 1979, to celebrate the fiftieth anniversary of the Derby. Bobbi waved off fifty-nine planes with a red-and-white checkered flag. All planes were piloted by women. She was impressed with the difference fifty years made. In Bobbi's day, all the planes had tail skids; in 1979, all the planes had tricycle landing gear. Sophisticated instruments, electric starters, and the latest in navigation equipment were not even thought of in Bobbi's era. The modern pilots did not wear helmets, goggles, breeches, or heavy boots. Instead they were attired in smart slacks and shirts; pilot and co-pilot usually alike. The planes were valued from thirty thousand dollars and up.

Future, present and past

Members of a unique "Women in Aviation" forum —representing 50 years of aerospace, general and commercial aviation—examine a vintage aircraft model at Northrop University's Hall of Aviation History in Los Angeles, site of the recent Hughes Airwest-sponsored panel. From left are: Rhea Seddon, a U.S. space shuttle astronaut candidate; Julie Ames, Hughes Airwest first officer; Wally Funk, the first and only woman investigator for the National Transportation Safety Board; and Bobbi Trout, a contestant with Amelia Earhart in the country's first women's air derby in 1929. The forum also announced contestants for the Hughes Airwest Air Race Classic which Trout flagged off in Santa Monica on June 16.

Gathering of the Hughes AirWest Air Race Classic participants.

Bobbi flagged off the Hughes AirWest Classic.

CREDIT: GLENN BUFFINGTON

Pre-flight party for Hughes AirWest with the last two living participants of the first Women's Air Derby: Bobbi (l) and Mae Haizlip (r).

Flag-off August 21, 1979 of the Angel Derby, the 50th anniversary flight of the first Women's Transcontinental Air Derby, dubbed the "Powder Puff" by Will Rogers. (from left) Doris Minter, Bobbi, and Jean Ferrell, who was killed at the South Pole.

Group picture of Charter 99's on the 50th anniversary party of the group.

Louise McPhetridge Thaden
(1905-1979)

Louise Thaden, stalwart Charter Member of The Ninety-Nines, passed away November 9th in the evening at High Point, N.C., following a heart attack. A private memorial service was held.

With license number 1943, Louise wasted no time in hanging up many records starting in 1928 and proved an inspiration to this writer and a multitude of others over the years. Much of her memorabilia and awards is housed at the Thaden Library, a log cabin adjacent to the Beechcraft Staggerwing Museum at the Tullahoma, TN, Northern Field planes she helped to make famous by flying them in competitions.

Within the past month, Louise wrote she had cancelled her trip "up North" three times because she didn't feel equal to it. She had planned one of her many visits with her daughter, Pat, at Leesburg, VA and son, Bill, in the Boston area. Pat is now renewing her interest in flying and Bill is a pilot for Eastern Airlines.

LMT lamented the fact she was unable to attend 50th Anniversary celebrations this year at Milwaukee, Albany, Atchison, Cleveland, San Diego and Valley Stream. She wrote of the invitations, "Of course had to reply negatively—I can only hope that The Ninety-Nines know my lack of participation is not from disinterest."

In correspondence over the years, I adopted Amelia Earhart's habit of ending her letters to Louise with the closing 'Cheerio'. In her autobiography, *"High, Wide and Frightened"*, Louise wrote regarding Amelia, and it is most appropriate for quoting (with poetic license) at this time: "Eternal life, I think, is a life so lived that its deeds carry on through the ages. Louise has carved a niche too deep to ever be forgotten. She will live. So I have said no farewell to her . . . I say to her, 'Cheerio'!"

Glenn Buffington

Friendly rivals in California 1935 (l. R) Florence (Pancho) Barnes, Amelia Earhart and Louise Thaden

CREDIT: MRS. RALPH CARTER

Early photo of Louise in the 1920's.

5-22-79

Dear Bobbi
Shortly before Phoebe died two lady writers were to help her finish the book she'd been working on for years. About two years ago I wrote each of them & the letters were returned "stamped" address unknown". Sooo. — Phoebe had sent me portions from time to time to edit & make comment & it was more about her various "politicking" efforts than biographical (personal) —; also pull of verbiage & on the whole uninteresting I'm sorry to say.

Blanche Noyes says you are working on a book. Good for you & much success with it. Are you also still "inventing"? Oops, Innovating! Have seen your face in the 99 NEWS & you look Gung Ho, which is the opposite of me.

Affectionately, Louise

One of the last letters Bobbi received from Louise.

One month later, as a charter member of the Ninety Nines, Bobbi was invited to Albany, New York, for the Golden Jubilee, their fiftieth anniversary. The event, held at the Empire State Plaza, was packed for the occasion. Bobbi's flight arrived late, just in time to catch the bus for the Plaza. She did not have time to change clothes, and again maintained her tradition of being the most comfortable person there, and attended in her slack-suit.

Bobbi flagged off the Angel Derby Race, officially commemorating the year and day of the first Women's Transcontinental Air Derby. It used almost the same route, and ended at Cleveland, Ohio, for the big racing events. It took twenty-three minutes to get all thirty-three entrants off in the Angel Derby.

At the 1976 OX5 Pioneers Reunion, Bobbi was awarded the OX5 Pioneer Woman of the Year Award. She met Neta Snook Southern at the reunion; they were both on the program. Neta, who received her instruction in 1917, learned to fly earlier than any other living woman, but is best known for having taught Amelia Earhart to fly.

In 1981, Neta and aviation historian Carol Osborne were guests of the Zonta women's professional organization and went to meet Professor Hatfield. Their visit ended with Neta being interviewed on videotape by Professor Hatfield. He donated his lifelong collection of pictures, books, inventions, and aviation memorabilia to the American Hall of Aviation History at Northrop University in Inglewood, California. For over fifty years, Professor Hatfield photographed and documented the history of flight. From some of his two hundred-fifty thousand negatives, he made thousands of eight-by-ten black and white enlargements. Using special paints, he carefully colored three thousand of these enlargements.

Opening of the new San Diego museum, Friday, June 18, 1979. (left to right) Bobbi, Betty Gillies, Melba Gorby Beard in front of a manikin of Amelia.

OX5 AVIATION PIONEERS

THIS IS TO CERTIFY THAT

Bobbi Trout

HAS BEEN SELECTED FOR THE

OUTSTANDING WOMEN'S AWARD

HER ACTIVITIES IN THE PROMOTION OF AVIATION HAVE EARNED OUR RESPECT AND ADMIRATION AND HAVE ENCOURAGED WOMEN THROUGHOUT THE WORLD TO PARTICIPATE IN THE FIELD OF AERONAUTICS.

By authority of Board of Governors and the undersigned officers of the OX5 AVIATION PIONEERS, THIS 1ST DAY OF October 19

By *(signature)* PRESIDENT

(signature) SECRETARY

Bobbi received the National OX5 Outstanding Women's Award in 1976.

1976 OX5 Banquet where Bobbi met Neta Snook Southern.

CREDIT: CAROL OSBORNE

The day Neta was interviewed on videotape by Professor Hatfield, Jan. 10, 1981.

Neta and Carol Osborne's story appears in the Lockheed Star.

LMSC employee enjoys once-in-a-lifetime trip with woman who taught Amelia Earhart to fly

The oldest woman pilot in the United States, who once barnstormed across the country, operated a flying school, and performed spectacular aerial stunts, is best known as Amelia Earhart's flying instructor, not for her own flying feats.

That is fine with Neta Snook Southern, a Los Gatos resident and friend of Carol Osborne, a logistics analyst in 87-84. "I wouldn't court fame," said the feisty 85-year-old Southern, adding, "Amelia never wanted fame either."

Memory of Famous Pupil
It was the memory of her most famous pupil that took Southern to Los Angeles earlier this month.

Southern   Osborne

She and Carol were guests of Zonta International, an organization of executive women who gather annually to observe Amelia Earhart Day. The day commemorates Earhart's first solo flight from Honolulu to the mainland.

The group established the Amelia Earhart Fellowship Award for Graduate Study, which grants $5,000 annually to women entering or continuing full-time graduate study in aerospace-related science and engineering fields.

Carol took with her parchment copies of a letter that Earhart—who flew Lockheed Vegas and Electras—wrote to a friend asking about Neta.

Meeting Amelia
While in Los Angeles, Neta and Carol visited the Donald Douglas Museum. While there, Neta reminisced about meeting Earhart, then 24 years old.

"It was a hot December day in 1920 when I first saw Amelia," Southern said. "She walked up to me and said, 'I'll come right to the point. I want to learn how to fly and I understand you teach flying'."

Southern, then 25, gave Earhart lessons in a Canadian training plane, the Jenny. Southern retired from flying before Earhart's first solo flight.

Southern used to build her own flying machines in those days, she said. And when an airplane broke down, she repaired it.

"I was always interested in engines, that's what got me interested in flying," she said.

Dollar A Minute Lessons
To earn money during the summer, Southern would don goggles and a long leather coat and take passengers for rides for a dollar a minute. At county fairs, she performed aerial loops that amazed the crowds, once they learned that a woman was at the controls.

Her only frightening experience in a plane occurred while she was performing one of those loops. "The owner of a flying circus in Santa Monica asked me to test a plane for him," she said. "He told me to take the plane up to 5,000 feet and make a loop."

Southern said she was unsure of the plane's reliability, but she performed the maneuver. "At the top of the loop, the cushion I was sitting in fell out and left me dangling by my seat belt."

Interviews, Visits, Memories
Neta and Carol visited North Hollywood Park where there is a statue of Earhart. Neta thought the statue was a good likeness, but the "cheeks were too drawn, not quite full enough."

Neta was interviewed several times by writers and researchers. On the flight from San Francisco, she was invited to the cockpit. More questions. What was Earhart like? How did she fly?

For Carol it was a once-in-a-lifetime experience. She met many luminaries in the world of aviation, including Dr. Anna Lee Fisher, a NASA astronaut. Some pictures Carol took of old photos in Neta's scrapbook were given to the Douglas museum. The museum plans to dedicate one entire wall to Neta.

Neta Snook Southern is part of aviation history. She has answered and will continue to answer questions until first-hand details, and the only living account, die with her.

CREDIT: LOCKHEED MISSILES & SPACE COMPANY

IN MEMORIAM

David Daniel Hatfield
1903-1981

COWBOY—RANCHER—PILOT—MECHANIC—ENGINEER—INVENTOR—HISTORIAN
EDUCATOR—PHOTOGRAPHER—ARTIST—RESEARCHER—AUTHOR...GOOD FRIEND!

We have had a rare privilege, the privilege of loving, working with, and enjoying a truly remarkable, extraordinary and unique man.

David Hatfield was born in a covered wagon around the turn of the century in the Oklahoma Territory. As for his birthday, July 1 1903 , he picked it. To him, it satisfied anyone's asking and it did not detract from other important events.

David's love for aviation started in the '20's as a barnstorming pilot, mechanic, engineer and business-man. His dream for preserving aviation history started at the same time; his knowledge of photography made it a natural. The American Hall of Aviation History at Northrop University is a testament to David and his dreams becoming a reality. The collection consists of over 300,000 negatives and photos, magazines, books, reference materials and film that no longer exist except in his collection. David is internationally known and respected for his first-hand knowledge, his lifetime research and experiences in the development of aviation.

He was recently appointed chairman of the committee to select the world's major airlines for the Franklin Mint Silver Insignia Collection.

He worked continuously with film companies, magazines and authors, providing detailed information on aircraft companies and personalities. He also found time to author a series of books on aviation history which have become collectors' items.

Of his many awards, some of the notable ones are the Robert Wanamaker Award, the Southern California Outstanding Citizen's Award, the OX5 President's Citation, the Air Force Association Appreci-ation Plaque, and currently, he has been nominated for the Aviation Hall of Fame.

David was active in the Los Angeles Breakfast Club, the OX5 Club, the Quiet Birdman, the American Society of Photogrammetry, the Society of Automotive Engineers (SAE), the Experimental Aircraft Association (EAA), and many others.

His monumental project to chronicle man's flight was almost complete. He left 2,000 hand-painted photographs of the history of flight from myth to modern day and 160 hours of video cassette film documentary.

David had picked a location to retire. It was a small place on the New Mexico - Arizona border in New Mexico. He had surveyed this area in the '20's. It has an old house which he

intended to rebuild with adobe, having learned the art of working with adobe as a teenager. He intended to generate electricity from the wind. He had researched windmills and knew exactly how they would be con-structed to achieve maximum effect. He had determined that pure, clean water was available; he intended to have a vegetable garden to supply his needs. He would plant the fields in clover. The clover would have purple blooms; from the air it would look like a blue sea. His friends would come and visit. They would land their airplanes in the clover field.

If you have tears, let them be tears of joy; if you have a heavy heart, let it be uplifted, for I believe David has his dream. I believe David has his landing field of clover; I believe David is with his friends. Can you imagine the reception committee: Roscoe Turner, Jack Northrop, Fish Salmon, Don Douglas, Charles Lindberg, Tiny Broadwick, Amelia Earhart, and Major Bong? And I will lay odds that the clover field is covered in purple blossoms!

Eulogy delivered
June 29 1981
by Joseph C. Miles
Director Institute of Technology

Eulogy of Professor Hatfield

Carol spent hours researching information and photographs with Professor Hatfield. Carol's interest in aviation, its personalities, and the tremendous knowledge Professor Hatfield had in aviation history, resulted in their becoming good friends. The professor was alone and did not know who would be right to carry on his love of the history of flight. Since museums are usually not moneymaking projects, Northrop University wanted to curtail expenses, which deeply disheartened Professor Hatfield. Six months after meeting Professor Hatfield, Carol was notified her good friend had passed away, on June 21, 1981. To her shocked surprise, she was named executrix and heir to his personal memorabilia and videotape equipment.

Carol found it necessary to contact Bobbi Trout for some information. They soon became good friends. During one of Bobbi's visits to Santa Clara, California, Bobbi suggested they continue what Professor Hatfield started in 1977: interviewing and video taping aviation pioneers for history. Bobbi suggested they go to the OX5 Aviation Pioneers Reunion at San Francisco Airport, which also included the Early Birds of Aviation, Inc. What better opportunity to catch them all in one place? It was just before the reunion that their good friend, Early Bird Tony Stadlman, died. It dawned on

Bobbi and Carol that if they did not get these pioneers on videotape very soon, while they are "breathing and mentally alert," it would be too late. Bobbi and Carol have been working hard ever since. They were invited to become associate members of the Early Birds of Aviation, Inc. by Early Bird President Forest Wysong.

CREDIT: CAROL OSBORNE

Bobbi—76 (l), Tony Stadlman—96 (c), and Neta Snook Southern—86, being honored at the Santa Clara County Fair, Aug. 11, 1982.

CREDIT: ESTELLE MANBECK

One of the last gatherings of the W.A.R. (standing left to right): Bobbi, Dr. Kit Quinn, Ethyl Tobin, Viola Curley, Jo Weiss Backus, Monte Orman, Edie Curtis and Patty Willis. (seated left to right): Estelle Sherman Manbeck, Melba Beard, Jane "Kelly" Quick.

Bobbi and Carol have interviewed hundreds of pioneers and special personalities who have related extremely interesting experiences of first-hand information that will be of utmost interest to coming generations. Some of the recollections Bobbi has are about friends like Jimmie Mattern. Jimmie, who is a renowned around-the-world flier, is responsible for Bobbi joining the OX5 Aviation Pioneers organization.

Bobbi often talks about one of the first interviews with R. Glenn Osborn. Osborn was about ten years old when his big sister, Agnes, met and began dating Orville Wright. Agnes and Orville played chess in their spare time. Osborn died January 27, 1986, at the age of ninety nine. In the interview, Osborn said,

> "I was the only person allowed upstairs, above the bicycle shop, where they did their inventing. Being the little brother of Orville's girlfriend, you get privileges that you wouldn't ordinarily get. Orville didn't dare run me out. . . . I had an 'in' no one else had. I used to see all types of kites mounted on the wall and I wondered what grown men were doing monkeying with kites."

Bobbi also remembers the day she and Carol interviewed Early Bird A. Walt Claverie. Among many of his experiences, Walt told about Julia Clark, who enrolled at the Curtiss Flying School in San Diego in 1912. Julia received her pilot's license on May 19, 1912. She was in the class just ahead of Claverie's. Only one month later, she became the first American aviatrix to be killed in an airplane crash.

Bobbi loves to relate about the interview she and Carol made of Edna Gardner Whyte, in 1983. Edna, who had been teaching flying more than sixty years, told how she started Friendly Aero Valley Airport in Roanoke, Texas. She told how she began in March, 1970. When she went to the Small Business Administration in Dallas, Texas, to apply for a five thousand dollar loan to build a hangar on her twenty-four acres, to her surprise, she was turned down: because she was "too old," sixty-eight; she was a woman; and building and running an airport was too risky.

That was the wrong thing to say to Edna. Edna found the money elsewhere and built the hangar and a small apartment for herself. It took ten years of hard work, but today her logo is "Growing Without Federal Money." Her airport houses three hundred sixty airplanes and three flight schools.

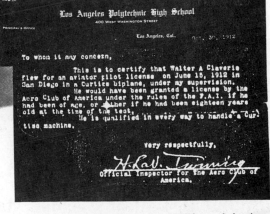

Early Bird Walt Claverie's Aero Club letter regarding his aviation qualifications.

Julia Clark, first American aviatrix to be killed in an airplane crash. This rare photo was autographed to her good friend, Walt "Kiddo" Claverie in May, 1912, and within a month of her death.

Clema M. Granger, pioneer aviatrix, succumbs at 89

Former valley resident was fearless flier

By SUSAN MORA WOOD
Desert Sun Staff Writer

Obituary of a dear friend, Clema Granger, on June 29, 1983.

Her pilot's license was signed by Orville Wright. She palled around with Amelia Earhart.

She was Clema M. Granger, a pioneer aviatrix and fearless flier who helped break new ground for women — by soaring in the air.

Mrs. Granger, a former Coachella Valley resident, died Tuesday at Palmdale Hospital in Palmdale. She was 89.

No services are planned.

Born in Oskaloosa, Iowa, she moved with her family to Pasadena in 1909. Two years later she met and married James E. Granger.

In 1926, the Grangers bought a World War I surplus "Jenny," leased a hangar at Santa Monica Clover Field and went into business. During that time there was no license required to teach flying. So, with little experience, they opened for business with Jim Granger doing the teaching and his wife running the office for the Pacific School of Aviation. They were also the West Coast distributor for Swallow airplanes, used for sport and training.

The couple graduated hundreds of students, including some of Hollywood's brightest stars — Spencer Tracy, Hoot Gibson and Ruth Elder among others.

Mrs. Granger took up flying in 1929, earning a pilot's license signed by none other than Orville Wright. She performed such aerial stunts as shutting off the engine in midair and then landing without power.

The Grangers passed on their love of flying to their three sons. By the time each boy was 16 years old, he had been taught to fly. By 1933, the family was known as the "Flying Grangers."

Although the Grangers' business prospered during the Depression, they later supplemented their family income by performing stunts and aviation scenes for motion pictures. Their work appeared in the first "Dawn Patrol," "Wings," "The Yellow Ticket," and many Hoot Gibson westerns.

It was during this time Mrs. Granger became involved in air racing. She raced in the Air Derby of 1930, 1931 and 1932. In each race she competed against and befriended Amelia Earhart, Gladys O'Donnell, Bobbi Trout, Pancho Barnes and many other aviation notables. Mrs. Granger also came into contact with Palm Desert developer Cliff Henderson in her flying days.

The couple remained in Santa Monica until Granger's death in 1934 which occurred during the testing of a race plane. With her husband's death, Mrs. Granger's flying days also ended.

She sold the business and moved in 1934 to Palm Springs, where her family had spent many a happy weekend.

She built a small apartment complex and went into

real estate sales, handling the operation of both businesses until the mid-1970s when she sold the buildings and moved to Palm Desert to be near her son, Norman. Later, due to poor health she moved to

CLEMA M. GRANGER
. . . dead at 89.

Palmdale to live with her son, Harry.

Mrs. Granger was a member of the Ninety-Nines, a national club of female pilots that formed at the National Air Races in 1929. She was secretary-treasurer of that organization when Amelia Earhart was its president.

She was also a member of the OX5 Club and she was solely responsible for the original Aviation Breakfast Club in Palm Springs which began in the mid-1930s. The club began in her living room.

Mrs. Granger was honored in 1977 as the honorary starter of the 30th Powder Puff Anniversary Commemorative Flight from Palm Springs to Tampa, Fla.

Her aviation career has now caught the imagination of Bob and Margie Glover of Sylmar who are currently researching the flying pioneers and hope to produce a fictional television production of the 1929 Air Derby Races. The Glovers intend to base one of the major characters of the production on the events in Mrs. Granger's life.

She is survived by her three sons, Norman of Yucca Valley; Harry of Palmdale, and Jim Jr. of Lakeside; one sister, Blanche Long of Palm Springs; and 10 grandchildren, including Public Information Officer Tom Granger of the California Highway Patrol's Indio station. Other survivors include 33 great-grandchildren and three great-great-grandchildren.

Arrangements were handled by The Neptune Society in Burbank. •

Dr. Emma Quinn; First Female Medical Examiner

Obituary of another dear friend, Dr. Emma McNair Kittridge Quinn who died on Jan. 3, 1984. She was a friend from W.A.R. days.

Emma Kittredge Quinn, the first woman ever to be named an aviation medical examiner and a practicing physician in this area for 50 years, died Jan. 3 in her Los Angeles home after a lengthy battle with cancer. She was 81.

Dr. Quinn, who earned her medical degree from Women's Medical College of Pennsylvania (one of the few universities in the nation then accepting women) in 1929, came to Los Angeles to intern at Los Angeles County General Hospital and in 1932 became the first anesthesiologist hired as a permanent staff member at California Hospital.

By then she was an ardent flight enthusiast and had been doing medical research on such women aviation pioneers as Amelia Earhart, Pancho Barnes and Bobbi Trout. That work led to her being named medical

examiner for Southern California in 1934, the lone woman in the country then qualified to conduct physical examinations for pilot licenses and renewals.

In 1936 she married the late William F. Quinn, a surgeon, and became his anesthesiologist.

Among her many avocations was a 25-year alliance with the American Bureau for Medical Aid for Free China. As West Coast chairman of that group she helped underwrite hospitals, clinics and ambulance services for Taiwan while training Chinese doctors in this country. Mrs. Quinn was credited with the construction of a hospital there and for her work was given the Order of the Chrysanthemum, the highest honor Taiwan bestows on a non-Chinese.

Until she retired in 1982 she had served as campus physician at Pierce College.

Bobbi being inducted into the OX5 Hall of Fame, October 13, 1984, by President Paul McCully (l). Mrs. Cliff Henderson (c), former actress Marian Marsh, presented her deceased husbands traditional gift to every Hall of Fame inductee, a gold card.

In 1976, Bobbi had been named "OX5 Woman of the Year," which was an honor for any aviator. October 13, 1984, Bobbi was inducted into the OX5 Aviation Pioneers Hall of Fame, the highest honor the OX5 Aviation Pioneers bestow on any of their members. She is now in the company of Charles Lindbergh, Amelia Earhart, Jimmy Doolittle, Jimmie Mattern, Barry Goldwater, and many more.

Bobbi and Carol videotaping at Keuka Lake, New York, Oct. 14, 1984.

Bobbi videotaping property once owned at the turn of the century by Flora Lockheed.

Bobbi celebrated her fifty-fifth anniversary of the first Woman To Fly All Night, on February 11, 1984. She flew in Jim Nissen's OX5 Jenny, from Meadowlark Field in Livermore, California. The event was covered by John Fullmer on NBC television. Nissen took Bobbi up and let her take the controls of his Jenny, the first time she had been at the controls of a Jenny since 1928.

January 7, 1986, Bobbi celebrated her eightieth birthday on ABC's KRON-Telecopter 4. They hovered above the Golden Gate Bridge as Bobbi was interviewed by Bob McCarthy.

CREDIT: CAROL OSBORNE

Bobbi with telecopter reporter, Bob McCarthy, who interviewed Bobbi on her eightieth birthday as the helicopter hovered over the Golden Gate bridge.

CREDIT: CAROL OSBORNE

Bobbi and helicopter pilot, Will Prater, before Bobbi's big ride on her birthday, January 7, 1986.

Major Tom Moncure from Maxwell Air Force Base, Alabama, contacted the Smithsonian Institution to identify a living aviatrix who might be eligible for the "Gathering of the Eagles" annual celebrations. The planning for this celebration was a year in the making. On May 28, 1986, Bobbi and Carol arrived at Maxwell Air Force Base for the "Gathering of the Eagles." There were eighteen "Eagles" honored by the graduating class. The military gave them officers' quarters with all amenities. The first two days found all the "Eagles" autographing one thousand five-hundred lithographs. These lithographs sold for sixty-five dollars each to help pay the expenses of the annual gathering. A four-year set recently sold for four thousand dollars, not a bad investment.

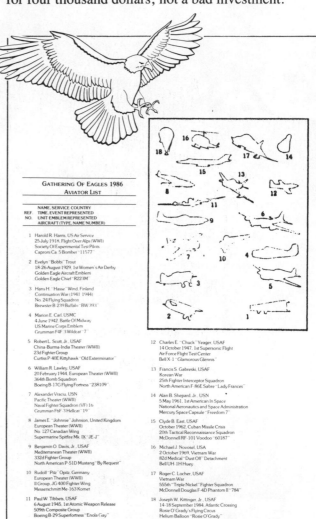

GATHERING OF EAGLES 1986
AVIATOR LIST

REF. NO. NAME, SERVICE, COUNTRY
TIME, EVENT REPRESENTED
UNIT EMBLEM REPRESENTED
AIRCRAFT (TYPE, NAME, NUMBER)

1 Harold R. Harris, US Air Service
25 July 1918, Flight Over Alps (WWI)
Society Of Experimental Test Pilots
Caproni Ca. 5 Bomber "11577"

2 Evelyn "Bobbi" Trout
18-26 August 1929, 1st Women's Air Derby
Golden Eagle Aircraft Emblem
Golden Eagle Chief "R223M"

3 Hans H. "Hasse" Wind, Finland
Continuation War (1941-1944)
No. 24 Flying Squadron
Brewster B-239 Buffalo "BW-393"

4 Marion E. Carl, USMC
4 June 1942, Battle Of Midway
US Marine Corps Emblem
Grumman F4F-3 Wildcat "7"

5 Robert L. Scott, Jr., USAF
China-Burma-India Theater (WWII)
23d Fighter Group
Curtiss P-40E Kittyhawk "Old Exterminator"

6 William R. Lawley, USAF
20 February 1944, European Theater (WWII)
364th Bomb Squadron
Boeing B-17G Flying Fortress "238109"

7 Alexander Vraciu, USN
Pacific Theater (WWII)
Naval Fighter Squadron (VF) 16
Grumman F6F-3 Hellcat "19"

8 James E. "Johnnie" Johnson, United Kingdom
European Theater (WWII)
No. 127 Canadian Wing
Supermarine Spitfire Mk. IX "JE-J"

9 Benjamin O. Davis, Jr., USAF
Mediterranean Theater (WWII)
332d Fighter Group
North American P-51D Mustang "By Request"

10 Rudolf "Pitz" Opitz, Germany
European Theater (WWII)
II Group, JG 400 Fighter Wing
Messerschmitt Me-163 Komet

11 Paul W. Tibbets, USAF
6 August 1945, 1st Atomic Weapon Release
509th Composite Group
Boeing B-29 Superfortress "Enola Gay"

12 Charles E. "Chuck" Yeager, USAF
14 October 1947, 1st Supersonic Flight
Air Force Flight Test Center
Bell X-1 "Glamorous Glennis"

13 Francis S. Gabreski, USAF
Korean War
25th Fighter Interceptor Squadron
North American F-86E Sabre "Lady Frances"

14 Alan B. Shepard, Jr., USN
5 May 1961, 1st American In Space
National Aeronautics and Space Administration
Mercury Space Capsule "Freedom 7"

15 Clyde B. East, USAF
October 1962, Cuban Missile Crisis
20th Tactical Reconnaissance Squadron
McDonnell RF-101 Voodoo "60187"

16 Michael J. Novosel, USA
2 October 1969, Vietnam War
82d Medical "Dust Off" Detachment
Bell UH-1H Huey

17 Roger C. Locher, USAF
Vietnam War
555th "Triple Nickel" Fighter Squadron
McDonnell Douglas F-4D Phantom II "784"

18 Joseph W. Kittinger, Jr., USAF
14-18 September 1984, Atlantic Crossing
Rosie O'Grady's Flying Circus
Helium Balloon "Rosie O'Grady"

Gathering of Eagles 1986
Original Painting by Jay Ashurst

Autographed lithographs of the famous Eagles of Aviation.

Bobbi stopped autographing four times for interviews on two television stations and two radio talk shows. Each evening and several afternoons were spent attending elegant luncheons and banquets. In their free time, Bobbie and Carol videotaped other "Eagles." The big event was on Saturday evening, with ceremonies straight out of Hollywood. The eighteen "Eagles" walked in behind bugles blowing and flags waving to sit on the stage before approximately fifteen hundred people, mostly graduates of Maxwell Air Force Base. The cream of the military, these officers will be our future military leaders. Bobbi was again herself, wearing traditional evening slacks.

After a three minute slide show on each "Eagle," the "Eagle" was presented in spotlights and before cameras. General Harold R. Harris, ninety-one, was presented first and Bobbi, at age eighty, was second. About midnight, after the ball was over, they were escorted to their quarters. Bobbi and Carol came home with over ten hours of videotaped interviews of General Harold Harris, General Paul Tibbets, General Marion Carl, General Benjamin Davis, Jr., General George Vaughn, Colonel Clyde East, and Admiral Alan Shepard.

CREDIT: CAROL OSBORNE

General Harold Harris and Bobbi.

CREDIT: CAROL OSBORNE

Bobbi and Alan Shepard at The Gathering of Eagles at Maxwell AFB, Alabama, May 31, 1986.

CREDIT: CAROL OSBORNE

General Paul Tibbets, his son Gene, and Bobbi.

CREDIT: PERRY COLEY

The Eagles (front row, left to right): Michael Novosel and wife, Johnnie Johnson and wife, Francis Gabreski and wife, General Paul Tibbets, Roger Locher and wife Patty, Mrs. Benjamin Davis Jr., Rudolf Opitz, and Bobbi. (Back row, left to right): General Harold Harris, Mrs. Vraciu, General Robert Scott, Alexander Vraciu, Mrs. Lawley, Admiral Alan Shepard, William Lawley, Hans Wind, Mrs. Marion Carl, Mrs. Wind, General Marion Carl, General Benjamin Davis Jr., and Colonel Clyde East.

Alan Shepard and Carol, Bobbi's videotaping partner, at the banquet, May 31, 1986.

CREDIT: CAROL OSBORNE

Major Ann O. Smethurst, Bobbi, and Major Susan Neugebauer, at The Gathering of Eagles banquet, May 31, 1986.

In sixty years, Bobbi saw remarkable changes. Planes flew sixty miles per hour, had open cockpits, and a piece of iron for tailslids. An airplane with a compass was called an "instrument airplane." Today's airplanes fly hundreds and thousands of miles an hour, have luxurious air-conditioned cockpits, sophisticated brakes, retractable landing gear, automatic pilots and heavily instrumented cockpits. It was quite a change from the days when solo pilots were happy to have a compass. It was a change from Bobbi's first Women's Transcontinental Air Derby, in 1929, when she flew her beautiful Golden Eagle Chief monoplane.

CREDIT: CAROL OSBORNE

Celebrating Bobbi's eightieth birthday, January 7, 1986, with friends (standing from left) Tom Wilson and David Giver. (seated from left): Kelly and Joe Wendeln, Jo Ann Peakes, and Fran Woolley.

CREDIT: CAROL OSBORNE

Bobbi's birthday, Jan. 7, 1984 at Lake Tahoe, trying to win the jackpot, an airplane!

Epilogue

Preserving Aviation History

DR. David D. Hatfield, Aviation Historian of Northrop University started videotaping aviation pioneers in 1977. Four years later he passed away, willing his video equipment and personal aviation memorabilia to Carol Osborne. Through Dr. Hatfield, Bobbi met Carol. They are currently working to continue Dr. Hatfield's videotape interviews and trying to preserve a part of aviation history.

CREDIT: CAROL OSBORNE

Bobbi interviewed Ed Lund, Howard Hughes co-pilot on their record breaking round the world flight in April 1984.

Ed as the camera records his biography, Easter Day, 1984.

CREDIT: CAROL OSBORNE

The videotaping began with several friends. They attended the 1982 Reunion of Early Birds and OX5 Aviation Pioneers, and were busy taping during the whole event. Since, they have taped at all of the reunions, driving many miles to interview and tape other famous pioneers including:

Jimmy Doolittle (retired WWII General), Paul Garber (Historian Emeritus, Smithsonian), Forrest Wysong (Early Bird President), Neta Snook Southern (learned to fly in 1917, longer than any living woman), Tony LeVier (Lockheed test pilot during the 1930's), Ed Lund (Howard Hughes' copilot on 1938 record flight), Muriel Earhart Morrissey (Amelia's sister), Edna Gardner Whyte (eighty-four years of age and instructing the last sixty years), John Lockheed (Allan's oldest son), Tony Fokker (nephew and assistant to Anthony Fokker in the 1930's), and Ed Heinemann (the famous combat aircraft designer for Douglas Aircraft).

Bobbi wishes to document all she knows. She has a wealth of knowledge and knows many of the pioneer aviators personally. Bobbi and Carol are proud of their accomplishments during the past five years. Since the fifth Early Bird and OX5 reunion, they have conducted two hundred thirty-three different interviews. It is only a start to where they are going. Bobbi and Carol formed a non-profit corporation and hope to get a grant to carry on this work so that each one of the aviation pioneers, their memories, and their experiences will live on in aviation history.

CREDIT: CAROL OSBORNE

Lester and Kay Maitland, August 31, 1986 Les Maitland and Al Hegenburger were the first to cross the Pacific, a great feat only two months after Lindbergh flew the Atlantic.

Edna Gardner Whyte, who is still teaching flying after more than sixty years, taken in September, 1983.

CREDIT: CAROL OSBORNE

CREDIT: CAROL OSBORNE

Combat aircraft designer, Ed Heinemann, in October, 1985, when Ed was inducted into the OX5 Hall of Fame. Here he is enshrined by J. Max Freeman, International OX5 President, of 1986.

Bobbi and Muriel Morrissey visiting with Neta Snook Southern in her Los Gatos home, March 1983.

Bobbi and Muriel Earhart Morrissey, Valentines Day, 1983.

Jimmy and Joe Doolittle the day Bobbi video taped them in their home, February 27, 1984. What a delightful day with a beautiful couple who have been happily married since 1917!

Index